Denis Carroll

Unusual Suspects
Twelve Radical Clergymen

the columba press

First published in 1998 by
the columba press
55A Spruce Avenue, Stillorgan Industrial Park, Blackrock, Co Dublin

Cover by Bill Bolger
Origination by The Columba Press
Printed in Ireland by Colour Books Ltd, Dublin

ISBN 1 85607 239 8

For Orla

Acknowledgements

Thanks to: The Linen Hall Library, Belfast; the staff of the manuscript room at TCD; Fergus Brogan; Archbishop Donald Caird; Margaret Carroll; Mary and Jerry Caroll; Déaglán de Bréadúin; Dorine Davin; Douglas Gageby; Betty Hilliard; Martin Hilliard; Peadar Kirby; Brian Murphy (Dublin); Fr Brian Murphy OSB; Eugene McCartan; Terence McCaughey; Sheila McCormack *(Church of Ireland Gazette);* Fergus McGarry; Brendan Ó Cathaoir; Thomas O'Dwyer; Felicity O'Mahony; Stuart O'Paidin; Brenda O'Riordan-McGaley; Ml O'Riordan; Fr Ml O'Sullivan SJ; Risteárd Ó Glaisne; Cathal O'Shannon; Rev Alfred Williamson (Belfast).

Contents

Foreword

In his essay 'Reconciling the Histories: Protestant and Catholic', political scientist Frank Wright argues that a legacy of antagonised history entraps us all. In Ireland, historical perceptions have 'magnetised (us) towards antagonism and rivalry'. Although this is not an exclusively Irish phenomenon, it is particularly true of our situation. Today, we are perhaps aware of the need for reconciliation across our religious and political traditions. This reconciliation is not simply a polite wish. It is a moral imperative. Even more, it is a socio-political necessity. New international configurations will either wither the old antagonisms or entrap us in a time warp. How much better if, moving beyond ancient hatreds, we could face the third millennium with energies devoted to solving new problems which inevitably will arise in an expanding Europe?

In a divided society (divided at many levels – religious, political and economic) we need to know the history not only of our own tradition but those 'events which have become central to the antagonistic histories' still potent in our society. That is to say, we need to know each other's histories and somehow enter the mind of 'the other'.

The fascinating thing about Irish history is that many unlikely people tried to reroute a long chapter of division and social disruption. Examples can readily be found. In the 1860s, Protestants like James McKnight (editor of *The Banner of Ulster*) and William Sharman Crawford (an extensive landowner) opposed government measures which they deemed offensive to Catholics. Together, they denounced Coercion

Acts seemingly favourable to the Protestant interest as 'the violence of property'. Crawford referred to eviction as 'extermination' of a people. On the other hand, the Catholic nationalist, Charles Gavan Duffy, defied sensitivities within his own tradition by collaboration with a noted Orange figure (Sam Gray) in establishing the Tenant League. Here are instances where a 'trans-sectarian class alliance' was attempted, even though, for extraneous reasons, it did not last. Here are men who addressed their own tradition but in doing so endeavoured to understand the world of 'the other'. On the surface they were ineffective, since their project did not survive. Yet, they are significant for our own day – they show that there can be innovative 'angles of vision' in the midst of prevalent hostility. There are precedents for 'tangents' to long-standing antagonisms

This study examines the work of clergymen from diverse traditions whose social and, sometimes, theological views made them 'unusual'. Without exception they incurred 'suspicion' either from their own authorities or from the organs of state. By 'unusual' I do not suggest that priests or ministers who contested social injustice were few and far between. Rather, I believe that the approach of the people studied here had an unusual radicalism or courage. At times, they were misguided or hasty or driven by personal idiosyncrasies. On the whole, they were ineffective. They did not bring their own tradition with them, much less the antagonistic traditions which marked their day.

With honourable exceptions – particularly the Society of Friends – the churches of all traditions seemed to shore up the antagonism. Today there is a perception that, on the whole, the leadership of these churches was either committed to the *status quo* or simply a conduit of bitter sectarianism. While the perception is understandable, it is not the whole story.

From a purely academic point of view, this exercise could be termed 'meandering'. My choice of individuals can be contested. It is undoubtedly subjective. Yet, it is not without rationale. Although history sheds few tears over 'losers', one has to ask about the definition of 'loser'. I believe many of the people examined here fashioned our history, although they were not 'winners' in the conventional sense. Their thought and their conviction go some way towards 'disintegrating the seeming coherence of antagonistic patterns'. To recall their work can have a power to heal in the present. To reconsider them now is not idle self-indulgence but rather to look at our past from different, sometimes ill-aligned, perspectives. Frank Wright's words splendidly express my reason for examining the thought and work of clergymen from different traditions: 'Insofar as the national conflict in Ireland is between groups dominated by "religious" identity, it is a question of searching for a history of ecumenism before the time when anyone thought of using that word.'[1]

I am aware that women are not represented here. The only reason for the omission is that, unfortunately, women were not ordained as clergy in any of the traditions at the times under study. My admiration for Mary Ann McCracken and for Margaret Anna Cusack (The Nun of Kenmare) renders me particularly aware of this limitation. In regard to the material which follows, I hope it is responsible history, written with the intention of manifesting that, in our diverse traditions, there were ministers of religion who cared for justice, for inclusion of all our people in the definition of a worthwhile society. Thus I hope to show how 'pessimistic judgements about the other, born out of real experiences, turned into righteous causes'[2].

1. In *Reconciling Memories,* ed Alan Falconer, Columba, 1988, pp 68-84. citations at pp 82 and 84. The extensive references here to Frank Wright's essay is accompanied by an enthusiastic endorsement of the thrust of his fine article.

PART ONE

The Eighteenth Century

INTRODUCTION

A Gathering Storm

Ireland of the 1790s was a dangerous place. More exactly, it was a precarious country for everyone outside the ascendancy class. 'Ascendancy' denoted Protestant ascendancy. Or, again to make a precision, it meant Anglican ascendancy. A declaration by the Corporation of Dublin spoke of ascendancy as 'A Protestant (Anglican) King of Ireland. A Protestant Parliament. A Protestant Hierarchy. Protestant electors and government, the benches of justice, the army and the revenue through all branches and details Protestant and this system supported by a connection with the Protestant realm of England'. There was, in essence, a triple ranking: Anglican, Dissenter and Catholic. State and polity were defined in terms of Anglican establishment.[1]

Penal laws, more or less severe, stood against Catholics and Dissenters, mainly Presbyterians. By definition, Catholics and Dissenters were excluded from higher offices of state and from upper ranks of the army. To be Anglican was to be 'in'; to be Catholic or Dissenter was, in different degrees, to be 'out'. Hence, in regard to eighteenth-century Ireland, there was a yawning divide between Catholics (the vast majority of the people) and the apparatus of state in the hands of the ruling Anglican 'elite'. Ascendancy presupposed a tactical alliance with Presbyterians against Catholics and was underpinned by confidence of British official support. Whenever there was a hint – as in the 1790s – that the Anglican-Dissenter alliance was under strain, the unfailing tactic of Ascendancy was to forestall Catholic-Dissenter alliance by sectarian innuendo. And if it appeared that British government was irresolute in defining Irish citizenship along Anglican lines, the Ascendancy resorted first to complaint and then to repression.

Sociologically, the circumstances resembled the *ancien regime* of pre-revolutionary France. In economic terms, late eighteenth century Ireland was indeed a 'distressful country' for the vast majority of the people. The 'settlement' of 1690 had consolidated an arrogant, selfish ruling class in a country devastated by a century of war. Through the eighteenth century this class built up its fortunes at the expense of the dispossessed. A further element was the virtual disqualification from political influence of anyone outside the Anglican communion. Many Presbyterians emigrated to America where they played a major role in politics – something denied them in Ireland. Young men of Catholic background emigrated mainly to France, Spain and Austria seeking advancement either in the army or the church.

By the 1790s, although Dublin wore a 'gorgeous mask' and Belfast showed signs of prosperity, a vast disenfranchised population remained hungry, ill-clothed, sick and diseased. Lacking civil and economic rights, they were at the mercy of landed magnates who retained the power of life and death over them. These circumstances were discounted by the relatively prosperous middle classes and the egregiously rich aristocracy. According to one historian, the rich 'maintained their equanimity, like people in Calcutta or New York today, by becoming blind to the sight of perpetual poverty and callous to the suffering involved'. Nevertheless, despite the apparent quiescence of a brow-beaten people, radical ideas coming from America and France suggested that change was possible given the right circumstances.[2]

Since 1782 College Green had been the seat of an autonomous Irish legislature. However, the Dublin parliament was in the pocket of a dominant clique whose rapacity matched its contempt for the larger population. Rabidly anti-Catholic, College Green underwrote the virtual exclusion of Presbyterians from the polity. In regard to religious emancipation, it continued to devise 'means of maintaining itself against a population to which it was clearly alien.' Led by Henry Grattan, a Whig party maintained opposition to the Castle administration but without much enthusiasm and, certainly, without much success. Irish Whigs feared Catholics as an unknown force which could not be trusted with political or civic power. On parliamentary reform, Whig politicians endeavoured to conciliate middle-class opinion but remained obdurately protective of the existing land 'settlement'. With Grattan, they acquiesced in harsh emergency laws after the commencement of England's war on France, even to the point of disbanding the Volunteers. From that date (1793), the 'war effort' caused grave hardship for the poor. Also, it induced hostility to government since people (by no means revolutionary) either sympathised with the French or disowned the war as none of Ireland's business.[3]

From the Williamite settlement there remained a minority of Catholic aristocrats who had avoided dispossession. At their head were the conservative Lords Kenmare, Fingal and Gormanstown. However, their co-existence with the authorities did not spare them the studied contempt of government. Nor, at this stage, were they respected by a newly confident group of middle-class Catholic spokespeople who regarded Kenmare's timid prudence as no better than servility. In fact, by the 1790s the Kenmare group was merely an aristocratic rump suspicious of radicalism and inveterately attached to the old system of deference. The emergence of a Catholic middle class proved an important factor in the turbulence of the 1790s. Prosperous businessmen like John Keogh and professionals such as Dr Wm McNeven vigorously demanded full Catholic emancipation. In a dramatic gesture, amounting almost to a secession, they hired Theobald Wolfe Tone as professional secretary of the Catholic Association. Tone's energy impelled a radical process of election to a Catholic Convention eventually held at Tailors' Hall, Dublin (December 1792).

Although such middle class radicalism should not be over-estimated, it is of considerable moment. Approving of the French Revolution (at least in its earlier stages), middle class Catholics were enthusiastic about democracy – provided it did not go too far. With Tone's help, they organised an expression of Catholic grievances by 'democratic' consultations throughout the parishes of Ireland. In the winter of 1792-3 Catholic activism and the emergence of liberalism in Ulster had made it probable that parliamentary reform might triumph.[4] It is noticeable that the Catholic Association had lessened the power of the aristocrats and bishops, to the great discomfiture of the latter two groups. Perhaps most significant of all is an emergent readiness on the part of many lay Catholics to co-operate with northern Dissenters in the demand for parliamentary reform and religious emancipation. Here, one can discern the influence of Tone and perhaps of Tone's new friend, Thomas Russell.

Such influence brought with it an openness towards comprehensive religious emancipation, viz. the removal of disabilities still affecting Protestant Dissenters such as Presbyterians and the Society of Friends.

Apart from disadvantages mentioned above, the situation of the great body of the people is far less clear. The Catholic 'nation' had been dispossessed after the treaty of Limerick. Now, people held small plots of land at the whim of a new and despised aristocracy. Memories of better times fuelled agrarian resistance. In the countryside were groups such as 'Ribbonmen' and 'Defenders'. In the towns, people worked in menial tasks either for the new 'aristocracy' or in even less inviting situations. Dublin, now second only to London in imperial prestige, was beset by widespread poverty. In the Liberties, in the Coombe, in the alleyways near Dublin Castle ('Hell'), the usual accompaniments of deprivation prevailed – appallingly bad housing and endemic disease. For the poor, the institutional church seemed to do little. Perhaps it could not do much more. Yet, a symptom of ecclesiastical conservatism is the reservation of seats in chapel for 'better class' Catholics while 'inferiors' were rigidly precluded from occupying these honoured places.

Many of the poor (discerning that even their own church deemed them second-rate members) did not attend Mass. Episcopal references to 'lower orders' (apart from acquiescing in the class-distinctions of the time) locate the mentality of these bishops, viz. warily but not uncomfortably alongside the *status quo*. In the course of the 1790s, radicalism gained increasing purchase with both urban and rural poor. Through the countryside (in the northern counties, in east Leinster, in parts of Munster and in Connacht) Defender lodges proliferated. An evidence of this is the repression visited on the west of Ireland in 1796 by Lord Carhampton with the connivance of Camden, the viceroy. In the cities, particularly after the Convention Act forbade assemblies, workingmen's clubs and philanthropic societies became an effective cover for meetings of a more radical kind. The overspill from revolutionary France (which some bishops termed 'the French disease') meant that in Dublin people called each other 'citizen' and cropped their hair in the style of the French Jacobins.

Among priests there is evidence of some openness to democracy. Nor is this surprising since from their training on the continent many had become acquainted with democratic ideas. Having witnessed the exactions, evictions and cruelties of the Camden regime, the priests gained new understanding of the need for reform. When Wm Corbet, an informer to Dublin Castle, drew up his report on the political stances of Catholic clergy in Dublin, it is surprising how many priests he could label 'violent democrats'. In such context at least two of our 'Unusual Suspects', Frs Coigly and Prendergast, can be understood. To the Archbishop of Dublin (Troy), and the equally conservative Bishop of Ferns (Caulfield), all this was a symptom of 'the French mania'. Dublin priests had called for 'a new Catholic reformation', for optional celibacy, for election of the clergy by laity. In 1792, Fr Robert McEvoy, a curate in

Swords, Co Dublin, decided to marry while remaining in his ministry.

Just as the linkage of Catholics and Presbyterians represented the worst nightmare of the Camden regime, for the bishops such 'unsoundness' among priests was the harbinger of ecclesiastical disintegration. And so, Fr McEvoy was excommunicated. Dire warnings against disaffection were uttered in Troy's *Duties of Christian Subjects* – a compendium of the most reactionary theology. The bishops were indeed engaged in local strategies – for Troy, a chief priority was to set up Maynooth College. Yet, episcopal stances also reflect Roman interests – Papal and British interests were at one in opposing the French. As loyal servants of the institutional church, the bishops pursued these interests even to the cost of identifying Catholicism with counter-revolution and, sometimes, to the cost of their own flocks.[5]

And what of the north, where several of the following chapters are set? In Ulster, there was a powerful ascendancy both civil and ecclesiastical. From 1793, they obdurately discountenanced reform. The Knoxes (Lord Northland), the Chicesters (Lord Donegall), the Stewarts (Lord Londonderry), the Hills (Lord Downshire), viewed talk of parliamentary reform and Catholic emancipation with suspicion, albeit in various degrees. Due to the nature of government, these families had easy access to the highest offices in the land. With immense power and little accountability they resembled the corrupt aristocracy of pre-revolutionary France. R. R. Madden describes the context in dramatic terms : '… the great landed proprietor, who was not only lord of the soil, but, virtually, the lord of the law also, was, in reality, the supreme arbiter of life and death in his locality, … at every period when a pretext was made for … consolidating their own privileges.'[6]

Beneath these, the countryside was ruled by squires and parsons of the Anglican ascendancy. The squire or 'secular gentleman' lived off rents collected from struggling tenants while the vicar or 'religious gentleman' lived off tithes extracted from the same people.[7] It boded ill for Christian faith that parsons were frequently magistrates hated by the poor. Often, too, they were the agents of landed magnates with vested interests in the exaction of rents and tithes. Decades later, Thomas Moore criticised a church establishment which:

'armed at once with prayer books and with whips,
blood on their hands, and Scripture on their lips,
tyrants by creed and torturers by text,
make this life hell, in honour of the next.'[8]

Yet, there were presages of change. Through the 1780s the Volunteer movement showed increasing openness to religious emancipation and, even, parliamentary reform. Lords Charlemont and Moira had expressed sentiments which in the context of the time seemed promising. Even Robert Stewart, Lord Londonderry, was perceived to be of the reforming party. In relative terms, democracy was in the air. By the 1790s among the urban middle classes there was guarded enthusiasm for the French Revolution. This lessened as Robespierre's France moved towards 'the Terror'. Nevertheless, Dublin, Belfast and other parts of the north had dangerous potential from the government's point of view. The mercantile community at Belfast, mainly Presbyterian and therefore outside the Ascendancy, had interests in the reform instituted by the American revolution and now by the French.

Culturally developed and economically prosperous, they nonetheless found themselves relegated to the margins of political influence. Their fortunes had been made, or were in process of being made, in distilling, tanning, weaving and milling. Already Samuel Neilson had amassed a considerable fortune which he ploughed into the liberal newspaper the *Northern Star*. Others – for example, the McCabes and the Simms – manufactured cotton, linen, and textiles. As well, there were smaller businesses: carpentry, ropemaking, chandling, etc. An improved harbour, linking Belfast to Europe and America, was the base for the town's continued prosperity. From among Belfast families – the McCrackens, the Simms, the McCabes –

radical thinkers emerged and, as the decade progressed, leaders of the United Irish society. The town had its problems but they were those of a community in process of expansion. It still was congested and dirty, 'with dunghills a constant nuisance in the streets and pigs wandering at will'.[9] Belfast, nonetheless, had an extremely active cultural life – from 1791 it boasted the successful *Northern Star* while the radical works of Paine, Priestly, Godwin, Voltaire and Rousseau were available through *Northern Star* publications and the Belfast Society for the Promotion of Knowledge.

One can say, then, that the political temper was distinctly 'advanced' if not radical. Perhaps due to its Presbyterian temper, the Belfast community 'disliked prelacy, aristocracy, privilege and the entire hierarchical system central to eighteenth century government and society'.[10] The Revolution in France had an especial impact due to extensive trading links with that country. Quite naturally, the new ideas of free trade and middle class influence in politics were favoured by merchants and tradespeople. Democracy and republicanism, the ideals of liberty, fraternity and equality, were valued to the point that Belfast was termed 'the Athens of the north'. Nevertheless, these were middle-class values untested by conflict. Such 'transcendental politics' did not encompass the plight of excluded classes like the tenants, the workmen and day-labourers. In France, the *sans culottes* had yet to emerge as a political force. In America, there was studied neglect of black people's rights. It would take several years and the consistency of a Mary Ann McCracken, a James Hope, a Thomas Russell, to apply the new ideas for the benefit of the labourers, the domestic servants, the small tenant farmers. Despite this reserve, it should be noted that a Whig club in Belfast was generous enough to resolve (Oct 1790): '... the Protestant dissenters ... will on all occasions support their (the Catholics') just claim to the enjoyment of the rights and privileges of free born citizens, entitled to fill every office, and serve in whatever station their country may think proper to call them to.'[11]

In Ulster, many poorer people were of Presbyterian faith.
Throughout the north, weavers, cottiers and tenant farmers
eked a difficult existence, all too frequently harassed by agents
of landlord or parson. A common Protestantism was sometimes used to unite tenant and landlord against Catholic
worker or tenant or middleman. When this happened it was
usually to the benefit of landlord or parson. When it came to
emolument or rent or civil office, Presbyterians felt themselves disadvantaged almost as much as their Catholic neighbours. In such a context, Russell, Neilson and other United
Irish leaders stressed that divisions benefitted only the establishment. Their remedy was 'a cordial union of all Irishmen'.
Or, as Fr James Coigly noted, it was 'of great utility to the
Irish government that religious disputes should exist between
Dissenters and Catholics'.[12] For radicals, no political progress
could be made until Catholics and Dissenters united 'to iso-
late the Irish executive and overthrow the power of the
Anglican Protestant Ascendancy'.[13]

How far they were successful in forging such unity remains
a matter of debate – the cordial union of Irishmen was a distant ideal when the United Irish society was founded in
October 1791. Yet, discontent with government, poor living
conditions, rents and tithes, brought many Catholics and
Presbyterians into sympathy with French ideals as well as
some understanding of each other's situation. Thomas Russell
noted this sympathy and commented: 'When the majority
feel themselves slaves they will resist ... Information being diffused will produce this'. Presumably, he meant the sophisti-
cated means of popular instruction then under way among
the northern United Irishmen. and propagated by the
Northern Star.[14] By 1794, the temper of the country was
changing towards radicalism. The Reverend Edward Hudson
(Jonesborough, Co Armagh) noted in August of that year:

'The change in the natives here is truly astonishing.
Formerly a newspaper would have been a phenomenon
amongst them. At present they vie with the northerns *(sic)*

in their thirst after knowledge. He who can read has generally a large audience about the door of his cabin, whilst he
is endeavouring to enlighten his countrymen.'[15]

For an understanding of late eighteenth-century Ireland, the
especial role of the Presbyterian minister should be noted.
More fully identified with his congregation, he was corres-
pondingly more likely to join in their complaints against government. It has been argued that, independent of the views of
individual ministers, the eighteenth-century Presbyterian
ministry was itself a subversive institution. Since it was not an
'established' institution it could retain detachment from the
'stake in the country' mentality. Certainly, many Presbyterian
clergymen were involved with the radical politics of the 1790s:
Porter (Greyabbey), Barber (Rathfriland), Warwick (Kirk-
cubbin), McMahon (Hollywood), Birch (Saintfield), Kelbourne
(Belfast) and Steel Dickson (Portaferry). Yet, while noting
such radicalism, one should not exaggerate it. It has been argued that the majority of Presbyterian ministers were conservative in outlook, viewing rebellion 'as the sin of witchcraft'.[16]

From 1795 presages of storm multiplied. There was resentment among a hard-pressed tenantry at exactions by landlords (rents) and parsons (tithes). Repression in Connacht
(1796) and Ulster (1797) could be declared legal only because
the law was revised to legitimate such repression. Sectarian
riots in Armagh, the favouritism of biased magistrates, and re-
current shortages of food added to the misery. And there was
naked fear – to his credit, Dr Dickson, Anglican Bishop of
Down, protested that drunken soldiers and yeomen were visiting women and children with 'every species of indignity, brutality and outrage'. About the same time, General Sir Ralph
Abercrombie denounced the state of the soldiery and, for his
pains, was replaced by the martinet General Gerald Lake .[17]

Hence, one better understands Thomas Russell's comment
that people joined the 'system', viz. the United Irishmen, as a
refuge from the distress now visited on the country. If many

people looked to France and even spoke of French intervention, it was not from admiration of Robespierre or the
Directory which replaced him. All the indications are that
Russell and, even, Tone were lukewarm about French intervention. They mistrusted French rule as much as they detested
Dublin Castle or Whitehall. The question was how French
intervention could be limited to assistance rather than hegemony. When the storm broke in 1798, loyalist publicists set to
work on explaining it in terms convenient to loyalism. For Sir
Hector Langrishe, the country was happily and justly governed – 'the country was prospering, the poor were lightly
taxed'. While Richard Musgrave blamed the Catholic Church
– even Troy of Dublin – for the outbreak, Langrishe saw the
problem in the 'jargon of equality ... diffused through a de-
luded multitude by designing men ... to break the bonds of
society and set up the capriciousness of the popular will
against the stability of settled government'.[18]

Against such background, James Porter of Greyabbey and
William Steel Dickson of Portaferry are situated. Their bitter
criticism of a corrupt and often brutal establishment lies
within the context of exaction and repression. Their closely
reasoned theologico-political stances have been sadly neglected
in more recent times. Yet Porter's *Billy Bluff* swept the north
for more than one generation. Steel Dickson has been termed
'the most influential United Irishman of the North' (Brendan
Clifford). On the Catholic scene, Fr Coigly's enthusiasm for
French help and the welcome shown by Fr Prendergast to
Humbert's landing at Killala (August 1798) should also be es-
timated as a brave, if desperate, attempt to contest a systemic
injustice. There were, of course, many 'unusual suspects' – at
least fifteen ministers and nine probationary ministers of the
Presbyterian church; sixty Catholic priests were implicated
(nine were killed in action); one Church of Ireland priest,
Henry Fulton, was accused of sedition in 1798.[19]

CHAPTER ONE

THE IRISH-BRITISH-FRENCH TRIANGLE

Fr James Coigly (1761-1798)

James Coigly (also O'Coigley, Coigley, Quigley and O'Quigley) was born in August 1761 at Kilmore, Co Armagh where his family had farming and weaving interests. His background, therefore, is that middling group which despite the no-popery laws could prosper and even become rich. Families such as Coigly's were vividly conscious of earlier plantations and penal laws which made them non-citizens in their own country. Access to the professions was extremely limited. There were indeed such prosperous Catholics as the Sweetmans of Wexford, the Teelings of Lisburn, the McGennises of Dromantine (Newry) and John Keogh of Dublin. Their wealth had been acquired in commerce and, almost by accident, in landed interests. As well, there were people such as Dr William McNeven who had attained prominence as a medical doctor. Nevertheless, penal laws designating Catholics as inferior remained not merely unrepealed but even were reaffirmed. Catholic schools might be opened but only with the permission of a Protestant bishop. Land could be acquired freehold but only where such tenure had no political effects. As to political office of any significant kind, for Catholics and Protestant Dissenters this was out of the question.[1]

In these circumstances, it is not surprising that families such as Coigly's should retain memories of their connection with the old Gaelic order. At the end of his life, Fr Coigly wrote of his family's role at the battle of Aughrim and in the siege of Derry. Aspiring young people of Coigly's background looked either to the church or to foreign army service as outlets for their talents and enthusiasm. Major sacrifices were made to acquire education in hedge schools and in some secondary colleges. In this context, James Coigly was sent to the Dundalk Grammar School for higher studies. Here he was introduced to classical studies and, particularly, Latin. The possibility that this was a Protestant school may account for his later appreciation of the common interests of many Catholics and Protestants. Likewise, it is notable that he consistently refused to equate criticism of Orange depredation with hostility to Protestants as such.

After his studies in Dundalk, Coigly entered the priesthood in the archdiocese of Armagh. In January 1785, he was ordained by the Coadjutor Bishop of Armagh, Richard O'Reilly, at Dungannon. Later in the year he set out for the Lombard College in Paris, then a centre for Irish students. This college, a constituent of the University of Paris, had passed to Irish control by letters patent from Louis XIV in 1677. In the early eighteenth century it had become the sole college for Irish students in Paris. Some of these were preparing for church ministry while others concentrated on law, medicine or surgery. Still others aspired to army service with the Irish Brigade. Coigly's status as an ordained priest gave him access to the College des Lombards. He could procure some income through Mass-stipends and other services in the surrounding churches of Paris.[2]

By the 1780s the college was directed by John Baptiste Walsh, formerly of the Irish College at Nantes. The history of the college discloses a fractious student body always ready to protest at derogation from its rights. There is some evidence that Walsh maintained a harsh discipline which was resented by the students. Fr Coigly's enthusiastic temperament soon led him to organise opposition to the college regime. Likewise, he actively litigated about a burse which, he believed, had been unjustly denied him. He seems to have regarded a form of class distinction as the reason why the bursary was given to another student. During a lengthy dispute which reached the French courts, he was more than once

threatened with imprisonment.[3] Eventually, the dispute led
to Coigly's departure from the Irish College after five years'
studies in philosophy and theology.

For a while, he lived privately in the city and there is some
suggestion, although unverified, that he took part in the capture of the Bastille on 14 July 1789. Certain it is that another
student of the Lombard college, James Blackwell, led a detachment from the Faubourg St Antoine in that historic
event. The outbreak of revolution had drastically altered the
situation of most clerics, whatever their views. The memoir
written by Fr Coigly shortly before his death tells of a narrow
escape from 'lanternisation' by an angry crowd who mistook
his clerical garb for royalist sympathies. It has been shown
that indiscreet behaviour by Irish students on the Champ de
Mars incurred hostile attention to the Irish College on the Rue
des Carmes.[4] For reasons none too clear, Fr Coigly quit Paris
in October 1789. Travelling by Dieppe and Brighton he
reached Ireland in the closing months of that year.

When James Coigly returned, he became part of a larger
body of Catholic clergy whose education had benefitted by
six or more years in France. Of them, Lecky later wrote: 'no
subsequent generation of Irish priests have left so good a reputation as the better class of those who were educated in
France … they brought with them a foreign culture and a foreign grace which did much to embellish Irish life'.[5] Coigly
was not the only French-trained priest to bring with him an
openness to social and ecclesiastical change, a mistrust of the
society of deference then prevalent. Although he had left revolutionary France in haste, it is clear that he was imbued with
its egalitarianism and its insistence (at least in the Revolution's
early stages) on the disestablishment of a comfortably en-
sconced church. It is frequently overlooked that many Irish
Catholic priests and friars did not share the pragmatic conservatism of prelates such as Troy, Moylan and Caulfield. These
bishops, perhaps for strategic institutional reasons, lost no opportunity to denounce Defender activities and to protest

their abhorrence of the French revolutionary system. Thus one can read the denunciation by Bishop Caulfield (Ferns) of 'the unnatural business of uniting' as an attempt to distance institutional Catholicism from the rising of 1798. Nevertheless, the careers of clergymen such as Coigly, Martin, McGinnis, Prendergast and others would suggest that there was an ideological pluralism among the Catholic clergy on the question of radical social change.

Dundalk

In the 1790s, Dundalk, though a relatively small town, enjoyed civil and ecclesiastical importance. At most, Fr Coigly worked for three years in directly pastoral ministry although it is unclear what ecclesiastical duties he performed. Later allusions to his practical charity and the affection he had won in Dundalk, suggest that some of his work lay among the poor of the area. A rapid involvement in political activities may have caused him to leave settled work in Dundalk. As was the case with nearby Drogheda, Dundalk's social and political reference leaned northwards to Antrim, Down, Armagh and Tyrone. Since the political travail of those counties had spilled over into Louth and Meath, both Dundalk and Drogheda were important centres of Defender activities. At this stage the Defenders were in process of national, as distinct from purely local, reorganisation. It seems that Coigly introduced the Dublin activist, James Napper Tandy to Defender leaders in the Dundalk area. Certainly, Tandy was sworn as a Defender at Castlebellingham, Co Louth, before the end of 1792. Insofar as he had forged such links, Coigly had already gone beyond the official stances of his church which condemned Defenderism in the most hostile terms.[6]

Recent studies show that Defenderism was a more complex phenomenon than presented heretofore. Defenders were not always rural brawlers perpetrating mindless 'outrages'. They did, indeed, work by overt intimidation and were guilty of more than one murder. Yet, as its name suggests, 'Defenderism' was reactive to land expropriations in earlier plantations. At least in part, it was a form of resistance by the dispossessed who had been declared non-citizens in their own land. While there had been many forms of agrarian unrest during the earlier part of the eighteenth century, Defenderism was most active wherever landlords' arrogance, magistrates' partiality and, from the mid-1790s, Orange harassment were at their height. Through the 1790s, Defender groups were particularly energetic in Armagh, Tyrone, Monaghan, Cavan, Louth and Meath. Likewise, they operated in those parts of Down where Lord Hillsborough owned extensive lands. Defenderism was also widespread in Leitrim, Galway and Roscommon.

The savage repression of those suspected of Defenderism means that evidence about the movement comes from self-interested informers or from official reports. Invariably, Defenders were represented as bloodthirsty ruffians whose creed was mayhem and whose objective was murder. In July 1795, Camden's extended memorandum to Whitehall secured *carte blanche* for repression of Defenderism. The atrocities of Lord Carhampton in Connacht drew horrified comment from the United Irish leader Thomas Russell. Despite the tensions between Defenderist emphasis on Catholic grievance and the United Irish gospel of non-sectarianism, it is clear that from the mid-1790s the two organisations were closely allied. As to Defenderism, an outline political and economic programme began to replace what had been uncoordinated expressions of resentment. In opposition to a now ferocious regime, in desire for change, and in openness to French help under certain conditions, United Irishmen and Defenders entered a common cause. Despite this communality, there is some evidence that the United Irish leaders tried to curb Defender activity lest it issue in premature revolution.

Coigly's readiness to contest perceived injustice is already clear from his brief but turbulent career at the College des Lombards. On his return home he identified with the Catholics of Ulster whose security was minimal and whose disqualifications were multiple. It is, perhaps, understandable that he established cordial links with the Defender society of which his cousin, Valentine Derry, was principal for Co Louth. 'Switcher' Donnelly, a prominent Tyrone Defender, was his first cousin while a Captain Quigley, prominently involved in the battle of the Diamond (September 1795), is reputed to have been his brother.[7] From his base in Dundalk, Fr Coigly increasingly entered the politics of social change, viz. relief of Catholic disabilities and some measure of parliamentary reform. Personal connections with members of the Catholic Committee gave him access to a radical middle-class group hostile to both the conservative bishops (Troy, Moylan, etc) and the Catholic aristocracy led by Lord Kenmare. In the north-east, people like Charles Teeling (Lisburn), John Magennis (Newry) and Bernard Coyle (Armagh) had begun to link social reform and revolutionary politics.[8]

Coigly's main contribution may well have been to cement an alliance between the United Irishmen and the Defenders. He seems to have had major influence in persuading radicalised Catholics towards 'a cordial union of affection' among Irish people of whatever religious persuasion. This activity marked him out for attention by government. Thus, John Foster, speaker of the House of Parliament, later spoke of him as 'busy and meddling'.

Contact by this group in the Louth/Armagh district with Belfast radicals and several Presbyterian clergymen in Co Down was producing a formidable coalition. It was an axis which eventually led to that 'nightmare of the Establishment', the Jacobinising of the secret societies.[9] The evidence is strong that Coigly enjoyed the trust of Belfast radicals as well as of Defender leaders. Of Presbyterian United Irishmen he later wrote: 'They were lovers of liberty and republicans by religion and descent, their concurrence in the system (i.e. United Irish) was not unimportant ... Covenanters in numbers became United Irishmen, and the most active promoters of the system'.[10] The inveterately hostile Richard Musgrave claims

that Coigly was a member of the United Irish council for
Ulster and was sufficiently deep in the confidence of the national directory to have access, in January 1797, to their assembly in Dundalk.[11] The priest's importance in the northern
United Irish organisation may well date from the first wave of
arrests in Autumn 1796 which robbed the association of its
most determined leaders. According to McEvoy, Coigly was
sworn into the United Irish society at Merrion Street, the
Dublin home of Valentine Lawless. His association with
Arthur O'Connor and Lord Edward Fitzgerald gives a clue to
his proximity to the society's deliberations on the question of
French intervention.[12]

Writings

Fr Coigly seems to have shared the literary proclivities of
radical activists like Russell and Neilson. Most probably, he
wrote the pamphlet attributed to 'J. Byrne' detailing outrages
against Catholics in Co Armagh from 1784 to 1791.[13] This
pamphlet had a political thrust similar to that developing at
Belfast among the Presbyterian radicals. Like the United Irish
leaders, Coigly believed that in Armagh there was a virtual
civil war with 'religion made the pretext'. And like the United
Irishmen, he diagnosed that such divisions suited an increasingly oppressive regime. On this he had some authority since
in 1791, 1792 and 1793 he had travelled through Randalstown,
Maghera, Dungiven, Newtown and Magilligan on 'uniting
business'.[14] Here is a further indication that from the early
1790s Coigly was acquainted with the United Irish leadership
at Belfast.

At the height of sectarian violence during 1795 Coigly's
family home in Armagh was burned by what he later termed a
'King and Church' mob – an epithet for marauding Orangemen. His own library (his 'choice collection of books') was
destroyed. Among his papers was material for a history of the
1641 rebellion in Ireland. This gives insight to his preoccupation with the history of Catholic dispossession, so much part
of Defender motivation.

Links between Covenanters, Defenders and United Irishmen

As already noted, some years after the priest's death, Richard Musgrave bitterly described his influence among both Defenders and United Irishmen. Some uncertainty persists about the date of Coigly's recruitment to the United Irish society. Brendan McEvoy places it 'probably in May or June 1796'. (A collateral descendant of Fr Coigly's argues that the priest was not in fact a member of the society although closely sympathetic to its work.) This is the period when a merger took place between Defenders and United Irishmen. It is worthy of note that some of the negotiations for the merger were conducted in Dundalk, Coigly's town of residence. Historians of the period give Russell, Tandy and Coigly a pivotal role in the amalgamation. From radically different backgrounds, these men occupied an important place in the spreading movement for social and political change.

From 1795 to 1797 Fr Coigly operated in the triangle from Dundalk to Tyrone and thence to Belfast. According to his *Life*, his travels through the area were incessant. When, in 1797, the Armagh freeholders petitioned the reigning King for redress in the wake of Thomas Birch's murder by Orangemen, Coigly visited towns and villages enjoining on people 'to do their duty'.[15] At this time, too, he assisted the campaign mounted by United Irishmen to defend small farmers and weavers charged under the Insurrection Act. During 1797 a pamphlet entitled *A View of the Present State of Ireland* re-echoed the United Irish line on the need for a 'union of affection', on the history of sectarian division, and on criticism of military repression. James Hope later wrote of this pamphlet that it 'contained more truth than all the volumes I have seen written on the events of 1797 and 1798'. Réamonn Ó Muirí has cogently argued that the pamphlet is from the pen of Coigly.[16] Ó Muirí sees the pamphlet as 'an argument for civil rights in Ireland and Britain, an end to repressive measures, a call to freedom and democracy'. 'Observer' – the nom-de-plume of the pamphlet's author – praises United Irish efforts

to reconcile Irishmen and to bring the Defenders to good relations with Protestants. As well, he details the chain of atrocities committed against Catholics by Peep o' Day boys,
Orangemen and the military itself.

Activity in England and France

Fr Coigly's growing prominence met a proportionate –
and very hostile – attention from the state authorities. Feeling
that he was in danger from Castlereagh, Beresford and
Annesley, he moved in Summer 1797 to Manchester. After arrests in Dundalk, Coigly was warned of his own danger.
Despite an initial hesitation, he quit Dundalk, went to
Liverpool, and thence to Manchester. This course of action
should be linked to what Marianne Elliott had termed 'a
minor exodus' of United Irish leaders dissatisfied with their
executive's procrastination on the matter of a rising.[17] Fr
Coigly's decision to settle at Manchester perhaps was motivated
by the existence of sizeable disaffection among the Lancashire
textile workers. It has been noted that his views on social
change went beyond many of his colleagues in the United
Irish society. Unlike the somewhat patrician leadership of the
Dublin branch, he argued for 'a union of all the underprivi-
leged against their social superiors'.[18] While there are re-
echoes here of Thomas Russell, Henry Joy McCracken and
James Hope, the urgency on Coigly's part to link radical elements in Ireland, England and Scotland is of especial significance.

At Manchester, Coigly helped to extend the Society of
United Britons. This urban-based movement represented a
new departure among the English working-class for objectives defined by themselves rather than upper-class radicals.
Coigly seems to have worked with considerable effectiveness
among the United Britons throughout the north-east of
England. Meanwhile, he retained contact with the advanced
wing of the Belfast United Irishmen. By the end of Summer
1797 he had left Manchester for London where the United
Britons (meeting at Furnival's Inn in Holborn, London) en-

deavoured to co-ordinate English radicals with their counter-
parts in Ireland, Scotland and France. Elliott remarks: 'As in
Manchester, the main impetus behind the London organisation had come from Coigly.'[19] Thus, Fr Coigly had helped to
propagate the democratic or republican system in Bolton,
Stockport, Warrington, Nottingham, Liverpool and
Birmingham as well as in London.

With the Reverend Arthur MacMahon, erstwhile Presbyterian minister at Hollywood, Co Down, Fr Coigly travelled, first to Hamburg (where there was a sizeable group of
Irish exiles) and thence to Paris. MacMahon's association with
those who in 1797 had argued for a rising even without
French help, raises the question of whether this was Coigly's
view also.[20] On the continent, Coigly became embroiled in
the troubled relationships among Irish republicans. The relationship of Wolfe Tone and Napper Tandy, never cordial, had
deteriorated gravely in their competition for leadership of the
Irish group. In December 1797, these intrigues among the
emigrés led the French directory to deny further passports to
Irish people. The dissensions at Paris reflect both the flam-
boyance of Tandy and the sensitivity of Tone. Coigly seems to
have supported Tandy with whom he had earlier worked in
Dundalk. Tone wrote of 'these dirty little intrigues ... which I
scorn to commit to paper'. As a result, Tone's opinion of the
priest became extremely jaundiced and only altered – even
then ambiguously – after Coigly's death.[21]

Coigly's visit to France was certainly about United Irish af-
fairs – he submitted a memorial to the Foreign Ministry at
Paris. Yet, it can also be linked to his work among radicals in
England. It may be no accident that his visit to Paris over-
lapped with the presence of the Scottish radical, Thomas
Muir, who had escaped from imprisonment in Botany Bay.
Muir was now claiming to speak for republicans in England,
Scotland and Ireland; likewise, he was pressing for a French
expedition to Scotland rather than Ireland.[22] At the end of
1797 Coigly returned to Ireland. During a brief stay in Dublin

where he lodged at Usher's Island, he presented a report on the Irish group in Paris to Lord Edward Fitzgerald. Unknown to him, and doubtless to the other Irish emigrés, Samuel Turner was forwarding detailed reports to Dublin Castle. As a result, it is likely that Coigly was being shadowed by Castle officials from the point of his entry to the country and during his stay in Dublin.

In Dublin, feuding was rife between the United Irish leaders. It centred on mistrust of the Irish delegates already in France. As well, while some of the leaders were anxious for a rising, others were unwilling to sanction armed rebellion. The disagreement mirrored tension between the northern United Irish and those in Dublin. In that disagreement Coigly shared the more militant view that further delay spelled disaster. On these lines one may suppose that the object of an ill-organised trip to France in February 1798 by Fr Coigly, Arthur O'Connor and John Binns was to secure French help through an invasion of Ireland. O'Connor had been designated by the militants to replace Samuel Lewins, now the object of suspicion. Through January the enigmatic O'Connor had dallied in London; it was only on Coigly's arrival in February 1798 that the journey to France was put under way.

Margate and Afterwards

In the London house of Valentine Lawless, Coigly, O'Connor and – fatally – Samuel Turner settled the details of the mission to France. On February 27, Coigly and O'Connor set out by separate routes for Margate where they were to embark for the continent. The circumstances of this return to France remain enveloped in the mists of subsequent tragedy. Certainly, Coigly had made contact with United Britons in London and, probably, with Irish republicans in the city. Unknown to him, Bow Street Runners, the police of the day, were on his trail even in London. Travelling in rudimentary disguise, Coigly (Captain Jones) and O'Connor (Captain Morris) proceeded without hindrance as far as Margate. O'Connor's behaviour, never discreet, gave rise to suspicion that he, as well as Turner, was an informer. The arrest of 'Captain Jones' and 'Captain Morris' along with their 'servants' took place early on February 28 1798 when Bow Street Runners swooped on the King's Head Inn. Unfortunately for Coigly, his 'blue spencer greatcoat' (which lay on a chair in the breakfast room) contained an address from the United Britons as well as his own pocket book. The document (specifically from Benjamin Binns) pledged support for the French directory in the event of an invasion of Britain. Floridly and with some exaggeration, the document put it: 'Already have the English fraternised with the Irish and Scots ... a delegate from each now sits with us ... and United Britain burns to break her chains ... we now only wait with impatience to see the hero of Italy and the brave veterans of the great nation.'[23]

Coigly, O'Connor and three companions were taken to the Watch House at Margate where they were indicted for treason. Some days later (6 March) they were lodged in the Tower of London and separately examined by the Privy Council. A month later (7 April) they were returned to the county jail at Maidstone for trial by special commission. On 10 April, a Grand Jury of the commission returned them for trial which eventually commenced on 21 May 1798.

Pre-Trial Incidents

The weeks before the Maidstone trial disclose more than one happening instructive on the nuances of Irish and British politics. Correspondence between William Wickham (Whitehall) and Edward Cooke (Dublin Castle) shows the administration's determination to stamp out radical movements in Ireland and England no matter the cost. Towards mid-March Wickham informed Cooke of a passport found in Coigly's luggage. The passport, used by the priest during his sojourn in France in 1797, tells us in broad outline of his physical appearance: 'height, five feet four inches; hair and eyebrows, greyish; nose, medium; eyes, blue; mouth, medium; chin, round; face, round and full'. On the other hand, years later

Valentine Lawless later described the priest as 'striking in appearance and tall'.[24]

Although his activities were disconsonant with official stances of the Catholic hierarchy, Fr Coigly seems at no stage to have been remiss either in his sacerdotal obligations or his commitment to the Catholic faith. Indeed, the opposite appears the case, given his anxiety to obtain the services of a Catholic priest during his imprisonment. His request for such ministration occasioned unseemly manoeuvres which do little credit to the civil power or to the hierarchical leadership in the London area. Wickham informed Cooke on 21 April 1798 that much would depend on the choice of priest to visit Coigly and that 'as pains are taking to make it a good one I have hopes that Coigly will make a full disclosure of everything'.[25] The priest chosen was a Father Griffiths who more than amply justified Wickham's hopes. Griffiths had already colluded with government in breaking the naval mutiny of the Nore. Now, he seems equally pliant to government by insisting that Fr Coigly make full 'discoveries' (about O'Connor and the radical movements) before absolution could be given. Such compliance approaches professional misconduct for a priest. It contrasts with the reaction of Archbishop Troy who, for all his co-operation with Dublin Castle, brusquely refused the Castle's suggestion that the confessional be used to 'pacify' the people. Griffiths, by using his leverage as a confessor to elicit information, caused needless trouble for Coigly. Fr Coigly's own words reflect both chagrin and an exemplary charity: 'A certain venerable and pious-looking brother was dispatched from London to attend and assist me in the spiritual way ... during nine days he stayed with me ... to engage me to make what he called important discoveries ... I have not been able to obtain his absolution as yet, nor will I have it on such terms.'[26]

Trial at Maidstone
The trial of Coigly, O'Connor and their associates remains full of inconsistencies. O'Connor was acquitted after charac-

ter references from leading Whig politicians who hoped by
his acquittal to gain political capital in the House of Parliament. Immediately afterwards, he was spirited from the court
by his friends. Coigly, however, was left to his own devices
and even Dublin Castle officials commented wryly on the de-
sertion – 'there was no one to speak for him'. After a hostile
summation by Judge Buller, Fr Coigly was sentenced to death
with the lurid accompaniments of drawing and quartering.

An aura of miscarriage has surrounded his case, reminiscent of many subsequent political trials. Informers in the
United Irish Society were at work but could not be produced
in court. Thus, in regard to evidence, there was glaring insuf-
ficiencies which would be fatal to a present-day prosecution.
A Bow Street policeman gave inconsistent evidence on the
document alleged to have been in Coigly's overcoat An informer of little credibility, Frederick Dutton, 'proved' Coigly's
handwriting from a ticket allegedly signed by the priest for a
charity lottery at Dundalk. An English Whig, Lord Holland,
would later aver: 'O'Coigly *(sic)* was condemned on false and
contradictory evidence.'[27] Another politician, subsequently
Lord Chancellor Thurlow, is quoted: 'if ever a poor man was
murdered it was O'Coigly'. As to the document of the United
Britons – which convicted the priest – there is a suggestion it
was planted on his clothing. Over forty years later, O'Connor
claimed 'there was not legal evidence that the paper found in
Coigly's pocket was Coigly's'. Yet with typical ambiguity on
his allegiances he also wrote: '(Coigly) never made a secret to
his fellow-prisoners that he got that paper from a London society'.

The closing hours of Coigly's life are full of poignancy.
They disclose at once his courage, his humour, his attachment to his priesthood as well as his dedication to liberty and
justice. John Binns, a fellow prisoner, remembered Fr Coigly's
refusal to inform on him even though promised a reprieve:
'Though heavily ironed, he pushed the gentlemen out of his
cell, when he there lay under sentence of death.'[28] Fr Coigly

was executed at Penenden Heath, Maidstone on 1798. Though largely overlooked in studies of Irish republicanism, (with the exceptions of fine work by Frs Raymond Murray and Brendan McEvoy), he is remembered in a stained glass window and plaque at St Francis of Assisi Church, Maidstone.

A Forgotten Critic of Injustice

History, we are told, sheds few tears over losers. That judgement is exact, especially in regard to many academic histories. They tend to honour winners and discredit losers. It has been said that academic historians frequently judge things from the standpoint of the chanceries, the big houses, the place behind the coachman. This is because most of the documentation available is written from such a standpoint. However, the sensibility of unwritten history, of popular remembrance, is otherwise. Here, a certain feeling for the losers credits noble motives, envisages lost possibilities. Frequently, although by no means always, an 'hermeneutic of suspicion' subjects the official versions to a much needed critique. In regard to the 1790s this alternative consideration is given to 'the glorious pride and sorrow (which) fills the name of '98'. Such 'pride' and 'sorrow' is part of Fr Coigly's remembrance. Indeed, the account of his own life-work, written during his last weeks, is both interesting and frustrating for that very reason. One gets the impression of an energetic, sincere, turbulent figure who existed on the margin of the multiple skeins of Irish life in the late eighteenth century. Yet in that marginal position he intersected, sometimes tragically, with the most significant events in Irish politics of the time.

Judged by narrower standards, James Coigly was, indeed, a turbulent priest. Judged by the prudential norms of an Archbishop Troy, he was infected by 'the French disease'. His years at the College des Lombards discloses a man sensitive to, and ready to resist, personal slights. Nonetheless, clerical life of the time was far less monolithic than the more staid pattern of today. And the difficulties of the Paris college must be judged by criteria of the period. In his writings, Coigly shows a deep reverence for the church of which he was a minister. His stern criticisms are not of policies forwarded by the Irish hierarchy or by the Roman authorities. They are reserved for injustices perpetrated by a state apparatus which used religious differences as means to its own end. Nonetheless, it is clear that after Coigly's return to Ireland in 1789 his activity diverged radically from his church leadership and possibly from the majority of his fellow priests. Hence, perhaps, comes the overtone of isolation one senses in Coigly's life. Yet, in this very divergence there is a hint that not all priests were ready to follow their bishops in equating Catholicism with counter-revolution.

A scholar of Irish history, Fr Coigly was keenly aware of the evils of sectarian division. He detailed the tragedy for poor people in allowing themselves to be pitted against each other. The writings attributed to him fit well within the programme fostered by the Belfast leadership of the United Irishmen. His own efforts to unite Dissenters and Catholics would represent the nightmare of both the Dublin Castle and church establishments. Yet, despite this, one discerns an unease in his relations with the higher ranks of the United Irishmen. Tone came to mistrust him, not for political reasons, but because of the unfortunate proclivity of the United Irish leadership to personal quarrels. It is likely that Coigly's acquaintance with Napper Tandy led him to adopt ill-judged stances within the ramifications of these quarrels. Tone's ungenerous reference in the aftermath of Coigly's death perhaps explains the mounting impatience by the French in face of endemic Irish quarrels.

A feature of Coigly's work is its linkage of political to social reform. Reform was worth little if it did not address the problems of weavers and small tenants. All too few in the United Irish leadership (with exceptions like Russell, McCracken and, perhaps, Emmet) understood that the political crisis had a socio-economic base. Or else they were unwilling to envisage radical change in socio-economic relationships within the country. Coigly had a natural sympathy with the poor – whether Catholic or Dissenter – and consistency in employing it in his political analysis. Likewise, his efforts to connect with radical societies in England is instructive. In Manchester, Liverpool and London he nurtured the first shoots of English republicanism. Coigly seemed to realise the necessity for radicals in Ireland, Britain and France to co-operate. Such triangular link-up did not consolidate. As Marianne Elliott has shown, the project rapidly disintegrated.

Bibliography

Archives des Affaires Etrangeres, pol. ang. 592 fol 43 (memorial of O'Coigley and MacMahon, 4/10/1797).

Bergeron, Louis and L.M. Cullen, *Culture et Pratiques Politiques en France et en Irlande XVIeme – XVIII eme Siecle,* Centre de Recherches Historiques, Paris, 1990. (Article by L.M. Cullen 'Late Eighteenth Century Politicisation in Ireland', pp 137-157).

Carroll, Denis. *The Man From God Knows Where. Thomas Russell 1767-1803*, Gartan, Dublin, 1995.

Cloncurry, Lord (Valentine Lawless), *Personal Recollections of the Life and Times of Valentine, Lord Cloncurry,* McGlashan, Dublin, 1850.

Elliott, Marianne, 'Irish Republicanism in England' in *Penal Era and Golden Age. Essays in Irish History 1690-1800,* (eds. Thomas Bartlett and D.W. Hayton), Ulster Historical Foundation, Belfast, 1979, pp 204-221.

Fitzpatrick, W.J., *Life, Times and Contemporaries of Lord Cloncurry,* Duffy, Dublin, 1855.

Fitzpatrick, W.J., *Secret Service Under Pitt,* Longmans, London, 1892.

Keogh, Daire. *The French Disease. The Catholic Church and Radicalism in Ireland 1790-1800,* Four Courts Press, 1993.

Madden, R.R., *Lives and Times of the United Irishmen,* Third Series, Vol 2.

Miller, D.W., *Peep O'Day Boys and Defenders,* PRONI, Belfast, 1990.

Ó Muirí, Réamonn, 'The Killing of Thomas Birch' in *Seanchas Ard Mhacha,* (1982), pp 267-320.

Ó Muirí, Réamonn, 'Fr James Coigly', in *Protestant, Catholic and Dissenter. The Clergy in 1798,* Columba, 1997, pp. 118-164.

Simms, S., *Fr James O'Coigley,* Belfast, 1937.

CHAPTER TWO

BILLY BLUFF AND THE SQUIRE

James Porter (1753-1798)

The Reverend James Porter's writings – satires, lampoons and songs – are his most lasting contribution to radical Irish politics. A generation before Thomas Davis he showed the effectiveness of well-crafted satire on the collusion of church and state. Porter's lampoons are classics of resistance literature while his *Billy Bluff and the Squire* remains in print two hundred years after its composition. Arguably, it is still unrivalled as an exposition of hypocrisy in Irish politics. For this reason, Porter has been deemed 'one of the most sparkling Irish political satirists ... '[1] Whether or not he was formally a United Irishman is irrelevant. Porter's chief significance lies elsewhere – the damage he inflicted in print and pulpit on the credibility of landlords, magistrates and parsons.

James Porter started life as a farmer and miller in Tamna, Ballindrait, Co Donegal. Having ceded the farm to his younger brother, he became a schoolmaster for almost a decade in Dromore, Co Down. In 1780 he married Anna Knox and shortly afterwards the couple moved to Drogheda. Here, again, Porter taught school. Through the mid-1780s (circa 1784-86) he attended Glasgow University to study for the Presbyterian ministry. The link with Glasgow should be noted since the 'New Light' (more liberal) theology was preponderant there. Thus, at Glasgow – if not before – Porter would have come in contact with the Enlightenment in its Scottish Presbyterian form. Throughout his subsequent career he was deemed to be on the liberal wing of theology. Events would also show that he had imbibed Francis Hutcheson's emphasis on the close connection between political, social and theological questions. In Porter's view, social questions were ultimately moral ones and therefore of professional concern to ministers or theologians.[2]

From 1786 Porter was licensed as a probationary minister by the Bangor presbytery. On 31 July 1787 he was ordained for Greyabbey, Co Down, after his candidacy for his home congregation in Donegal was unsuccessful. With a small annual income (£60), he resorted to part-time farming as supplement. Here, with a natural ability perfected by his earlier work as a miller, he turned his technical skills to help local farmers revise their methods and thus increase their income. Classon Porter, author of an excellent memoir on the minister of Greyabbey, refers to a workshop set up for 'improved models of ploughs, carts and other agricultural instruments'. In his *History of the Irish Rebellion 1798*, Charles Teeling refers to Porter's science lessons: 'unostentatious but adorned with a native simplicity of eloquence which riveted the attention of his auditory'.[3] Clearly, the minister of Greyabbey had an innovative energy which he generously devoted to a practical end.

At Greyabbey, Porter joined the Volunteer movement, probably (like Wm Steel Dickson) as chaplain. In essence a citizens' militia, the Volunteers (founded in 1778) were to be a defence force during the American Revolution. Along with Henry Grattan, great landowners such as Lords Charlemont and Moira were its most notable officers. Although there was some posturing about uniforms, arms and parades, nonetheless Volunteering coined a worthwhile language of patriotic and civic responsibility. On major issues of the day, volunteer assemblies often tended towards liberality. More worrying for Dublin Castle was an ambivalent sentiment for the American Revolution. Not until the 1790s did the break occur in Irish politics between cautious reformers (like Charlemont and Moira) and radicals like Tone, Napper Tandy and Russell. As to James Porter, there is scant evidence of his political attitudes during the 1780s.

In view of later events, one notices with surprise that Porter
was a frequent and welcome visitor to Mount Stewart, home
of Robert Stewart (Senior), later to become his determined
enemy. Certainly, the daughters of the Mount Stewart house-
hold attended some of Porter's scientific lectures, and in 1798
tried to save him from execution. It is perhaps another irony
of Irish history that the notorious Castlereagh – Robert
Stewart, the younger – may well have entertained Porter at
Mount Stewart before their paths so radically diverged. Such
friendship with the lords of Mount Stewart may perhaps be
read in terms of Porter's engaging personal traits. Nevertheless
it should also be noted that in the late 1780s the Stewarts were
associated with reform politics and at that stage enjoyed the
support of other radical clergymen, notably Wm Steel Dickson
(minister at Ballyhalbert and then Portaferry) and of Thomas
Ledlie Birch (minister at Saintfield).

With the declaration of war on France in February 1793
the polticial situation caused a dramatic split, even among
hitherto reformers. The Chancellor, John Fitzgibbon (later
Lord Clare) had contemptuously rejected Catholic demands
for relief on the specious ground that Protestants would not
tolerate such emancipation. With the outbreak of war, attempts were made to neutralise Catholic pressure by granting
limited relief. In reality, this was a stratagem to prevent union
between Catholics and Belfast radicals. A Convention Act
was rushed through parliament to prevent assemblies such as
the Catholic Convention which in December 1792 had met at
Tailors' Hall. The act effectively suppressed the Volunteer
movement – strangely, with the assent of Grattan. At this point
'advanced' democrats parted company with their erstwhile
Whig collaborators. Many, amongst them Porter, felt de-
barred from working openly towards reform and moved into
closer alliance with the United Irishmen. Others – prominently,
the Stewarts of Mount Stewart – became unremitting opponents of radical ideas and perfervid supporters of government
policy.

Throughout the country, but particularly in Ulster, a new militancy went step by step with governmental repression. The Militia Act, in essence a conscription law, caused noticeable alienation from the army. Through the summer of 1793 there were riots at Belfast and at Lisburn. In an incident which points up the tensions, Thomas Russell, himself an ex-officer, had a near fatal street affray with the military in November 1793. From this time one notices – for example, in Russell's *Journals* – a growing scepticism about reform by constitutional means. With hope of conciliation dashed on the rock of Fitzgibbon's obduracy, the option of physical force seemed all the more attractive. About this time, Porter began his contributions to the United Irish journal, the *Northern Star.* Through 1794-95 he published several patriotic songs, among them 'The Exile of Erin' which entered the canon of radical ballads (cf. *Paddy's Resource,* published in 1796). When Lord Fitzwilliam's recall signalled entrenchment of the College Green ascendancy, a more savage era of repression commenced. Lord Camden, the new viceroy, a relative of the Stewarts, lost no time in introducing the younger Robert Stewart (Lord Castlereagh) to the centre of power at Dublin Castle.

Popular Literary Campaign for Reform

Since the minister of Greyabbey now joined the United Irishmen in a protracted literary campaign, it will be useful to notice that this was an essential part of extra-parliamentary opposition to government. Already, in the England of the 1760s, popular mobilisation was attempted by what one commentator has termed 'the commercialisation of politics'.[4] Here, radical followers of John Wilkes addressed the people at large through pamphlets, broadsheets and caricatures. In this way, the monopoly of political discourse by aristocrats was broken, at least for a while. In pre-revolutionary France, the same phenomenon can be observed. Such productions attempted to break the vice-grip of the oligarchy on political thought, to democratise political culture, and, in the words of

Thomas Addis Emmet, 'to make every man a politician'. This was the great fear of the ascendancy – that every man might exercise political judgement rather than abide by the instructions of his 'betters'. Implicit in the dissemination of such literature were two conceptions of the political 'nation' – the one defined narrowly by the ascendancy and the other, very much broader, defined by those who challenged that ascendancy. Here, perhaps, lies the difference between the sympathisers of the United Irishmen and the Grattan Whigs, who could not forsake the old conception of 'ascendancy'. Squire Firebrand, the central character of Porter's famous lampoon, bemoaned the new situation: 'Oh, how times are changed, and all for the worse. Your Catholic college, your Catholic schools, your Catholic emancipation, your Sunday schools, your Charter schools, your book societies, your pamphlets, your books and your one hell after another are all turning people's heads and setting them thinking about this, that and the other' (*Dialogue Two*, 18.7.96).

A variety of methods was used to disseminate the 'alternative' literature: distribution at chapel gates, discussion in reading clubs; cheap editions of Paine's *Rights of Man*. As Porter hints, Sunday schools, local meetings, even masonic conventions, became occasions for spreading 'uniting' principles. Thomas Russell was spotted in Portarlington (1793) distributing handbills from a phaeton. These methods, so difficult to control and multiplied by immense ingenuity, worried government and its agents. An instance of this alarm is A Charles Murphy's letter to Dublin Castle in 1794. Murphy complained that United Irishmen were using every device to promote their aims: 'Addresses, odes, songs – in short every species of literary mischief is resorted to and circulated ... to every part of the kingdom and amongst all the lower orders of the people'.[5]

Perhaps the most successful means of radical dissemination was Neilson's *Northern Star*. Not only was its circulation extraordinarily wide, it also put the most successful articles into pamphlet form which then had successive reprints. During the mid-1790s, the *Star*'s most popular contributors were William Sampson, a barrister, Thomas Russell, librarian at the Belfast Society for the Promotion of Knowledge and, perhaps the most influential of all, James Porter. From their pens came three works which have endured as classics of political satire: *Billy Bluff and the Squire* (Porter), *The Lion of Old England* (Sampson and Russell), and *The Trial of Hurdy Gurdy* (Sampson). Along with the United Irishmen, James Porter now addressed weavers, small farmers, and artisans. His purpose was to stimulate their awareness that they too had rights which at present were denied them.

Billy Bluff and The Squire

Billy Bluff is the compendium of seven letters to the *Northern Star* from 30 May 1796 to 2 December 1796. Later, the *Star* pamphletised them as *Billy Bluff and the Squire (A Satire On Irish Aristocracy)*. Thus, Porter's influence was destined to continue for generations after his death. As to the pamphlet, even sympathetic reviewers such as R. R. Madden found their conservatism assailed by its virulence. In his study of Porter, Madden primly observes: 'if that violence of language which was the foolish fashion of the day, had been a little moderated, the thoughts which are clothed in it would have suffered no injury'.[6] Madden's fastidiousness takes insufficient account of the satire's object and the detailed arrogance of an establishment which provoked the minister of Greyabbey to such wrath.

Entertaining from beginning to end, *Billy Bluff* is nonetheless a deadly critique of the political context. It is reminiscent of the 'Junius' letters which in the 1790s had major impact in London and other places. It ridicules 'the system of espionage and feudal tyranny which was then undoubtedly present' (Classon Porter). By way of counter-point, it represents the desirability of union between Protestant, Catholic and Dissenter to attain reform of a corrupt system. The main objects of the satire are Squire Firebrand, Billy Bluff and Lord

Mountmumble. Firebrand is probably the Reverend John
Cleland, rector of Newtownards, a rabid loyalist and agent for
Lord Londonderry.[7] Billy Bluff is Wm Lowry, bailiff of the
Greyabbey estate, while Lord Mountmumble is Lord
Londonderry, father of Lord Castlereagh. Bluff's hectoring
reports on his neighbours give valuable insight to the actual
course of events during the mid-1790s. In the background is
'R', doubtless Porter himself, who merits the ire of the blimp-
ish Squire Firebrand. The satire closes with a confrontation
between 'R' and the Squire. Here, the tyranny of the established order is excoriated by 'R': 'I see when the Great cajole,
they want to deceive, when they smile, they want to betray –
when their own wickedness brought them into danger and
covered them with shame, they throw the blame on the innocent and unoffending, should they dare to complain.' As to
the emerging friendship between Catholics and Presbyterians,
which Firebrand deemed unnatural, 'R' says: 'It is not so new
– it has existed for several years; but it is not long since it
began to frighten their enemies.'

The first dialogue between Squire and spy discloses 'R' at
his customary occupation: 'railing at the war, against the
tythes, and against the game laws, and still reading the newspapers'. Even worse, he and 'the Popish priest' had drunk together last market day, had shaken hands, had toasted 'Union
and Peace to the People of Ireland'. In Firebrand's opinion
this was blasphemous: 'he who wishes union wishes ruin to
the country; and as to peace, 'tis flying the face of government
to speak of it – the d...l send the ruffians peace, till their betters chuse to give it to them'. Another liberal toast, 'Every
man his own road to heaven', provokes Firebrand to condemn
such a toast as fit only for republicans and sinners: '... it supposes all men to be on an equality before God, and supposes a
man may go to heaven, without being of the established
church, which is impossible'. Porter's second dialogue brings
out the full arrogance of the Squire. 'R' is setting people
thinking – 'filling their heads full of notions'. To Firebrand

this is monstrous. The country was happy before people started to think: 'Catholics thought of nothing but just getting leave to live, and working for their meat – Presbyterians thought of nothing but wrangling about religion and grumbling about tythes – and Protestants thought of nothing but doing and saying what their betters bid them.' Once, Firebrand's father could put someone in jail when he pleased, could horsewhip a tradesman when he presented his bill, could fancy a tenant's daughter, could shoot a dog for barking, could get a Presbyterian assassinated for voting against him in vestry. Firebrand complains that recently a tailor had the temerity to look him straight in the face: 'I saw the day that I could have had influence enough with the Judge and Jury to have him hanged for a less fault.'

The fourth dialogue brings to notice events which were happening in the everyday life of the mid 1790s. Billy Bluff's maladroit reports give a clue to the subversive import of songs, whistling of tunes, meetings to dig potatoes, funerals, etc. In Firebrand's view ''tis songs that is to be dreaded of all things'. For, trumpets Firebrand, 'singing infects a whole country and makes them half mad: because they rejoice and forget their cares ... and forget their betters'. Poor Billy Bluff reports on a collection of songs misnamed *Paddy's Race-Horse:* Firebrand corrects him on the title of *Paddy's Resource* (just published) and then adds, 'And I am glad it is the only resource Paddy has.' A skilful cut is made at the combination of Anglican ministry and civil magistracy when Firebrand lauds the Reverend Hawksneb for jailing three blind fiddlers, a ballad singer and a drunk who had sung and played tunes he disliked. Billy Bluff is told: 'there is nothing like making Clergymen Magistrates; it adds a double edge to the sword; shows the world the necessity of uniting Church and State; makes the dove bite like a serpent, and converts the lamb into the lion ...'. The contempt of the Squirearchy for juries becomes clear: 'the D...l has got into the juries now, there is almost no packing of them ....trial by jury was a foolish invention, it puts so much in the power of the people, that a gentleman has some difficulty in getting a fellow hanged that he has a spite at'. In Squire Firebrand's mind the only hope was for a new act of parliament to abolish juries.

The lampoon extends to the rapid advancement of Lord Mountmumble (Londonderry) through the peerage. 'R's' caustic remark is quoted. It was, said 'R', wonderful to see in one day: 'Mr changed in to my Lord; Mrs into my lady; and all the little Misses turned into my Lady A. my Lady B. my Lady C. my Lady D. my Lady E.' Whereas Thomas Russell had spoken of the aristocracy as a 'fungus on society', James Porter changes the metaphor. The image now is of mush-rooms on a dunghill: the newly created race of Lords and Earls (have) 'rotten roots, filthy stems, spungy *(sic)* heads and start up when no one expects it'. The pretended grandeur of the upstart aristocracy is no more than vulgar foolishness: 'Then comes the coronet painted on the coach, on the har-ness, on the dishes and plates, on the piss-pots.' Even Firebrand's stolidity heaps further irony on the peerage as he lectures Billy Bluff: 'a Lord is a new creature; he can see through a stone wall ... he can see in the dark ... he can hear a whisper five miles distance ... a musket ball would not pierce his skin ... he is wiser than Solomon, and he never dies ... the man may die but the title lives for ever ... and his virtue, his fortune and his wisdom go along with the title'. All Billy Bluff can say is 'Your Honour, I did not know that.'

Porter is too skilful a satirist to give lectures. For example, on the war with France he introduces the popular song 'Billy's undone by the War', a send-up of William Pitt's war policy. Firebrand lauds Pitt in ridiculous terms: 'The most wise, the most virtuous, the most warlike, the most candid, the most economical, the most successful minister that ever carried on a holy war, for the liberties of the world and the glory of God'. Again, Pitt is 'the lord of Lords, the Creator of Lords: he could make a Lord of you, of me, or of a cabbage stock. O Billy, his power is unlimited, and his wisdom unfathomable' (*Dialogue Four*, 2 Sept 1796). In this comic reference, Firebrand's stupidity is accented while government policy on the war with France is lampooned. Again, Firebrand's *bete noir* 'R' is cited by Billy: 'You are a pretty set, said he, ... he meant me and you, your honour, and the rector, and the collector ... You cut a pretty figure, said he, about religion in the present war, when every body knows that delusion, hypocrisy, intrigue, ambition and temporal distinction are all that is thought of ...'(*Dialogue Seven,* 2 Dec 1796).

In *Dialogue Five,* the comic figure of another landowner, Mr Noddledrum, hints that not all think like Squire Firebrand. Lord Mountmumble was reputed to be 'in a devil's pother about the times'. To Firebrand's confusion, Noddledrum asks 'whether the Times brought on the circumstances or the circumstances the Times'. The confusion deepens when Noddledrum confesses to a toast with his tenants 'Union to Irishmen'. Boasting of a new security, he parts from Firebrand: 'I'll take chance with my country, and live and die in peace' (*Dialogue Six,* 11 Nov 1796). Already, somewhat ruefully, Noddledrum enumerated his services to the authorities – two men imprisoned for shooting woodcock, a farmer in the stocks for striking Lord Mountmumble's spaniel, a double fine off an old Quaker who had not paid tythes, promotion of 'the depredations of the Orangemen'. (ibid).

The Orange note continues with the introduction of Bryan O'Carolin who seeks redress for the burning of his house, the abduction of his daughter, the killing of his son and an attack on himself. O'Carolin names his attacker, an Orangeman called George Williams who is also present. Instead of redress, O'Carolin is accused by Firebrand for defending himself: '... you come under the act against Defenderism ... And as to the burning of your house, many a man has burnt his own house to get double the value of it off the county ... Who can tell that your daughter did not take advantage of the confusion, to make an elopement with some of the assailants ... Your wife, like other wives, may be fond of gadding, when she might have staid at home.' In the event,

O'Carolin is murdered by Williams and Bluff with the approval of the Squire. The dead man's family are remitted to the tender mercies of Lord Mountmumble for trial as United Irishmen. There are echoes here of Armagh magistrates who during the Orange riots of 1796 claimed that Catholics burned out of their homes had set fire to their own houses. About the same time, Chief Secretary Pelham averred that reports of Orange depredations were much exaggerated.

While there is some evidence that Porter felt his ministry prevented him from taking the United Irish oath, he enjoyed the confidence of the organisation's leaders. Although he is not mentioned in Russell's journal, it is probable that the two would have met either at the *Star* offices or at the Belfast Library. Porter's lecture tour on astronomy ('with his tiny battery and Montgolfier balloons') was seen by informers as an alibi for work in the United Irish cause.[8] What William Drennan termed 'mole work' was under way from 1795, viz. the reorganisation of the Society both in Belfast and throughout the north. Russell's many visits to his sister at Enniskillen may have been a front for the work so well remembered in Florence Wilson's ballad, *The Man From God Knows Where.* Wm Johnston wrote in alarm that Russell 'is said to be now near Sligo, no doubt promoting union among Irishmen'. James Hope is said to have organised a linen market in order to propagate United Irish principles at Creggan, Co Armagh. Another United Irishman, James Cochran, travelled with Masonic seals and medals, as a cover for the United Irish extension work. William Putnam McCabe was sucessively a preacher, a recruiting sergeant, a pedlar, a schoolmaster, in disguise of his real work.

Subversive Homily at Greyabbey

Today, 'Fast Days' have mainly religious overtones. Not so in Ireland of the 1790s. Then, Fast Days had overtones more political than religious. Proclaimed by government as to date and manner, they were obediently celebrated by church establishments. In circumstances of political dissent such obser-

vances found mixed reception. When a general fast was called
on 19 April 1793 to mourn the death of Louis XVI, Thomas
Russell entered in his *Journal*: 'The day of the fast, whenever
the King was prayed for, stand up. Drink the fate of Louis to
all crowned heads, George the last etc, etc.'[9] When a French
expedition foundered off Bantry Bay in December 1796, the
government cast the unprecedented storm in religious terms.
According to government propaganda, the storm was provi-
dential, an act of God directed not only against the French
but also their Irish sympathisers. A Fast Day of thanksgiving
was proclaimed for 16 February 1797 alongside more temporal
measures of repression such as suspension of *Habeas Corpus*
and a reign of terror by violently excited troops and yeomen.
Back in France, Tone remarked with scant exaggeration: '…
the system of Terror is carried as far in Ireland as ever it was in
France in the time of Robespierre'. Despite Thomas Pelham's
claim that the oppression of Catholics in Armagh 'had been
greatly exaggerated', drunken troops and yeomen were visiting men, women and children with what the Anglican Bishop
of Down termed 'every species of brutality, indignity and outrage'.[10]

Just as Russell had entertained subversive thoughts during
the Fast Day of April 1793, Porter expressed equally dangerous
sentiments in the Greyabbey pulpit on the Fast Day of
February 1797. His sermon of 'thanksgiving', like his earlier
Billy Bluff, is an outstanding example of how government
diktat could be turned against itself. The sermon, 'Wind and
Weather', is a tour-de-force of ironic political analysis.[10a]
Once again, one notes the discomfiture of R. R. Madden as
he deems the preacher 'so far forgetful of (his) sacred office
and function, as to make (him) subservient to political purposes'. Madden also notes the 'strain of grave sarcasm and
ironical loyalty, better suited for the pages of *Billy Bluff*, than
for the place where it was uttered'. The sermon is indeed sarcastic, most particularly on the war against France, the emerging repression in Ireland, and the anti-democratic thrust of

church-state collaboration. The irony is compounded by
Porter's initiative in having the text later printed at Belfast.
The reaction of Porter's congregation can hardly be surmised
– the sermon's letter is ostensibly loyal, yet the sarcasm is obvious. In the case of Steel Dickson and of Ledlie Birch, 'seces-
sions' by those who disagreed with their radicalism had already taken place. Hence, one may assume that Porter's congregation not only grasped his purpose but also agreed with
him in essence. Given that he was already under suspicion,
the sermon – and, particularly, its publication – will have
made him even more a figure of odium to the local gentry and
to Dublin Castle authorities.

   'Wind and Weather' is indeed solemn. Replete with scriptural references, it has the portentous style associated with
sermons of the time. It has to be taken as a whole and there is
risk of distortion in selecting its elements. Yet, one notes
Porter's ironical disquisition on the changing nature of Fast
Days to suit government's purpose: 'they are wisely contrived
to change their nature as circumstances require; and those
who have the power of appointing the time of worshipping
God, have the goodness to appoint the manner also'. Porter
implies that the fast is not about religion as such. It is rather
to benefit government – to show how the administration are
friends of religion, that they serve God, that they hate cant
and hypocrisy. If anyone should doubt this, he is motivated
'by treason and infidelity'. Again, such fasts indicate 'the support which the state, on emergencies, can draw from the combined prayers of those who occupy the superb palaces, the extensive demenses, and the splendid chariots, for the meek and
lowly teachers of the religion of Christ'. Here is a barb directed
against the stipendaries of the Anglican Church. Clearly referring to the disabilities of Dissenters and Catholics, Porter
avers that all these benefits would be lost if the various sects
were allowed to choose their own mode, time and place of
worship. As to abstinence from food, he observed that church
dignitaries show by 'the profusion of their tables, and the del-

icacies of their wines ... that the practice of fasting is not very
strictly enforced upon themselves'.

Turning to the storm, the preacher again develops his ironic
vein. For three months before the storm, an unhealthy calm
had prevailed, pestilence had raged, 'the yellow fever advanced to our very doors'. Then came the storm which blew
for seventy two hours, 'without any variation from the SSE
... with a velocity of fify miles per hour ... accompanied ...
with an almost continual fall of sleet and snow'. While ad-
verting to the death and destruction caused by the storm
throughout Ireland, Porter nonetheless adheres to his remit –
to give thanks. In view of the repression under way through
1797, there is fine sarcasm in Porter's joy that since the storm
'We hear of neither sickness nor death amongst us – fear has
fled – every countenance looks blithe – and every heart pants
with joy.' By the dispersal of the French fleet, 'the invasion of
this country hath been providentially prevented'. When
Porter investigates the meaning of 'country' it emerges that
what the administration means by 'country' is not what the
people meant. By 'country' the government meant simply itself. The Fast Day was government giving thanks for its own
preservation.

Thereafter, Porter concentrates on the war with France:
'we are confident that nine tenths of the people of Ireland,
neither wished for the commencement nor continuance of
the war with France'. It was England's quarrel with a neighbouring power. The political realities were that '... should
England exhaust herself of men, money and reputation, and
permit her minister to plunge her into an abyss of ruin, we
must exhaust ourselves of men, money and reputation, and
permit her minister to plunge us into an abyss of ruin also'.
The benefit to Ireland was scanty – an invasion. Ireland was
now ordered to pray. And after praying, Ireland was solicited
to fight the French. Irony becomes lampoon when Porter de-
clares: 'And should a powerful and daring foe e'er again insult
our coasts, and threaten an invasion, we must not forget our
obligations to the weather'.

Here, the minister of Greyabbey exposes the administration's double standard. On the one hand, it was thanking God for deliverance and implicitly allying God to its cause. On the other hand, it reiterated the continuing threat from France and from those in Ireland sympathetic to French ideas. Hence, people should return thanks while noting government's purposes: 'Wise and grateful must the administration be which directs our thankfulness ... regulates our religion ... and forces us to sing together for joy.' Citing the Bible, Porter recommends his audience to rejoice with trembling. The storm, although great, was not great enough: 'Though it dispersed, it did not destroy: though it scattered, it did not annihilate.' It softened its fierceness and allowed the French ships with one exception to reach safety at home. In Paris, 'the proud commander ... forms new plans of enterprise and revenge'. Should the French return, it would be too much to hope for another storm. Yet, people should remember that were the British fleet defeated 'we can trust in God, who can of the air form wooden walls for our protection'. Official 're-joicing' is further questioned as Porter remembers that 'the lives and properties of foreigners and natives were promiscuously destroyed by the noisy guardian of our peace'. Given that many British ships also foundered, Porter then implies that the storm was no more than an 'unexpected friend and fickle ally'.

As the sermon approaches a conclusion, plain speech replaces satire. Porter stands on the bridge between the old volunteering spirit and the newer United Irish thrust. Here, he speaks of thoroughgoing reform rather than insurrection and seems implicitly to refer to Grattan's party as well as to United Irishmen. Instead of reliance on a storm, there should be a united people confident of each other and proud of their country. Yet, in present circumstances, this neither existed nor could exist: 'Here and there a few are chosen ... and exclusively instructed with the means of protecting our constitution and our country, while the great mass of our people, unarmed, in dismay and fear, stand alarmed at invasion from without, and are filled with jealousy at their protectors within'. While legislative reform was denied, repression and division would persist. Porter refers to men 'of distinguished rank and talents' both in Britain and in Ireland who saw legislative reform as the only means of saving the 'constitution and the country'. Many of these had opposed the war at its outset and in its progress, they had asked for reform both in Britain and in Ireland. Some were exiled, some tried and acquitted, and 'many immured in dungeons, without prospect of trial and relief'. (It should be remembered that since September 1796 Thomas Russell, Samuel Neilson, Charles Teeling and others were imprisoned in Newgate and Kilmainham.)

In his peroration, James Porter rebounded the administration's blame of reformers back upon itself. Government exculpated itself from all fault in the troubles of the day:

'Not unto us, say the contrivers and abettors of the war – not unto us be the shame and the odium of this disgraceful war – Not unto us be the exhausted treasury, the discontented people, the stagnation of commerce, and the approaching ruin of the country – Not unto us ... the provoking of a powerful and desperate invasion, the bringing carnage and war upon our native land.'

Yet such exculpation led nowhere except self-incurred disaster:

'As for us, should the flame which we have kindled in Europe spread to the British empire, should it involve our country, our king, our constitution and ourselves, we will cheerfully perish in the conflagration, provided the blame be laid upon those who atempted to prevent us from kindling it, or to extinguish it when kindled'.

Repression Evokes Reaction

Unfortunately, the reforms spoken of in 'Wind and Weather' did not eventuate. Through 1797 the administration seemed purposely to goad the people into rebellion. Repression and reaction mounted spirally right into 1798. Warnings came from sources less radical than Porter. Lord

Moira told the House of Lords in November 1797: '... I speak
of what I myself have seen in Ireland, the most absurd, as well
as the most disgusting, tyranny that any nation has ever
groaned under ... I have seen ... the most wanton insults, the
most grievous oppressions practised upon men of all ranks
and conditions, in a part of the country as free of disturbance
as the city of London.' In Summer 1798 came the inevitable
explosion – the seven days in June when 'summer soldiers' (A.
T. Q. Stewart) facing army, militia and yeomen gave determined battle in Antrim and Down. Due to earlier arrests, in-
competent political leadership, and sheer bad luck, that rising
was unsuccessful. Decades later, Mary Ann McCracken described it with typical appropriateness: 'In considering the
unsuccessful struggle in which my brother was engaged,
many are too apt to forget the evils of the time: the grinding
oppression under which the people laboured; the contempt in
which public opinion was held; the policy which prevented
its expression and intimidated the press. The only means then
existing of stemming the torrent of corruption and oppression was tried, and they failed, but the failure ... was not
without its beneficial effects.'[11]

James Porter is reputed to have disapproved of the rising in
the form it took. Here, he was not alone – United Irish leaders like Robert Simms felt reluctance for a rising insufficiently
co-ordinated. Yet, for someone of Porter's notoriety it was difficult to remain aloof. Whatever his views on the rising,
Porter took part only to a small degree, if at all. On Saturday 7
June, the opening day of the rising, Greyabbey insurgents
who intended to join the main force at Newtownards requested a blessing of their minister. They enquired about officers
to which Porter is alleged to have answered laconically that
they would find leaders near Newtownards (at Conlig and
Scrabo). On Sunday 8 June, according to a charge levelled
against him, Porter was amongst insurgents who detained a
messenger travelling from Captain Matthews, the army commander at Portaferry, to Colonel Stapylton at Comber. It was

further charged that when the messenger (McChesney) was deprived of his dispatch, Porter read its contents to the rebels. That was all.[12]

Yet, Porter was arrested and imprisoned at Newtownards. If one follows the account of his son (also James Porter), he did not expect arrest, having committed no crime. Another account claims he was arrested in hiding, at a cottage 'among the Mourne mountains on the verge of his parish'. At his court-martial on 30 June, Porter was charged with Treason, Rebellion and Sedition. His prosecutor was Lieut. the Reverend John Cleland, the Squire of Billy Bluff. The president of the tribunal was a Captain Singleton of the Monaghan Militia. Years later, Porter's son remembered: 'To his dismay he perceived that the Earl of Londonderry had taken his seat among them and he found, as the trial proceeded, how potent was his influence and how fearfully it was brought to bear upon him.'[13]

Porter, rebutting the charge, cross-examined the witnesses. One, a former United Irishman, had turned King's evidence and unconvincingly testified against Porter. The court, however, was convinced and its verdict was swift. The minister of Greyabbey, guilty of Treason, Sedition and Rebellion, was to be hanged. His closing address to the court, related by Classon Porter, contains interesting references to the failure of McChesney to identify him, and the production of a 'renegade and notorious paid informer'. The speech is dignified, without hint of special pleading. Porter emphasised that he had never concealed his sentiments throughout his life and 'expressed the honest convictions of his mind, verbally and in writing, upon all occasions when he thought the interest of his country was concerned'.[14]

Before Porter's execution, there followed another strange incident which shows the bitterness he had incurred from the leading ascendancy figures. Mrs Jane Porter asked the Stewarts to procure mitigation of her husband's capital sentence with its attendant barbarities of drawing and quarter-

ing. While Lady Londonderry and her daughter Lady
Elizabeth Stewart (herself terminally ill) were ready to inter-
vene with General Nugent, Londonderry (Mountmumble)
himself forbade it. It should be noted that Nugent did com-
mute the grisly elements of drawing and quartering. On 2
July 1798 James Porter was executed at Greyabbey, on an
eminence between his home and his meeting house where,
over sixteen months before, he had preached 'Wind and
Weather'.

James Porter the younger has written:

> 'On the morning of the day which terminated my father's
> life he got into a carriage at the hour of 11 o'clock and was
> conducted under a guard of cavalry from Newtownards to
> Greyabbey. A temporary gallows was erected on a small
> hill which overlooked the meeting house where he had of-
> ficiated as pastor for ten years. My mother rode with him
> to the place of execution. ... Arrived at the fatal spot, my
> mother kissed him for the last time. When she arrived at
> the manse, the children were all at the door, waiting for
> her arrival. She did not sit down. In an hour after, the body
> she had left in health and strength and all the pride of
> manly beauty, was delivered to her a corpse.'[15]

Doubtless, the hostility evoked by Porter's writing and
preaching had ensured his death. Although Cleland had
claimed – not in court – that Porter was a United Irish colonel
for Co Down, it is probable that his criticism of government,
of Lord Londonderry, of the Reverend John Cleland and of
the whole church-state alliance brought about his execution.
Two other Presbyterian clergymen were hanged later in the
Summer – Robert Gowdy, minister at Dunover, and Archibald Warwick, a probationer clergyman at Kirkubbin, some
miles from Greyabbey. There is no definitive evidence that
James Porter had taken the United Irish oath. Yet, his ideas
were those of the United Irish leaders on constitutional and
religious matters. Indeed, as a whole, his attacks on government's mismanagement were even more telling than those of

his fellow-contributors to the *Northern Star.* One also notices the continuity in his writing with the more radical Volunteers from the 1780s. For there were people, even in the 1790s, who continued to espouse parliamentary reform and religious emancipation without being members of the United Irish Society. And so, while it is absolutely clear that Porter was one of the most effective voices for radical reform, one has to take seriously his son's claim that he did not approve of the uprising when it came.

Further reading

For Porter's *Billy Bluff* cf Brendan Clifford's *Billy Bluff and the Squire,* Athol, Belfast, 1991.

Also:

Classon Porter, *Irish Presbyterian Biographical Sketches,* 1883.

Stewart, A.T.Q., *The Summer Soldiers,* Blackstaff, Belfast, 1995.

Teeling, Chas., *History of The Irish Rebellion 1798,* Irish University Press, Dublin 1972.

Article

Tesch, Pieter, 'Presbyterian Radicalism' in Dickson, Keogh and Whelan, *The United Irishmen,* Lilliput, 1993, pp 33-48.

CHAPTER THREE

ON THE RUN IN CONNEMARA

Myles Prendergast OSA

As James Porter had warned, the French did return. In August 1798 General Jean Joseph Amable Humbert led more than a thousand men into Killala without hindrance from 'Wind or Weather'. An earlier plan to land at Killibegs had been thwarted due to bad weather off Donegal. Humbert's intention was to link with another expedition under General Hardy, co-ordinate with United Irish forces in the north, and eventually take Dublin City. In the event, such plans came to nothing and Humbert's expedition proved the last campaign of the 1798 rising. In north Connacht, popular reaction was enthusiastic and many hailed the French as liberators. Hundreds came to join or assist the expedition. Local councils were inaugurated on republican lines. A 'Republic of Connaught' was declared. An 'auxiliary' army was created from the hundreds who came from surrounding farms and villages. A number of Irish officers who had served in continental armies placed themselves at the head of this ill-fated contingent. Colonel Matthew Bellew and, later, General Blake provided the leadership for the Irish 'auxiliaries' of Humbert's army.[1]

Among the first to land at Killala was a Mayo priest, Fr Henry O'Kane. With the rank of Captain, O'Kane functioned as translator and aide-de-camp to Humbert. Fr O'Kane took an active part in the fighting at Castlebar where his exertions on behalf of local Protestants were generously noticed and later recorded by Bishop Joseph Stock. Another Mayo priest, Fr Michael Gannon of Louisburgh, offered his services and became became *fournisseur general* to the invading army. According to the hostile Richard Musgrave, Gannon exhorted the residents of Castlebar from the window of Humbert's apartment in the town. From remote parts of the county several other priests brought scores of parishioners to augment the French arrivals. Thereafter, they acted as translators, guides and sometimes fighters in Humbert's inexorable push eastwards through Crossmolina to Castlebar and thence to Longford.

One 'recruit' to the French army was an Augustinian, Fr Myles Prendergast. At this time Prendergast was Prior of Murrisk Abbey, on the shores of Clew Bay, a few miles from Westport. Augustinian friars were active in the west of Ireland – in Galway, Roscommon and Mayo. An Augustinian colleague, Fr Owen Killeen (who also came to join Humbert) had been a United Irish organiser in Sligo and Mayo. As to Prendergast, little is recorded of his earlier career. His name appears on the house books of Ballyhaunis Augustinian Friary for 1791.[2] According to his own claims, he worked in parish ministry at Westport for some five years as well as two years in the parish of Oughayour, (Aughagower?) near Westport. It is possible that such work was from a base at Murrisk Abbey – he is spoken of as Prior of the community during the 1790s. In addition, he was a travelling missioner 'in all the towns and county chapels all over the county of Roscommon'.[3] As with his confrere, John Martin, such work could well have provided a cover for another missionary endeavour, viz. propagation of the United Irish Society in several counties of the province.

The involvement of Catholic priests in the Killala expedition has been obfuscated by partisanship in subsequent writing. Richard Musgrave undoubtedly exaggerates in his argument that the 1798 rising was a murderous sectarian jacquerie where the Catholic clergy played a leading role. On the other hand, Catholic bishops strove desperately to underscore their loyalty by isolating rebel priests as drunken ruffians with a grudge against all authority. More recently, S. J. Connolly has suggested that those priests who welcomed Humbert did so 'in the name of confessional and dynastic loyalties of the *ancien regime*'.[4] Yet it is unsafe to limit clerical involvement with the French expedition to 'reluctant rebel' or 'drunken ruffian' stereotypes. Nor, for that matter, is such involvement explicable simply in terms of dynastic loyalties. There are signs of a 'principled motivation' in the enthusiasm with which these men brought their followers from remote areas of the province. To all appearances, these were not a group of frustrated curates or drunkards. As Keogh emphasises, the patterns of their activity 'reflect the radicalised society from which they emerged'.[5] In regard to Fr Prendergast's own motivation, one notices his close relationship to Johnny 'the Outlaw' Gibbons. This may indicate sympathy with Defenderism and, perhaps, resentment evoked by Lord Carhampton's repression of Connacht two years earlier.

At first, Humbert's expedition routed all before it – in popular lore 'the races of Castlebar' refers to the precipitous flight of British forces before the French. Only at Ballinamuck, Co Longford, was the incursion halted when government troops under Lord Cornwallis easily defeated the French and Irish. Casualties were high. Atrocities were committed on surrendering rebels, particularly the Irish irregulars. At Shanmullagh Hill five hundred people were summarily executed. While Humbert and his officers were generously entertained at the Mail Hotel in Dublin, people like Fr Prendergast were either executed on the spot or detained to face later courtmartial. On 5 November, General Power Trench offered a reward of fifty pounds for information on 'Rev Myles Prendergast, friar of Westport, Rev Ml Gannon of Louisburg, Rev Myles Sweeney, Newport, priest' on head of high treason in aiding and assisting the late invasion of the country.[6] Hence, shortly after the defeat at Ballinamuck, the Augustinian prior of Murrisk Abbey found himself in Castlebar jail with exceedingly dim prospects for his future.

However, the imprisonment was short – not due to acquittal or release, but because Myles Prendergast, John Gibbons and Austin Gibbons effected their own escape. A key was smuggled to the prisoners by a Dr Prendergast and in the actual escape a prison guard, Brighouse, was killed by Myles Prendergast.[7] By December, the three had reached the fastnesses of Connemara joining many others from Leinster and Ulster who had escaped the debacle in those provinces. Magistrates like 'Humanity Dick' Martin turned a blind eye to the newcomers. In Fr Prendergast's case, Martin later endeavoured to secure him a pardon. In March 1799 Captain Taylor, aide de camp to General Trench, reported with some alarm that J. J. McDonnell, an adjutant of Humbert, had conferred with John Gibbons, Fr Myles Prendergast and Fr Ml Gannon at Ballynakill, Co Galway. McDonnell had spoken of the inevitability of another French landing and was investigating if people were still ready to join such an expedition. Meanwhile, according to Captain Taylor's report, 'A concourse of people, some of them armed and some unarmed, constantly kept watch on the shore – a report having been put about that King's troops were coming from Westport.'[8]

Later in 1799, when Cornwallis's policy of reconciliation declared a 'grace and pardon' for those who had taken part in the rising, General Thomas Meyrich excluded named persons from the amnesty, on account of 'the magnitude of their crimes'. Fr Prendergast and Fr Cowley of Crossmolina were detailed with John Gibbons and J. J. McDonnell as remaining under sentence by court-martial. Five hundred pounds were offered as reward for apprehending McDonnell while two hundred pounds were offered for the arrest of the others. Also at this time, information to Dublin Castle declared that 'Prendergast the priest and principal leader of the Mayo rebels … is now in Cornamona organising the people. He has been seen near a place called Ardbear within five miles of Ballinahinch … holding a conference with an armed stranger … passing with great rapidity through the country.' The information is alarmist, emphasising the conviction of 'the gentlemen of the country' that the area would soon be up in arms and ready for 'the landing of the Enemy'. Particular hostility to Prendergast is evident: 'Prendergast is a notorious murderer as well as a most desperate rebel and in the late rebellion shot one of his own men dead on the spot for saying he was sorry he ever came among the party.' The information is also significant for its warning that arms were being imported into the area and that 'strangers appear ... armed in small scattered parties'. The intent is clear – measures are needed to 'enable the Loyalists to drive all strangers out of the country, keep down the smugglers and take up all arms ...'9

Thus, while Lord Cornwallis – doubtless for his own purposes – worked to mitigate loyalist revenge, there were many like Denis 'Hangman' Browne who remained inexorable in pursuing the remnant of the 1798 rebellion. On the other hand, Connemara proved a hospitable asylum for Prendergast and Gibbons as well as for many others who had joined in the French expedition. The poem of Anthony Raftery expresses well the feelings of those outside the ranks of loyalist gentry:

'If I got your hand it is I who would take it
But not to shake it, O Denis Brown
But to hang you high with a hempen cable
And your feet unable to touch the ground.
For it's many's the boy who was strong and able
You sent in chains with your tyrant's frown.
But they'll come again with the French flag waving
And the French drums raving to strike you down.
John Gibbons and our Father Myles
Are being guarded out in the bog'.
Under thirst and dishonour and the cold of night
They have not as much as a drop to drink
or dram to imbibe'.

Even in 1801, after the Act of Union, Denis Browne wrote to Dublin Castle that the rebel priest was abroad in the mountains of Galway and Mayo. Speaking of Prendergast as 'a desperate intelligent fellow ... very deep in the mischiefs of the country', Browne was now recommending that government should consent to his transportation for life. Browne's sibling, the Marquis of Sligo, was even more virulent about Prendergast: 'the friar is the only one to do harm, being a most daring character of desperate courage and some influence arising from his sacred function'.[10]

In the aftermath of 1798, despite major changes in political attitudes, many people remained alienated from the regime either of Dublin or Westminster. James Hope, the weaver of Templepatrick, had continued to provide a link between radicals in Dublin and Belfast. In Co Down, some Protestant Dissenters, like the Witherspoons of Knockbracken, were ready to answer Thomas Russell's call for a rising in 1803. A re-examination of Emmet's ill-fated rising shows it was not merely a brawl on the night of 23 July. In Wicklow, Kildare and Westmeath a network of former United Irishmen was ready to move if Dublin were captured by Emmet's more local insurrection. As late as 1805, reports to Dublin Castle show a virtual paranoia among loyalist gentry about an imminent French invasion. And from Thomas Russell's papers it emerges that Irish emigrès believed that Humbert was eager to return and avenge his earlier defeat by Cornwallis.[11]

Informers' reports are notoriously difficult to assess. Loyalist gentry frequently exaggerated due to their own insecurity. In some cases, a self-interested desire to raise militia forces caused them to magnify the smallest portents into threats of major disaster. In such accounts from Galway and Mayo, Fr Prendergast occupies a central position. His second escape from prison, this time from Galway, evoked a flurry of reports on sedition in that town. Suspected persons were named and located – at The Green (Ml Dugdale) and The Quay (Peggy Halloran). As to 'The Nunnery' at Market Street, an informant claimed 'this is a place where rebels have been concealed and Fr John Kirwan is connected with the concealment'. Reporting on others suspected of treason, an unnamed informer discloses 'they correspond with Prendergast the Priest'.[12]

Secret information from Connemara in April 1805 re-echoes the alarm: a great deal of French arms were being kept in good repair near the coast; McDonnell, Humbert's adjutant, had returned. Of Fr Prendergast it was said that he was concealed by Richard Martin's tenantry and was daily shifting from place to place with John Gibbons. Gibbons was alleged to have moved two French cannons into the mountains while Prendergast was reputed to be contriving plans 'to render the telegraphs useless'. Meanwhile, the tireless 'Dr' Trevor was alleging that 'An organisation has certainly taken place ... in Co Galway ... the officers appointed ... over a letter to be sent to Prendergast the priest through the Post Office ... under cover to Dillon'. Doubtless, it was little comfort for Dublin Castle to hear that 'The majority of the county magistrates do not wish to have anything to do with arresting John Gibbons, Prendergast or such persons, as it would entail certain destruction on their family for generations to come'. Thus both local tradition and documentary reports envisage Fr Prendergast's continued evasion of arrest through the sustenance of the indigenous population. As well, it seems clear that Richard Martin – now an MP at Westminster – made no move to procure his capture.[13]

Given his nomadic life, it is not surprising that Myles Prendergast left no political or personal testament. Hence, little is known of his views as the events of 1798 receded into the far background. Of the other Catholic priests involved with the Killala invasion, Fr Henry O'Kane and Fr Ml Gannon eventually reached the safety of France. O'Kane's military rank saved him from execution and he was repatriated along with other French military personnel. Thereafter, he maintained his connection with the French army while its republican phase lasted. Years later, O'Kane memorialised his experiences in 1798 for Dr Wm MacNeven. Fr Gannon eventually got to Spain and, thence, to France where he became the parish priest of St Germain-en-Laye. Both men retained links with the Irish emigrés in Paris, particularly Miles Byrne and Thomas Addis Emmet.

Myles Prendergast's evasion of capture through several decades argues to unfailing support by the inhabitants of Connemara and South Mayo. As already mentioned, Richard Martin's discretion played a large part in his continued liberty. In the years from 1807 to 1819 virtually nothing is heard about Prendergast or Gibbons. It is probable that Fr Prendergast's life 'on the run' had now become an established habit. About 1819 his religious order worked at Rome for remission of the ecclesiastical penalty incurred by his killing of the prison guard at Castlebar so many years earlier.[14]

Thus, documentary evidence on the priest's later years is sparse. A small corpus of letters, from a base near Clifden, shows his intermittent contact with Augustinian confreres. In itself, the correspondence provides a fascinating glimpse of ecclesiastical politics in the decade before Catholic emancipation in 1829. From 1799, episcopal pragmatism led prelates such as Troy (Dublin), Caulfield (Ferns) and, later Murray (Dublin) to emphasise Catholic 'loyalty'. Men like Coigly and Prendergast were disowned as aberrant exceptions. Nonetheless, the autonomy (albeit limited) of religious orders provided a niche where dissidents like Prendergast (and some other survivors of 1798) could shelter.

Fr Prendergast's surviving letters (mainly to the provincial superior, Fr Daniel O'Connor) are lengthy. Although written in a good hand and plentifully interspersed with Latin phrases, they show mediocre literary style. Frequent references are made to ill-health, due to a recurring leg-wound. Complaints are made about the rapacity of local clergy who preclude him from ministration of baptism, anointing or celebration of Mass, lest they should forfeit income thereby. Clearly, he dislikes the new Maynooth-trained priests because of their 'Antimonachal' stances (hostility to order priests). There is an overtone that he would wish to return to community life in an Augustinian friary, yet there are many feeble excuses to prevent Fr O'Connor visiting him. In a letter of March 1828 there is reference to an attempt by the son of the Knight of

Glin to obtain a pardon. More effectively, Richard Martin had now procured guarantees from government officials that 'no procedure would ever be taken against my freedom'.[15]

Despite his status as an outlaw and, for many years, a 'hunted priest', the Augustinian order kept contact with Myles Prendergast through several decades. There is a record of monies sent to him at various locations and under various covers. From 1835 to 1842 a modest but regular supply was sent. During 1836 several remittances of five pounds were acknowledged by the fugitive priest. One such stipend was sent by the Agricultural Bank while another was remitted through 'his friend Mr Darcy of Clifden'. On July 1840, five pounds cash was sent to the parish priest of the place where he was in hiding.

Nevertheless, Fr Myles Prendergast did not 'come in'. He remained 'on the run' in Connemara until his death in 1842. His life has given rise to a plentiful folklore about his exploits and popularity among the inhabitants of west Connacht.

In his *Sketches of the Irish Highlands,* Henry McManus refers to the activity, even during the 1830s, of those who fled to Connemara after 1798. Although his strokes are broad and by no means inerrant, he gives a worthwhile view from the standpoint of a visitor in the 1840s:

'Of these fully one hundred still maintained their military organisation and they were often seen in arms in the middle of the day, 'exercising' on Rosshill. Their captain was one Prendergast who had been prior of a monastery near Westport and by all accounts he became a desperate man. The band first drew their supplies of food from the surrounding localities, especially Co Mayo to which Prendergast sent out plundering expeditions. At last, however, this resource began to fail and then they resorted to levy a 'black mail' even on their hospitable friends in Connemara *(sic)* ... But happily for that country it was saved from spoliation by some companies of Highlanders whom the government sent down to the district. At the sight of them the insurgents fled; and Prendergast having

concealed himself near Clifden till the government proclamation of the amnesty, availed himself of its terms and
thus obtained a full pardon'.[16]

Bibliography
Primary Sources
Augustinian Archives (Ballyboden). File on Fr Myles Prendergast (some
letters as well as records of payments to Prendergast during 1835-1842).
Archives of Congregation of Propagation of the Faith (Rome). Udienza, 6
June 1819, 57 f.483,5; ibid. Udienza , 23 April 1820, 58 f 298. 3 (304).
National Archives (Rebellion Papers). 620/1/197; 620/7/76/7; 620/14/188/6;
620/14/189/1, 3-6 and 9; 620/46/83; 620/54/12; 620/56/48; 620/14/33.

Secondary Sources
Brady, John, *Catholics and Catholicism in the 18th Century Press,* Catholic
Record Society of Ireland, St Patrick's College, Maynooth, 1965.
Ford, Sean, *Annala Beaga O Iorruis,* Irish Authors Press (at Ballyboden
Augustinian Archive).
Hayes, Richard, *Last Invasion of Ireland,* Dublin, 1939 (*vide* 2nd ed).
Keogh, Daire, *The French Disease: The Catholic Church and Radicalism in
Ireland 1790-1800,* Four Courts Press, Dublin, 1993.
Kilroy, Patricia, *The Story of Connemara,* Gill and MacMillan, Dublin,
1989.
McManus, Henry, *Sketches of the Irish Highlands,* Hamilton Adams,
London, 1863.
O'Broin, Leon, *Slán Le Muirisc* (play), Oifig an tSoláthair, Baile Átha
Cliaith, 1944.

Articles
Carr, L.W., OSA, 'Friar Prendergast', *The Connaught Telegraph,* 5.7.1941.
Gibbons, J., 'Fr Myles Prendergast', *An Coinneál,* December 1980, pp 79-82.

CHAPTER FOUR

William Steel Dickson (1744-1824)

Modern Irish history is strangely mute on William Steel Dickson, a 'New Light' minister of the Presbyterian Church. Yet, along with James Porter, his writing and preaching had major influence on the politics of the day. His arguments for parliamentary reform and religious toleration are among the finest examples of Presbyterian generosity, while his political theology ranks high in Enlightenment thought. Some have argued that Dickson and Porter influenced events of the 1790s even more than Tone or Drennan. Whatever about this claim, it is indisputable that their politico-theological analyses were of major import, particularly in the north of Ireland. As to Dickson, his long career is marked by political integrity and religious toleration. Ultimately, his association with United Irish principles incurred prolonged imprisonment, exile and extreme poverty at the end of his life.

On Christmas Day 1744, Wm Dickson was born into a family of tenant farmers at Ballycraig, near Carnmoney in Co Antrim. His early education was given by Robert White, the minister at Templepatrick, who, to cite Dickson's own words: 'first taught me, not only to reason, but to think'. At seventeen, he entered Glasgow University to read economics, law, political theory and theology, the latter to doctoral level.[1]

Many Irish Presbyterian divines (especially from the north) did their foundational studies at Glasgow . Here, a radical tradition of political theology derived from Francis Hutcheson. Hutcheson was himself an Irishman and a son of the Presbyterian manse. His stance on the link between morals and politics has already been noticed. Political and social questions were ultimately moral issues. Hence, there was an obligation to work for a social order where 'the greatest good of the greatest number' would be served. While this was not a full-blown theory of republicanism, it was essentially anti-oligarchic. Even more radical was Hutcheson's tenet of a people's right to contest misgovernment: 'where the governor is plainly perfidious to his trust, he has forfeited all the power committed ...' Thus, some years after Hutcheson, Dickson was exposed to a version of the European enlightenment and a thorough-going system of Calvinist theology. Returning home after four years, he had imbibed 'advanced' political views through Hutcheson and other mentors such as William Leechman, John Millar and Adam Smith.[2]

In Irish circumstances, it was unpropitious for Dickson's future that he regarded aristocratic hegemony as invariably bad government. Specifically, and even less propitiously for himself, he saw administration by a faction or sect as equivalent to the rule of 'spies, informers and mercenary clerks'. Perhaps the influence of John Millar led him to prefer 'rational republicanism'. Nonetheless, he was not a doctrinaire republican since he believed there was little difference between limited monarchy and a well constituted republic. Thus, he held that where a constitution fostered political responsibility, it mattered little whether the ruler were called 'emperor, king, duke, stadtholder, consul or president'. The essential thing was that the chief magistrate should be 'elected by the state, and amenable to the laws under which he derives his authority'. Unfortunately, in late eighteenth-century Ireland such circumstances were notable by their absence .[3]

Ballyhalbert, Co Down

Urged by his old teacher, Robert White, Dickson presented himself for ministry in the Presbyterian church. In 1767, he was licensed as a probationary minister. Only in 1771 did he receive a call to full-time ministry of the Ballyhalbert (Glastry) congregation. Here, on the Ards peninsula, he worked in pastoral duties and, like James Porter, as an improving farmer.

Another similarity to Porter is that he enjoyed the friend-ship/patronage of Alexander Stewart of Mount Stewart. Many years later, writing in utter disillusion with the Stewarts, Dickson generously remarked on 'my esteem of the father of the family and my sincere gratitude for his kind at-tention paid me in early life'.[4]

Political Activity

From the late 1770s, Dickson became involved with na-tional politics. Due to convergent issues these years were a watershed in Ulster Presbyterianism – revolution in America, a general election (1776) and opposition to the exigencies of the Vestry Act. Most notable of all was the foundation of the Volunteer movement (1778). The primary objective of the movement was to defend the country from French invasion during Britain's war in America. Soon, armed Volunteer com-panies were drilling throughout the land and parading in re-splendent uniform. Given the sympathy of many Irish colo-nial 'patriots' for the American revolutionists and their more radical noises about free trade, Dublin Castle nervously re-garded its protectors. While government could do no other than tolerate the Volunteers, the prospect of an armed citizen-ry, albeit Protestant, was deeply worrying.[5]

By 1779, Lord Abercorn's agent in Strabane was sounding the alarm: 'the Volunteers are certainly driving at something more than defending us from invasion. The two companies of this town declared they would not serve under anyone who lived in England.' A year later, the same agent complained: 'the first cause for their associating is not even spoken of now, but (it is) openly declared to have the laws reformed to what they think right'.[6] Implicit here is that many Volunteers were infected by the spirit of parliamentary reform (later to be a central demand of the United Irishmen). Their other demand was essentially an anti-British one – the ending of discrimina-tion against Irish industry in the existing trade laws. There was talk of boycotting British imports and Swift's adage was heard: 'Burn everything British except her coal.' The climax

of this demand came in the historic parade at College Green
(4 Nov 1779) where two cannons were drawn up with the cap-
tion 'Free trade or This'. Here was the apex of Irish colonial
patriotism, an extension of the 'patriot Parliament'.

Involvement of clergymen in the Volunteers was considerable. Dickson himself later wrote: 'the rusty black was ex-
changed for a glowing scarlet, and the title of Reverend for
that of Captain'.[7] Anti-war sentiment was strong among
many Presbyterian divines. Such feeling did not arise from
pacifism but from kinship with the American revolutionists.
At Ballyhalbert, Dickson preached two 'Fast Day' sermons
criticising the government's 'unnatural, impolitic and unprincipled' war in America. In many ways these sermons run par-
allel to James Porter's more famous 'Wind and Weather'
homily of early 1797. In one (December 1776), Dickson called
for national repentance; in the other (February 1778) he again
criticised the government on 'the ruinous effects of civil war'.
The two sermons give a hint of Dickson's incisive mind and
keen political temper. They re-echo the deterioration in Irish
economy during the late 1770s when unemployment and
slumps became the order of the day. Yet, to loyalist ears they
sounded like treason and Dickson was denounced in many
quarters as a traitor. Such views and such trenchant expression may well have caused the secession from his Ballyhalbert
congregation when a 'seceder' church was formed at Kirk-
cubbin near Greyabbey, in 1777.[8]

Even more significant is Dickson's sermon to the
Echlinville volunteers in March 1779. Speaking as chaplain,
he called for parliamentary reform and admission of
Catholics to Volunteer ranks. On parliamentary reform he
spoke of a desired situation where 'The Benches of the House
would no longer groan under a cumbrous load of mutes and
nominal representatives nor would a man be revered as an
oracle because he could publickly express a few sentences
without degenerating into nonsense or absurdity'. On the of-
fence to Catholics by their exclusion from Volunteer ranks, he

told his congregation: 'To remove such injurious suspicions is an object well deserving your serious attention; and your conduct ought to show that ye have not taken up arms for that or the other denomination; but for your country ...' The sermon provoked both opprobrium and approbation. Later, Dickson referred to criticism by 'all the Protestant and Presbyterian bigots of the country'. Yet he published the sermon in its substance, adding that his original reference to Catholic fears was even stronger.[9]

The Stewart Interlude

Given the role of Lord Castlereagh (Robert Stewart Jr.) during the 1790s, it is at first surprising that Robert Stewart (Sr) was the reform candidate for north Down in the general election of 1783. William Steel Dickson was one of his most active supporters, to the extent of marshalling forty mounted freeholders in the Stewart interest. Robert Stewart was defeated by the candidate of Lord Hillsborough and shortly afterwards 'took refuge in a peerage' as Lord Londonderry. Seven years later, Dickson gave an equally spirited endorsement to the younger Robert Stewart whose radical sentiments were apparently sincere. This time, the future Lord Castlereagh was elected on a reform programme. The accelerating events of the 1790s would place Dickson and the Stewarts in bitter political enmity. It is a further indication of the subtleties of late eighteenth-century Irish politics that even up to 1790, Dickson, Porter and the Stewarts of Mount Stewart were in the same reforming camp of Whig liberalism.

Minister at Portaferry

Early in 1780 Dickson became minister of the Portaferry congregation. In June of the same year he was elected to the moderatorship of the General Synod of Ulster at Dungannon – an indication of his standing in the Presbyterian Church despite his radical leanings. Dickson's homily to the 1781 Synod (later published in *Scripture Politics*) provides a good example of his thought at this relatively early period. In hindsight, it

offers a clue to his subsequent development as a major figure
in reform politics. The address reflects Francis Hutcheson's
Glasgow lectures on government: all authority derives from
the people; their safety, happiness and protection are the
supreme norm against which all laws have to be judged . Even
now, Dickson will argue that 'All governments tend to despotism, and by degrees, more or less rapid, terminate in it'.[10]
One notices a developed view of the minister's responsibility
to offer critical comment – since religion and politics are directly related, 'we derive a political character highly important
and become dispensers of that knowledge which ... ought to
regulate ... political interests'. Clearly, Dickson argues for a
liberal spirit in religion: 'We should endeavour to banish that
blind and tyrannical daemon which can see no worth but in
the name of party, and under the name of liberty, is busied
only in the forgery of chains.' With evident approval, he declared: 'We have lately seen toleration extend her soothing
arms and offer an embrace unknown before'. Almost at the
end of the sermon, Dickson recommended the Synod to offer
a 'helping hand to extend toleration wider still'.[11]

Perhaps this 'toleration' refers to proposed concessions for
Presbyterians, although Dickson's generosity went beyond the
limits of his own church. Through the decade, government
concessions (notably repeal of clauses in the 1704 Test Act)
enabled Presbyterians to stand for parliament. Although
Robert Stewart (Sr) was defeated in north Down, a number of
reforming independents were elected in Co Antrim (John
O'Neill, Hercules Rowley and William Todd Jones). Nevertheless, more radical Presbyterians continued to insist on further parliamentary reform and (certainly in Dickson's case)
for Catholic emancipation. Ascendancy irritation is clear in
Lord Hillsborough's complaint that 'the Presbyterian parsons
are fomenting a turbulent spirit. There never was a worse
piece of policy than the rewarding of these incendiaries, for it
is impossible to gain them.' Writing to Pitt from Dublin
Castle, Edward Cooke remarked 'the Presbyterians are nearly

mad for parliamentary reform'. Even more robustly, Lord
Lieutenant Rutland observed that 'the province of Ulster is
filled with dissenters, who are in general very factious – great
levellers and republicans'.[12]

In view of his emphasis on democratic parliamentary reform and his regard for religious toleration, it is unsurprising
that Steel Dickson was among those who took the United
Irish 'test' in late 1791. The aims of the society – equal representation in Parliament, union among Irish people, removal
of all disqualifications based on religion – were exactly what
Dickson had written and preached for many years. According
to his own narrative (here one notes that Dickson's *Narrative*
has a very particular aim, viz. to rebut charges levelled against
him by colleagues), from this point onwards he endeavoured
'to elucidate the principles, prove the necessity, and diffuse
the spirit of union'. In this he saw himself as part of a wide social movement endorsed by his fellow Volunteers, his parishioners and even by his friends, the Stewarts. Through early
1792, he noted the widespread liberal spirit among his co-reli-
gionists and their welcome for the French Revolution.

Was this a miscalculation on his part? Certainly, Tone and
Russell already shared an extremely high estimation of the
new spirit in the north. On the other hand, the ever realistic
Samuel McTier had urged caution: '(Tone) mistakes the situation of this town and country round, they are still full of
prejudice, which only time can remove'. When it came to the
Bastille Day celebration of July 1792 – it is interesting that
Whigs, Volunteers and United Irishmen took part – McTier's
caution rather than the optimism of Tone or Dickson, appears to have been nearer the truth.

The celebration had been arranged for the Falls district to
highlight the demands for parliamentary reform and Catholic
emancipation.[13] Tone had come to Belfast with speech and
resolutions already prepared. From Dublin also came John
Keogh of the Catholic Committee with William Drennan,
one of the most outspoken in the reform party. During the

night of 13 July, Samuel Neilson informed Tone of attempts to
incite anti-Catholic feeling among Volunteer corps from the
countryside. Having overestimated the extent of United Irish
penetration in the north, Tone now had to face the fact of
anti-popery among Volunteers from Co Down. In the event,
the day proceeded satisfactorily for Tone: his pro-Catholic
resolutions, couched in implicit terms as matter of tactics,
were accepted. Tone's success may well have been due to the
endorsement of his resolutions by Presbyterian clergymen
amongst whom Dickson and Sinclair Kelbourne were prominent.

The argument was between 'gradual emancipation' on the
one hand and 'total and immediate emancipation' on the
other. The 'gradualist' argument forwarded by Henry Joy (a
barrister who would later defend Thomas Russell at Downpatrick) centred on the ignorance of Catholics and their in-
capacity for mainstream politics. Dickson rejected such positions as 'shameless pretexts, though equally unfounded, in-
sulting and blasphemous'. Speaking towards the end of the
meeting, he fastened on the weakness of gradualism: when was
emancipation to come? tomorrow? next month? next year?
next century? or happily in the next world? In his own
Narrative Dickson treats his intervention modestly:

> 'Something too warm seemed to pervade (the meeting) of
> which I feared the increase and the consequences ... I re-
> luctantly yielded to the impulse of adressing the meeting:
> and as argument was unnecessary, where there was noth-
> ing like arguments to answer ... I only hung a few rags of
> ridicule on the step-ladder of 'gradual emancipation',
> which were eagerly laid hold of ... and formed into a man-
> tle, under which 'Mrs time-to-time' looked so silly that her
> God-fathers were ashamed of, and abandoned her. In con-
> sequence, 'Lady total and immediate' was adopted, em-
> braced and cheered.'[14]

In Dickson's own view, the event gave new inspiration to the
friends of union among Irishmen. The public papers were, he

says, full of resolutions from every town, village and
Volunteer association in Ulster. These far outstripped 'the
toasts wet and dry, of the semi-patriotic societies denominated
"Whig Clubs" which embraced a great proportion of the no-
bility, and landed property of the province'. At this point
Dickson's *Narrative* is decidedly optimistic on the extent to
which United Irish ideals had spread, especially among the
non-official classes. Subsequent historians raise a cautionary
note about the Bastille Day celebration, especially about
Tone's success with aid of Dickson and Kelbourne. It is noted,
for example, that many of the country corps had left the
meeting before the end of the proceedings. Was this due to
disagreement with Tone's address? Or was it due to the long
journey home? Marianne Elliott comments: 'Whichever way,
there can be no doubt that opposition to the address would
have been greater had the Co Down volunteers remained.'[16]

Dungannon Convention

The months following the Belfast rally saw intense activity
by United Irish leaders. Neilson and Russell attempted to link
up with the Catholic convention at Tailors' Hall, Dublin, in
December 1792. Their purpose was to encourage the Catholic
leadership in demands for complete emancipation. As to
Dickson, his activity was cast in another direction – local meetings
preparatory for the Dungannon Volunteers Convention of
February 1793. He was present at meetings in Co Down and
was elected a delegate to the Convention representing the
Barony of Ards. Publicly and privately he urged his own policy
– 'to restore our paralysed constitution, conciliate the public
mind, and establish His Majesty's throne in the affections of
the people, and (to forward) the equal necessity of union
among Irishmen in order to obtain (or even) extort it from
the faction of the day'.[17] One notices here a divergence from
Thomas Russell's now explicit anti-royalism – on the 'fast day'
called to mourn Louis XVI's execution, Russell entered his
Journal: '... whenever the King was prayed for, stand up. Drink
the fate of Louis to all crowned heads, George the last, etc., etc.'.[18]

At the Dungannon Convention, Dickson spoke for parliamentary reform and full Catholic emancipation. It was something of a tour-de-force which was greeted enthusiastically. At the close of the meeting, the French war was reprobated almost unanimously (only '7 or 8 of the Down squires dissented'.) Two days later, Samuel Neilson wrote that 'Dickson of Portaferry attracted the applause of all parties and gave a sort of tone to the Convention ... I have never heard any man express himself to more purpose.'[19] Richard Musgrave, a more hostile chronicler, excoriated the minister's role at Dungannon. For Musgrave, Dickson – 'a noted demagogue and the leading orator there' – inveighed against militias and fencibles, criticised proposed reliefs for Catholics as shadow emancipation, reprobated the new laws introduced by parliament (e.g. the Convention Act) and condemned the war with France in severest terms.[20] In the same address, Dickson rounded on a 'friend of government' (perhaps the once radical John Pollock, now in government employ, or else the James Dawson mentioned in Neilson's letter) for offering 'a frothy collation of whip-sillabub ... instead of the substantial bread of reform ... which the voice of Irishmen so eagerly called for'.[21] After the Convention, Dickson addressed a religious service in a nearby meeting house. Musgrave notes the sermon, 'or, rather, the political discourse frought with phlogistick principles'. Here, once again, Dickson urged reform of parliament and Catholic emancipation as a demand of Christianity itself.

Parting of Ways

At Dungannon, Steel Dickson's liberalism seemed triumphant. The forthcoming publication of his *Scripture Politics* was announced with some ceremony and his influence seemed paramount. Yet, the victory may have been more apparent than real. The Dublin government either was – or pretended to be – alarmed by the unrest which they discerned first in the Catholic Convention and, now, the Volunteers Convention. A succession of Bills, nodded through by the Whig opposition, showed that the administration was in no mood for fur-

ther compromise. This point marked a watershed of constitutional pressure for reform. Among the Catholics, the conservatives (Lord Kenmare) and the pragmatically loyal (Archbishop Troy) were outflanked by more radical leaders (Keogh,
McNeven and Sweetman). Among reform minded Protestants
and Dissenters there was also a split. Deriding Grattan's feeble
opposition, Russell put it: 'we see him return once more to his
insignificant opposition … and again grinning and chattering
at the abuses of a ministry, which but for him would not now
exist'.[22]

In Dickson's view, the government had given itself up to
madness, directly contrary to the required liberality. Even worse,
a majority of those who supported reform at the Convention
now altered course. They became the Lord Mountmumbles and
the Billy Bluffs of James Porter's lampoon. Doubtless, at this
point the Stewarts converted to ultra-loyalism and, most probably, Dickson's and Porter's opposition to them commenced.
Although Dickson never speaks of underground activity, he
avows that, being frequently in Belfast, he was surrounded by
United Irishmen and 'the union of Irishmen was, on every
occasion, the common topic of conversation'.[23]

Three Sermons on the Subject of Scripture Politics
The forthcoming publication of Dickson's sermons had
been mentioned at the Dungannon Convention. Hence,
their publication (c. March 1793) cannot be linked directly to
the embittered relations which followed the Convention and,
more particularly, government's move against reform agitation. Indeed, the first of the sermons dates from the General
Synod of 1781. Yet, Dickson's influential book emerged
amidst several United Irish publications under the aegis of the
Northern Star. They may also be situated in the framework of
the Catholic Convention (early December 1792) which Neilson
(through Russell) had exhorted to persevere in the demand
for full emancipation. The incisiveness of Dickson's addresses
is matched by their appropriateness to the circumstances of
the time – sermon two was preached on Christmas Day 1792,

while the third was addressed, also to the congregation at Portaferry, on 13 January 1793.[24]

Christmas Day 1792

This sermon traces the patterns of religious bigotry from the state establishment of Christianity under the emperor Constantine (4th cent.). Thereafter, honours of state became associated with office in religion. Thus, religion was enmeshed by intrigue, its priests took seats among nobles, its gospel was perverted into 'a firebrand of discord'. With admirable consistency, Dickson applied this to all religious parties in Ireland and England. In England, 'as power changed sides, Catholic burned Protestant, Protestant persecuted Catholic, and the Presbyterians in their momentary triumph, denied toleration to both'. In Ireland, the same thing continued to happen: 'we see the devoted Catholics bound down ... by a body of laws which humanity views with horror, justice reprobates, and religion pronounces accursed'.[25]

At a time when Louis xvi was in danger and on the eve of hostilities with France, Dickson lauded the French Revolution as a harbinger of freedom. It had 'opened the temple of liberty for all at home and sent forth her arms not to destroy but to restore the liberty of the world'. Freedom was available to all who dared, and by daring deserved, to be free. Dickson was not calling for alliance with France at this point. Instead he urged that the necessity and horrors of revolution be precluded 'by seasonable and radical reform'. Referring to government propaganda to split Catholics and Presbyterians, ('now and lately inculcated among you') he criticised rumours which would 'revive and inflame mutual prejudice, jealousy and contention thus to perpetuate oppression, slavery and wretchedness'. Dickson cleverly showed his congregation that they too were being used by government. The argument about Catholic unfitness for emancipation was 'for your ears only'. To Catholics the same propagandists were saying that 'such is the ignorance, bigotry and illiberality of the Protestants, that nothing can be done for the Catholics without offending them'. Dickson's advice was peremptory: disregard 'the malicious whisperer's artful tale', 'the base insinuations of the crying sycophant', 'the false representations of the officious partisan'.[26]

Sermon of 13 January 1793

The third sermon, delivered less than three weeks later and virtually on the eve of the Dungannon Convention, seems a reply to criticism, perhaps of the Christmas Day address. Dickson here urges the right of a Christian minister to speak on political matters. No one objected to a minister's sermon on private morality. Yet when power was shamefully abused by governors or their agents, the minister was expected to stand by in 'slavish silence'. Dickson here exercises the freedom of the Dissenting tradition in contrast to state-established religion. Skilfully he elaborates the dilemma of established religion: ministers had little freedom to preach a critical word; monarchs were at the head of the church; political expediency was the dominant consideration. With evident irony he asks: 'shall the Priests and the Levites, who minister in the tabernacle of the state, and wax fat on the sacrifices of the people's substance, lift up their voices against the oppressions, which raise them to seats among the princes of the land?' Until principle became stronger than policy 'The Father of mercies will be solicited in prescribed forms, to become partner with the oppressor, the murderer, and the assassin of nations ...' There are presages here of James Porter's 'Wind and Weather' sermon, delivered almost exactly four years later.[27]

Even after two hundred years, Dickson's analysis of evangelical prophecy sounds radical. For him, the prophetic writings of the Bible are political in their entirety – they are about matters of public polity. When these texts refer to individuals it is to denounce tyranny of kings, corruption of government and rapacity of hierarchs. Towards the close of the homily, Dickson presented two options facing the country – radical reform or total revolution. That he had not despaired of reform is clear from his reference to the 'convulsions and horrors which attend revolution'. (In the Christmas Day sermon he had regretted that the the lesson of the French Revolution had had to be written 'in letters of blood'.) In Ireland, there was still time: although 'oppression sometimes makes wise men mad', yet reformers had proceeded with 'temper, moderation and order'. Nonetheless, the sermon finished with a note of warning: 'should division among the people tempt government to reject requisitions, founded in right, and sanctioned by religion, to loose the bands of wickedness, and break the yoke of oppression, something more expressive than requisition may be justly expected'.[28]

It would be irresponsible to claim that Dickson's activities in 1793 were more adventuresome than his *Narrative* allows. Nevertheless, it is evident that he persisted in his demand for the cessation of government abuses. At General Synod (Lurgan, June 1793), he reiterated the case for reform. The publication of *Scripture Politics* situates him within the growing campaign, led by United Irishmen, for thoroughgoing change. During summer 1793, the Militia Act, the Convention Act and the disbandment of the Volunteers, drove a wedge between erstwhile reformers. John Pollock, hitherto vociferous for reform, now became a government agent. Robert Stewart (Lord Castlereagh) opted for the administration and, under Camden, became a repressive Under-Secretary for Ireland.

After 1793, a determined strategy to incite sectarian antagonism was operated by ultra-loyalists. Rumours that one community had evil designs on the other were sedulously planted in order to prevent the dreaded unity of Catholic and Dissenter. From Tyrone, the army commander General Knox, wrote: 'I have arranged a plan to scour a district full of unregistered arms, or said to be so ... not so much with a hope to succeed ... as to increase the animosity between the Orangemen and the United Irishmen ... Upon that animosity depends the safety of the centre counties of the north.'[29] Dickson himself later described the ploy: 'private emissaries were sent abroad to circulate alarms and provoke jealousy.'

Around Portaferry, Catholics and Presbyterians were caught in the grip of panic: 'Presbyterians on one day and Catholics on another (ran) from house to house, under the alarm that a massacre was to take place on the succeeding night and that their neighbours, with whom they had lived in peace and friendship, were to be the perpetrators.'[30] Dickson tried to expose the trick, 'happily with success'. However, he did not go unscathed, for charges of sedition and threats of vengeance were made against him.

Dickson's safety was temporary and there were warnings of storms to come. Government spies amassed their evidence. Already there had been arrests in Belfast. From September 1796, Neilson, Russell, Teeling and several others had been incarcerated in Newgate and Kilmainham. Dickson's own colleagues could not hide their mistrust. Martha McTier, an ever astute observer, told Dr Drennan that 'a knot of ministers … envious of Dickson … and ready to catch anything that might throw odium on him, interrupted him too soon in a speech for their own purpose'.[31] More ominous was the arrest of several parishioners of Dickson's and the attempt to get one of them, a weaver named Carr, to incriminate the minister. Carr did not do so and the parishioners were freed at Downpatrick in Summer 1797.

Government surveillance of Dickson continued. Lord Londonderry, now unremittingly hostile, wrote of him as 'one of the most violent and seditious characters in the country'. When Dickson left for Dublin immediately after church service on Christmas Day 1796, the local landlord, Colonel Savage, informed Lord Londonderry. In turn, Londonderry wrote to Dublin Castle that Dickson 'who is supposed to be … very deep in the confidence and plans of those who have invited the French … on Sunday last was apprised that the French fleet was to be off Cork; and that evening, after preaching set off for Dublin'. Londonderry , surmising 'this journey can be with no good intention', recommended that Dickson be arrested in Dublin.[32] Dickson had indeed visited

Dublin and had visited the Belfast prisoners several times. Whilst there, he was informed in Kilmainham that 'everyone believed I was an United Irishman'.[33] However, the arrest called for by Londonderry did not take place.

Londonderry's estimation of Dickson's radical activity was not confined to the Stewart family. Lord Downshire also wrote to the Castle about Dickson's pivotal role in the United Irishmen.[34] Richard Musgrave later commented that in Summer 1797 Dickson 'gave political discourses which he entitled evening lectures to his congregation at Portaferry for the purpose, as he said, of enlightening them'.[35] The implication is clear: the minister was involved in seditious activities. Even more damaging for Dickson, the informer Nicholas Magin cast him as adjutant-general for Co Down.[36] In his own *Narrative,* Dickson neither affirms nor denies his part in the re-organisation of the United Irishmen during early 1798. The account of his own activity in late 1797 and early 1798 is suffused with mystery. Dickson adduces a succession of bilious attacks as the reason why he was not in public evidence through the winter of 1797. Early in 1798 he visited Scotland to transact business for his wife whose uncle had died. To government agents, this mysteriousness spelled implication with the United Irishmen whose earlier General, Thomas Russell, was now imprisoned at Newgate.

After return from Scotland, Dickson's luggage was impounded and minutely searched. Although nothing incriminating was found, he was given to understand that the magistrates of Antrim and Down suspected him of linking up with radical societies in Scotland. Even still there was insufficient evidence to arrest him. From April to June 1798 he was constantly riding through north Down. In May, he visited Newtownards more than once, as he put it, 'on sacramental duty'. There were several visits to Belfast, Saintfield and Ballynahinch. On the evening of 5 June 1798 he was arrested at Ballynahinch on foot of an order by Colonel Annesley.

Hence, when the ill-co-ordinated rising did take place, the

alleged General for Down was in prison at Belfast. North
Down did rise out under Henry Munro and there were battles
at Saintfield and Ballynahinch. At Belfast Dickson was imprisoned variously in the Donegal Arms, the Artillery Barracks
and the Provost prison. Attempts were made by John Pollock,
a government attorney, and by John Cleland, the Anglican
parson-magistrate, to incriminate him as rebel commander
for Co Down. At this point, Hughes and Magin were introduced, ready to swear against whomever the magistrates wished.
A poignant circumstance of Dickson's imprisonment is his
ministration to Henry Joy McCracken before the latter's execution in July 1798. As well, Dickson had to inform Mary Ann
McCracken that her brother's little daughter was then living
in the hills above Belfast.[37]

On his involvement with the events preceding and during
1798, Dickson's *Narrative* (written in 1812) does not lie.
However, it meets a specific purpose – to answer a resolution
of the Synod of Ulster that he had been involved in 'seditious
or treasonable practices'. His case is that, although bribery
and intimidation had been tried, government was unable to
prove its case against him. In such absence of proof the Synod
erred in finding against him. For this reason, one interprets
Dickson's enigmatic phrase with due caution – 'Yet I may have
been a General for aught that appears to the contrary; and I
may not have been a General, though people said I was. But
be that as it was, General or no General, it appears, that my
doom was predetermined, though, contrary to expectation, it
did not prove fatal. Perhaps ... as Mr Pollock said afterwards,
"had I been left to myself, it might have been otherwise".'[38]

Despite the hectoring of Pollock and Cleland, the required
evidence was not found, or else, to protect highly placed informers, it could not be adduced. Some weeks later, towards
the end of July, a version of the Kilmainham Treaty was presented to the Belfast prisoners for signature.[39] Dickson's personal reserve is evidenced not only by his refusal to sign a declaration but also by his resistance to the importunities of his

fellow-prisoners for a signature. Like Thomas Russell, he was unhappy at making avowals of guilt which he did not feel. Unlike Russell, he had the opportunity to put his unwillingess in writing: 'I (have) no compromise to make with government; and I (will) not sign any paper either implying that I was guilty of crimes that I (have) not committed, or admitting any thing, as a crime, which I (have) done as a duty'.[40] Some time later, he and several others were transferred to the *Postlethwaite,* a prison hulk on Belfast Lough. Here the extremely harsh conditions were borne with fortitude by Dickson and his colleagues through a hot summer and a biting winter. On 25 March 1799, without notice, he was transferred to the *Aston Smith* to join the Newgate and Kilmainham prisoners.

Of particular interest are specific notices which Dickson committed to his *Narrative:* good treatment by the escort to Fort George and, even more, the humane conduct of Fort George's governor, Colonel Stewart. Paying tribute to the behaviour of Stewart and his colleagues, he writes: 'when I contrast it with what I knew, witnessed and felt ... in what was my country, but now is or yet may be, I know not what, through the intrigues of an apostate (Castlereagh) and the enormities of a faction ... I feel praise too cool for their merits and language too feeble for the expression of my sensations.' Another interesting detail is Dickson's note on the religious composition of the prisoner group: four Catholics, six Presbyterians and ten Anglicans. From this he ridicules loyalist suggestions that 1798 was 'a Popish rebellion'. The very preponderance of Anglicans suggested that, where loyalty was left to itself, the gilded Protestant ascendancy had little cause to boast of loyalty.[41] This clearly hinted Dickson's contempt for the jobbery which had preceded the Act of Union.

Return to Ireland

Some months before the main body of Fort George internees, Dickson was released. In January 1802, he returned to a changed and very difficult context. During his imprisonment, illness, bereavement and impoverishment had struck his family – Dickson's son had died sometime in 1798 and his wife had become invalided. Many debts overhung the family and there was small prospect of his reinstatement to his ministry. Politically, another temper was in the air. The Londonderrys, the Clelands and the Pollocks were arrogantly triumphant. An erstwhile liberal, Dr Robert Black, had followed Lord Castlereagh into rabid loyalism and inveterate enmity to Dickson. Through Black's influence, Dickson had been disowned at General Synod (1799), for involvement 'in treasonable or seditious activities'. On the other hand was the extraordinary generosity of Wm Moreland, now minister at Portaferry, who offered to resign in favour of the returned internee. Yet, John Cleland's shadow fell over attempts to give Dickson an appointment, either at Portaferry or Donegore. Eventually, in March 1803, Dickson was 'called' to a secessionist church at Keady, Co Armagh. Here he ministered until his retirement in 1815.

Through the early months at Keady, Dickson was persecuted by government spies. In Summer 1803, Wm McGuire, (desiring 'to see Dickson's neck stretched'), alleged that he was awaiting a landing of French arms near Rostrevor. Another report detailed his visit to Dublin (July 1803) where he was seen by a Presbyterian minister 'in the company of Catholics and collecting money from them'.[42] Since the informant was living at Harold's Cross, the inference was that Dickson had endeavoured to link up with Emmet there or at Rathfarnham. Earl Annesley claimed to have issued orders for Dickson's arrest. Whatever about this involvement, Dickson was not idle during his years at Keady. In the 1805 election for Down, Castlereagh was opposed by a Colonel John Meade. Dickson's involvement is suggested by a tract from Caslereagh supporters about 'one who had led some of his own brethern to the rope' and who had barely escaped arrest during Emmet's rising. The *Narrative* shows Dickson's immense satisfaction at Castlereagh's defeat.

Other activities are reminiscent of Dickson's earlier work for 'a cordial union of Irishmen'. From 1810, Irish Catholics had begun to reiterate their demands for full emancipation. The old Catholic Committee, of which Tone was an erstwhile secretary, criticised the Dublin Castle regime under Lord Richmond as 'patrons of bigotry, intolerance and Irish slavery'.[43] A new campaign of petitions was spearheaded by Catholic laity (including Daniel O'Connell) and the Committee mounted public meetings in Dublin as well as throughout the country. Protestant reaction was mixed – some called for arrest of the organisers under the old Convention Act of 1793 while others supported the campaign. It would seem that Dickson was among the latter. In May 1811, he addressed a meeting of Catholics in Dublin, thus becoming 'probably the first Presbyterian minister in Ireland to address a wholly Roman Catholic gathering'.[44] In the context of propaganda designed to drive a deeper wedge between Presbyterians and Catholics, he emphasised that the great body of Ulster Presbyterians were sincere friends to Catholic claims. He also argued that Catholics had no cause to accept the rumours industriously circulated that Presbyterians had become enemies of Catholics. Again, on 9 September 1811 he attended another meeting of Catholics at Armagh. Returning to Keady he was beset by three men whom he suspected were Orangemen. With habitual forthrightness he gave utterance to his suspicions. The *Evening Herald* of 16 September decried his allegations. The *Herald* claimed he was 'beastly drunk' and that his blame of Orangemen was merely an alibi.

Apart from pastoral work at Keady, Dickson laboured to rebut the resolution of 1799 concerning his alleged 'treasonable or seditious activities'. His efforts were rewarded in 1813 when General Synod retracted the earlier resolution through the good offices of Reverend Henry Montgomery and Reverend Wm Porter. Keady itself was good to him – in an appendix to his *Narrative* (2nd edition) he notes with gratitude 'I have earned £312, in the abandoned and reprobated congregation of Keady, during the past nine years.' The congregation there had kept the Dicksons 'in decency and comfort'.[45]

On 27 June 1815 Dickson retired, deeming himself unable further to discharge his duties at Keady. Thereafter, he lived near Belfast in a cottage provided by Joseph Wright. It is interesting to note that he was helped financially by old United Irish families, amongst others, Francis McCracken, William Drennan, William Tennent and Adam McClean. A somewhat poignant notice is that a farm of his, near Comber, was sold on sheriff's order to meet a debt of £407-14-1 (*Belfast Commercial Chronicle*, 26 Jan 1814). There were few other public involvements although he published a further collection of sermons in 1817. A proposal to award him a chair of divinity was passed over by General Synod in 1816. During 1819, his long invalided wife, Isabella, died in Co Down. Five years later, on 27 December 1824, William Steel Dickson himself died. It is perhaps a sign of the changed times that less than a dozen attended his interment at Belfast's Clifton Street cemetery. Among those present was Reverend Henry Montgomery.

One can surely endorse W. D. Bailie's tribute to this often stormy character 'who had endeavoured to neutralise the poison of prejudice and bigotry, fostered the seeds of religious liberty and sought to promote union and harmony among his fellow countrymen of all religious persuasions'.[46]

Bibliography
Bailie, W.D., 'Wm Steel Dickson, D.D.', *The Bulletin of the Presbyterian Historical Society of Ireland*, No 6, May 1976.
Dickson, Wm Steel, *A Narrative of the Confinement and Exile of Wm Steel Dickson*, 2nd edition, Belfast, 1812.
Chart, D.A. (ed), *The Drennan Letters*, Belfast, 1931.
Clifford, Brendan, *Scripture Politics, Selections From The Writings of Wm Steel Dickson*, Athol Books, Belfast, 1991.

Stewart A.T.Q., *The Narrow Ground,* Faber and Faber, 1977.
Teeling, Charles, *History of the Irish Rebellion 1798,* Shannon, 1972.

Articles
Dickson, Wm Steel in *Dictionary of National Biography,* (Alexander Gordon).
Tesch, Pieter, 'Presbyterian Dissent' in Dickson, Whelan and Keogh, *The United Irishmen,* Lilliput, 1993.
David Kennedy, 'The Northern Whigs', in *Studies,* 1944, pp 263-9.
Irish Unitarian Magazine, Vol 2, No 10, pp 33-4.
Belfast Commercial Chronicle, 26 Jan 1814.

PART TWO

Nineteenth Century

Ireland Under the Union

The disappearance of the College Green parliament was re-gretted by few. Despite the sentimental canard that Ireland should have its own parliament, College Green was itself 'an alien thing, hostile to, and in craven fear of, the Ireland that waited outside its doors'.[1] The events of the 1790s went a long way to showing that it was irreformable as it stood. For some time, the Whig leadership at Whitehall had been laying the groundwork for a 'legislative union'. Apart from sections of the old ascendancy who trotted out nationalist rhetoric, most Presbyterians and Catholics felt that things could not be worse under direct rule from Westminster. Moderates like Henry Joy and William Bruce supported the union as provid-ing a better hope for gradual reform than the ascendancy Irish parliament.[2] Several United Irish leaders (e.g. Samuel Neilson) are reputed to have favoured the abolition of the College Green parliament. As well, testimonials from Catholic dioce-ses (e.g. Raphoe) pinned hopes for further relief on the Act of Union. Bishop Hussey of Waterford expressed preference for a union with 'the Beys and Mamelukes of Egypt to that of being under the rod of the Mamelukes of Ireland'.[3]

Meanwhile, the old ascendancy group argued for retention of the Dublin parliament. Ironically, many *ci-devant* loyalists became rabidly anti-Union. On 19 January 1799, their jour-nal, *The Anti-Union,* hectored northern electors in essentially nationalist terms: 'When your causes of complaint were trif-ling, you rent the air with your cries. Now that you are about to be sacrificed on the altar of British aggrandisement, a single murmur does not escape your lips'.[4] Wm Drennan caustically described an anti-Union meeting at Dublin's Royal Exchange: 'Orangemen, opposition men, democrats, Catholics and Presbyterians, the *omnium gatherum* of the day, forced by fear into a short cordiality'.[5] In fairness, it should be noted that Henry Grattan emotionally pleaded against the winding up of the native parliament. With bizarre logic, Francis Dobbs (former governor of North Carolina) adduced a treatise of millenarian arguments from the Bible to counter the dissolution of College Green parliament

In a very qualified sense, one can argue that the Act of Union was a 'triumph of failure' for the United Irish project. Doubtless, in framing the union, the purposes of Pitt, Castlereagh and Cornwallis were not those of the United Irishmen. While the aims of the latter remained to be achieved, nonetheless several of their objectives would be attained in the decades of the nineteenth century – religious emancipation (1829), amendment of the Tithe laws, disestablishment of Anglicanism (1869), land reform (1870-90). Even then, much remained to do and these reforms were attained only by sustained political pressure. Although a price of the Union was consolidation of the personal fortunes of John Fitzgibbon, Robert Stewart, John Beresford and their allies, yet the vice-grip of the old ascendancy was destroyed forever. New alliances would form. New political battles would be fought to change the social and economic face of Ireland through the nineteenth and into the twentieth century.

After the Act of Union, Ireland changed in many ways. Dublin became the capital of Ireland rather than of the Pale. The unlimited power of the anglo-Irish ascendancy was limited drastically. The richest of them departed for London. Taking their wealth with them, they lived ostentatiously as absentee landlords with little responsibility to the society from which they had abstracted such wealth. All they left was Dublin's splendid Georgian mansions which slowly degenerated into grimy slums. Of those who remained, many (although by no means all) withdrew into 'a hard, complacent dream life, glorying in their spectacular past' and affected to regard Irish life as

sad, stagnant and dreary. The exceptions have been documented by Hubert Butler's essays, e.g, 'The Big House After
The Union'; these exceptions are also notable in societies such
as the Gaelic Society (1806), the Iberno-Celtic Society (1818)
and the Ossiaic Society (1853).[6]

For a while, especially until 1815, middle-class interests
seemed best served in the 'New Order'. Thereafter, the hopeful vision of a cordial union among Irishmen relapsed towards
sectarian concerns. As to the grievances of Dissenters, these
were in part addressed by the *regium donum* to Presbyterian
clergy. Gradually, the radical voices of the 1780s and 90s, so
well exemplified by Dickson and Porter, were muted in the
theological divisions which racked Presbyterianism. While it
should not be assumed that the older radicals had all changed
their views, yet under Henry Cooke's influence, Presbyterianism
gradually aligned itself with conservative, land-owning interests
as a bulwark against perceived Catholic advances. In 1834, the
pragmatic alliance of Presbyterianism and the Established
Church could be solemnised in 'the nuptials of Hillsborough'.
Henry Cooke, although a dominant figure in Presbyterianism,
may well have reflected a widely-held view. By 1835, it was reported of Connor parish (Co Antrim) that although it had
been fully engaged in the 1798 rising '... their politics have
changed, and they now seem indifferent and careless on the
subject'.[7] Nevertheless, some Presbyterians continued to express their unease. In the 1860s the minister at Broughshane,
Reverend J. Rogers, criticised the Belfast Presbytery for its
'conventionalism and courtesy which had placed their principles in the dust and (made of once radical Presbyterians) mere
flunkies'.[8] At Belfast's Donegall St church, Isaac Nelson provided a lonely but persevering opposition to the new conservatism. Later again, several clergymen of the Presbyterian tradition represented the old radicalism in their defence of land
reform, opposition to the great landlords and espousal of liberal politics.

Nevertheless, one can hardly contest A. T. Q. Stewart's

claim that in early decades of the nineteenth century 'Many Protestants who had spoken up most vociferously for the rights of Ireland, then became fervent supporters of the British connection and left the national cause to the Catholic majority'.[9] Even former United Irishmen reread their own history. Decades later, James Hope put it forcefully: 'It is hard for a man who did not live at the time, to believe or comprehend the extent to which misrepresentations were carried at the close of our struggle; for, besides the paid agents, the men who flinched and fell away from our cause, grasped at any apology for their own delinquency.'[10] Despite earlier generosity, mutual suspicion was carefully fostered, so that collaboration in progressive politics became exceedingly difficult.

In regard to clerical leadership of Catholicism, there were many protestations of loyalty at the expense of a radical analysis of society. Unforgiveably, Bishop Caulfield of Ferns described Fr John Murphy and other radical priests as 'the faeces of the church'.[11] Maynooth College and the counter-revolutionary discipline subsequently imposed on diocesan clergy ensured that a sullen compliance was exacted from the rank and file of the people. Nonetheless, in the first decade of the century elements of the Catholic middle class remained in tension with the hierarchical leadership. Thus, a harried Archbishop Troy would complain to Rome that the laity 'torment the bishops'. Even in 1811, a Catholic pamphleteer could write of the 'National Will and Spirit of Erin' which, he claimed, terrified the government for its own rashness and folly.[12] Economic distress in the 1820s (there was a famine in 1819-20) led to disillusion – not confined to Catholics – with the government at Whitehall.

A political Catholicism began to emerge, popular and mass-based, led by the barrister Daniel O'Connell. Largely due to his political astuteness, the demand of the 1790s for religious emancipation was attained in 1829, albeit in a limited way. In the 'emancipation', the small-holders (the forty shilling men) who provided the backbone to O'Connell's movement found themselves disenfranchised. A century later, Fr Ml O'Flanagan remarked that emancipation applied mainly to the middle classes who could henceforth obtain employment from the British government. According to O'Flanagan, real emancipation had not been attained since it did not include ' the freedom of the rank and file of the people'.[13]

Orangemen determinedly opposed the Reform of 1829, although many liberal Protestants supported it. During the 1820s, the anti-Catholic Archbishop of Dublin, William Magee, pursued old hatreds even to the extent of banning Catholic funerals in Dublin cemeteries (then in Anglican hands). Whereas many clergymen were ready to work in harmony, Magee retained 'the hot No Popery blood of the Iniskilling Dragoons in his veins'.[14] The 'second reformation', launched with Magee's support in the 1820s and spearheaded by English evangelicals, drove a further wedge between Catholics and Protestants. By the 1830s 'Separation extended even to the grave' as disputes over cemeteries led Catholics to acquire their own burial grounds. The Catholic Defence Association of the 1850s was anticipated in a sectarian way when Protestant landlords founded the Protestant Tenantry Society (1841) – not for reform of land tenure but to replace evicted Catholic tenants by Protestants. Meanwhile, re-echoes of an earlier time were heard as Reverend Tresham Gregg, a virulently anti-Catholic clergyman, spearheaded the Dublin Protestant Operatives Association through the same decades.[15]

However, there were advances and presages in surprising quarters for a more enlightened social order. Responding to Lord Donoghmore's request for greater severity by government, Thomas Drummond, under-Secretary for Ireland (1835-40), reminded landlords that property had duties as well as rights. Further, it was past neglect of such duties which explained what Donoghmore had termed the 'diseased' state of society. Instead of the severity demanded by worried landlords, Drummond argued that 'better and more enlightened and more humane exercise of rights' would provide a permanent remedy to the disorders of which landowners complained.[16]

And what of the great mass of the people? In England and Ireland a post-Waterloo Tory repression set in and consolidated itself.[17] There were very few to protest injustice and even fewer to work for 'a cordial union of Irishmen'. As Roy Foster puts it, the Georgian radicals were either aged or already dead.[18] In 1812 it was said that the poor 'live in continual apprehension and have no confidence in their own situation; haunted with the terror of persecution, they feel they are without protectors (and) alive to the least alarm'. Valentine Lawless, an old United Irishman, observed in 1823 that the government 'think of no other remedy than the sword and the halter'. In these circumstances it is not incomprehensible that in the first thirty years of the nineteenth century Ireland was beset by recurring violence. Societies like the Ribbonmen carried on the Defender tradition with memories of earlier aspirations to republican separation from Britain. Now their aims centred on abolition of tithes and agrarian redress.

Alongside agrarian unrest and resistance to tithes, popular aspirations found expression through O'Connell's repeal movement. After emancipation, O'Connell's leadership of Catholic Ireland continued in his next project, viz. to reverse the Act of Union. Ironically, the days of a native Parliament were now regarded as an ideal age. In the repeal movement, clerical involvement was crucial, not in the sense of formal political leadership but in the ability of clergy to maintain popular support of 'the Liberator'. Conscious of the need for this clerical backing, O'Connell assiduously courted the bishops and priests. This he did with remarkable success. On the other hand, priests like Fr Kenyon and the Callan Curates were 'unusual suspects' since they framed their own strategies either in rejection of O'Connell (Kenyon) or by adapting his methods to protect vulnerable tenants (the Callan Curates).

As well, the famines of the 1840s brought catastrophic suffering and redefinition of social relationships. The great hunger of 1848 has been described as one of the most dreadful episodes of the nineteenth century, anywhere in the world. A careful judgement will admit that at this period Ireland was badly governed, far worse than England, Scotland or Wales. Social institutions were almost non-existent, poor laws were hopelessly inadequate and relations between landlords and tenants almost unmarked by minimal decency. So called 'relief works' (which made starving people labour on crazy schemes of public works), have been deemed '(an) insane economic experiment ... pursued long after its failure had become obvious'.[19]

In fairness, it must be remarked that clergy in the mainline churches (and, egregiously, the Society of Friends) made heroic efforts on behalf of starving people. The rector of Westport, Patrick Pounden, who had been giving more than half his stipend to the local relief committee, died of fever contracted in ministering to a stricken people during May 1847. C. L. Chavasse has recorded the heroism of the Reverend John Marchbanks, curate at Stratford-on-Slaney in Co Wicklow, who 'starved himself, giving his food away and when the fever seized him he ... died almost at once'.[20] There was some attempt at a 'theological critique', e.g. the list of famine deaths compiled by the priests of Derry, inscribed to the diocesan archive as follows: 'The records of the murders of the Irish peasantry, perpetrated in AD 1846-47, in the 9 and 10 Vic., under the name of economy during the administration of a professedly Liberal, Whig government, of which Lord John Russell was premier.'[21] On the other hand is the question of 'souperism', part of the so-called 'second reformation' which marked inter-church relationships for the worse and entered popular parlance for generations thereafter.

Accompanying these issues were questions of considerable import: the churches' relationships, disestablishment of Anglicanism, land reform, home rule for Ireland (from the 1870s). Inset to these issues was the emergence of separatist movements with both cultural and military overtones, viz. Young

Ireland and Fenianism. It has been observed by Garret Fitzgerald that, from the mid-nineteenth century, the movement for repeal of the union with Britain developed two wings. One was a parliamentary organisation for self-government, albeit within the United Kingdom. This was a line stretching from Daniel O'Connell through Parnell's Irish Party and on to John Redmond's ill-fated leadership in the early twentieth century. The other, more radical, wing sought full separation, by violence if necessary.[22] While it would be a mistake to define these differences in broad class or religious terms, it is true that nationalism had become a mainly 'Catholic' thing while unionism was largely 'Protestant'. The exceptions to this pattern are a fascinating reality. These exceptions are also a hopeful element for future resolution of age-old divisions. Some of our 'unusual suspects' are to been seen in this general context.

CHAPTER FIVE

THE 'PATRIOT PRIEST OF 1848'

Fr John Kenyon (1812-1869)

'Every priest believes he is bound to bow humbly to the decrees of his superiors. And the censure might come at some critical moment when the eyes of the people would be trained to him and then the people would be left distracted and disheartened'.
(Charles Kickham, 'Pulpit Denunciation – Priests in Politics', *Irish People*, No 44)

Kickham's words arise not from anti-clericalism but rather from bitter experience of clerical fulminations against the Fenian society. Hence his mistrust of priests who entered too closely to the society's plans. In a poignant way these words apply to Fr John Kenyon, so closely identified with the Young Ireland movement and yet reluctant to stand with it when, in 1848, his fiery recommendations about physical force were taken seriously. Kenyon's turbulent figure exemplifies the complexities of post-Emancipation Ireland. Fr Kenyon was at his most active even as 'Catholic nationalism' consolidated itself. His own stances reflect the tensions within a movement too frequently cast as monolithic. Kenyon's determined opposition to Daniel O'Connell, particularly on the question of physical force, anticipate many of today's disagreements among Irish nationalists. Likewise, it evidences the friction under the surface of O'Connell's apparently undisputed hegemony among Catholics, lay and clerical.

During Kenyon's active decades, the formative events of the century occurred. Pre-eminent is the famine period, the 1840s, when lethal hunger changed not only 'the face' of

Ireland but also its consciousness. Alongside the famine, although in no sense identically, is the 'Year of Revolution' – 1848 – when, for a brief period, middle class radicals toppled kings and princes in France, Italy, Hungary and Germany. Ireland had its attenuated version of this – a bungled rising in July 1848. Although Kenyon was high in the councils of those who fomented the 1848 rising, such as it was, and although his rhetoric contributed much to its plans, he refused to take part in it. Yet again, in the 1860s, when Fenianism occasioned bitter disagreement within Kenyon's church, we find him playing an active if oblique role. A sub-text to these events is the dilemma of priests with Kenyon's energy in a church becoming ever more conservative under the influence of Dr Paul Cullen, Archbishop of Dublin.

Background and Early Ministry

Whereas Irish diocesan priests of the time were mainly of farming background, John Kenyon's family was urban and middle class. Even by Irish standards, Limerick was not a metropolis. Yet it had a commercial and trading class. Kenyon's family was of this class – his father, Patrick, owned marble works and grocery stores in the city. John Kenyon himself became a student in Maynooth at a time when Catholic emancipation was about to benefit most especially the middle class Catholic.

Ordained for the Killaloe diocese (1835), Fr. Kenyon's first appointment was to the cathedral parish at Ennis. Three years later (after outspoken criticism of a rich family which had become Protestant) he was transferred to Silvermines in north Tipperary. Louise Fogarty, Kenyon's somewhat enthusiastic biographer, suggests that already he had incurred official displeasure for lack of 'a certain amount of self-effacement'. The same biographer notes his ebullient character: 'a strength of will and a decided tendency to bend others rather than to be bent'.[1] Descriptions of Kenyon corroborate this judgement. John O'Leary, for several reasons not uncritical of the priest, describes him as 'the first man of real intellectual eminence with whom I was brought in intimate contact ... he was sim-

ply the best talker, in whatever sense you use the word, that I
ever heard'. O'Leary's reference to Kenyon's eloquence – 'simple, natural and effective' – is echoed in tributes from other
colleagues. In physical appearance, he is described as above av-
erage height, athletic and given to field sports, yet with 'something of a student's preoccupied expression'. Other descriptions speak of his 'commanding appearance ... erect front ...
clear intellectual eye and powerful intonation of voice'.[2]

Templederry, Co Tipperary

In December 1842, John Kenyon was appointed curate in
the parish of Templederry. For the rest of his life he ministered here, as curate (1842-50), administrator (1850-60) and,
finally, parish priest (1850-59). Economically, this was pastoral
country – 'a fertile spot, situated among the Keeper hills'
(History of Ely O'Carroll). In 1837 it had a population of 1857
while the adjoining half-parish numbered 2236. In the parish
were several privately run schools – probably a continuation
of the old 'hedge schools', not yet effaced by the National
Education system. Although 'consolidation' by landlords exposed its people to unjust eviction, the area does not appear
to have suffered as badly as other parts during the famine
years. Some months after Kenyon's arrival in Templederry, he
took up the case of four men charged with the murder of a
land steward. Although the campaign was unsuccessful his efforts rankled with a police magistrate who, almost twenty
years later, mocked the 'ribald oratory which so well becomes
him (Kenyon)'.[3]

Templederry's hills and valleys provided an ideal surrounding for someone of Kenyon's predilection for the outdoors.
Local tradition recalls his love of horses and dogs as well as a
tame deer for which he cared. Doubtless, the very traits remarked by John O'Leary – wide reading, good organisational
ability and a touch of eccentricity – laid the foundation for
the priest's immense popularity among his people. Kenyon's
'eccentricity' is reflected in the presbytery which he built: an
exterior staircase provided the sole entrance to the house – at

roof level! The presbytery's main apartment was a sparsely furnished living room crowded with books on history, ancient classics and political science.

The Repeal Movement (O'Connell) and Young Ireland

At Templederry, Fr Kenyon found himself involved with Daniel O'Connell's repeal movement founded in 1840. Its object was reversal of the Act of Union and provision of an Irish parliament. Aided by a formidable body of lieutenants, O'Connell had fashioned the movement on the lines of his earlier campaign for religious emancipation. After a slow beginning, a mass-based organisation was built, committed to constitutional politics. It honeycombed the country (especially Munster and Leinster), relied on parochial clergy as organisers at parish level, and mobilised the poor through the penny rent to the association. As well as clerical support, the unexpected accession in 1842 of three journalists – Thomas Osborne Davis, John Blake Dillon and Charles Gavan Duffy – was central to the movement's consolidation. Their newspaper, *The Nation,* with its high-quality journalism, its ballads and its skilful advocacy of inclusive nationality, was immensely valuable to the repeal association. Kenyon himself wrote lengthy essays for the newspaper as well as poems under the pseudonym 'N.N.'. Under the aegis of the Repeal Association a network of local reading-rooms and even the skeleton of a welfare system were constructed in parishes throughout Ireland. Despite its abstract nature and lack of immediate effect for hard-pressed tenantry, repeal was in the air!

Shortly after his appointment to Templederry, Fr Kenyon attended a mass meeting held by O'Connell at the Hill of Grange, Nenagh (25 May 1843). Later in the evening, at a dinner for O'Connell, Kenyon seconded a toast to Fr Mathew, the temperance crusader. Given that so many priests were active in the Repeal association it is an indication of his growing influence that Kenyon was invited thus to speak. It is noticeable that the bitterness which led to his posthumous attack on O'Connell had not yet eventuated. Fifteen years later – long after an acrimonious split with O'Connellism – Kenyon remembered that with O'Connell at the Hill of Grange 'we renewed our baptismal vows of patriotism in Tipperary'. Even at the height of his disagreement with Conciliation Hall (headquarters of the Repeal movement at Burgh Quay, Dublin), Fr Kenyon could still refer to O'Connell's mind as 'bright and brave and buoyant'.[4]

Tensions Within Repeal Association

By 1845, tensions between 'Old Ireland' and 'Young Ireland' were beginning to surface.[5] Disagreement commenced after O'Connell cancelled his open-air meeting at Clontarf in face of government opposition. Gradually it became clear that 'Old' and 'Young' Ireland had different concepts of 'nation'. Views on how to obtain repeal began to diverge. O'Connell's tendency to personal arrogance counted for much in the divergence. Religious questions (for example, university reform proposals and the situation of Protestants within the desired 'New' Ireland) divided the Nation group from O'Connell. The Young Irelanders were 'political purists' who came to detest O'Connell's '... coarse populism ... truckling to British enemies and clerical friends ... jobbery, duplicity and outworn values'.[6] In the terminology of a later time, personality clashes began to multiply between Thomas Davis, John Dillon, Charles Gavan Duffy, on the one hand, and John O'Connell, Thomas Steele and Thomas Ray, on the other. The apparent self-seeking of the latter group irritated the Young Irelanders. To O'Connell's closest lieutenants, the *Nation* group seemed precipitative and recklessly unhelpful to the slow but careful politics of 'the Liberator'.

A major problem was Daniel O'Connell's ambiguity when in 1845 he seemed to adopt federalism rather than total repeal. Even more irritating to the Young Irelanders were mischievous allegations of John O'Connell that the *Nation* group were anti-Catholic and, even, irreligious. These allegations came to a head on the introduction of Robert Peel's 'Colleges Bill'. Misinterpreting the Catholic bishops, Daniel O'Connell

opposed 'godless' colleges and joint Protestant-Catholic education. For Young Irelanders, a central goal was union of
Protestants and Catholics not only in education but also in
loyalty to Ireland. In May 1845 long concealed divisions became evident. A bitter clash at Conciliation Hall revealed the
gulf between O'Connellites and Young Irelanders. Towards
the end of 1846, Fr Kenyon gave Archbishop Crolly a memorandum defending Young Irelanders from John O'Connell's
charges of atheism.[7]

Disagreement on Slavery

Divisions between Young Irelanders and O'Connellites on
the issue of slavery also betoken the association's woes. Here,
the ethical positions of Daniel O'Connell remain the more
admirable and suggest that Young Ireland criticisms of
O'Connell were not entirely justified. O'Connell sincerely regarded American money as tainted by slavery. Motivated by
horror of slavery, he may also have been anxious to court
Whig good opinion. Thus, he could say that if justice were
done to Ireland the country would help England 'pull down
and humble the proud American eagle in the dust'. John
O'Connell was equally strong in his opposition to slavery. Of
money from slaveholders, he simply recommended: 'Perish
the vile trash.' In April 1845, when moving a vote of thanks for
Irish-American contributions to the repeal association, John
O'Connell discouraged American aid 'if it came across the
Atlantic stained with negro blood'.[8]

Some weeks later, *The Nation* editorialised on 'America and
Ireland'. Here, pragmatism, not ethics, was in the ascendant:
American help was always welcome; disputes on slavery could
damage the repeal association (9 August 1845). For Young
Irelanders, repeal of the union with Britain, not abolition of
slavery, was the paramount issue. Even Thomas Davis, personally against slavery, had written: 'We court, and are most
grateful for the sympathy of America'.[9] These stances can easily be dismissed as self-interested pragmatism. Certainly, they

reflected badly on Young Ireland's ambiguity and left O'Connellites to occupy the 'high moral ground'.

'The slavery tolerating clergyman of Tipperary'

When, in 1847, John Kenyon gratuitously entered the dispute, his opinions were narrow and constricted. They contrast unfavourably with the stance then adopted in Belfast by another 'unusual suspect', the Presbyterian clergyman Isaac Nelson. They become all the more puzzling since in Dublin and Belfast well-publicised lectures had detailed the full horrors of slavery in the southern states of America. Even though Kenyon's lengthy missives to *The Nation* reflect Young Ireland's pragmatism, they do little credit to the priest himself or the movement of which he was part. Here, it is difficult to assess how far the influence of John Mitchel is at work. The two men had been friends for some time. Mitchel wrote: '... I reckon Kenyon the finest fellow, lay or cleric, that I ever knew'.[10] Mitchel's later endorsement of slavery is a reminder that Young Ireland's radical nationalism may have overlain a conservatism or, even, a retarded development on other moral and social questions.

The background to Kenyon's letters was a proposal by James Haughton, a member of the Society of Friends ('Quakers'), that the newly founded Irish Confederation should oppose capital punishment, foster teetotalism and reject slavery. On the first two issues there was no dispute. On slavery there was disagreement. The Confederation resolved to take money 'from whatever quarter of the globe good minds shall blow it'.[11] Fr Kenyon's *Nation* letters (19 Jan and 13 Feb 1847) are meant to support the Confederation's resolution. Unwisely discursive and polemical, they provided grounds for gibes about 'the slavery tolerating clergyman of Tipperary'. James Haughton had said he would 'indignantly refuse the blood-stained contributions of American slaveholders': John Kenyon 'would accept honest help from all, and think myself never the worse therefor'. Thus far, no more was stated than in the disputes of 1845.

Now, however, Fr Kenyon argues that the scriptures did not condemn slavery, nor did church tradition. (In a subsequent letter, he strengthens this claim: the scriptures 'do actually and, in form, acquit it (slavery) of all guilt'). Priests and bishops had maintained communion with slave-holders, had owned slaves themselves. While Kenyon did not covet their 'property', he 'would not condemn them for it either'. This faulty analysis is compounded by the suggestion that the issue of slavery was 'much exaggerated by fancy, perhaps by fanaticism'. For one who made impassioned speeches about Irish freedom, it was paradoxical that he could equiparate our common dependence on ('slavery to'!) 'tailors, snuff, washerwomen, quacks, policemen, umbrellas, London merchants, native millers ...' to another slavery – this time to slave-holders. Given that we tolerate the first, the latter slavery would not make 'our position ... very essentially deteriorated'. The argument concludes with the point at issue – refusal of American money would be 'such an Utopian remedy for the supposed evil as only homeopathists could countenance'.[12]

A few weeks later, Kenyon returned to his task. A letter of 13 April shows his blinkered view and perhaps disingenuousness. For example, 'If it be true (which I doubt) that the slaveholders of the Southern states are responsible for ... barbarities; or if it be true (which I also doubt) that they mistreat their negroes *(sic)* half as much as our poor Irish slaves are maltreated by their English masters, may God forgive them.' With peculiar insistence, Kenyon then argues that such transgressions do not convict the slavery system of evil any more than the cruelty of landlords proves that tenant farming is unChristian or family breakdown proves that marriage in unholy. Lamentably, Kenyon appeals to a Providence which has ordained inequalities: '... I have never seen a reason for excepting the condition of slavery, as if it did not enter like the others into the general dispensation of God's providence'. It was perhaps a wise editorial decision to end the correspondence, although the stated pretext was self-serving: '... Irish slavery is an abundantly large branch of the subject for our time and space'.

Secession from the Repeal Association

Among other difficulties, the disagreement on slavery had racked the association. In July 1846, barely nine months after the death of Thomas Davis, an outright split occurred. O'Connell tried to impose his 'peace resolutions' eschewing the use of force except for self-defence. Moral force was to be the exclusive method of the Repeal Association. By the end of the month, the Young Irelanders, led by Charles Gavan Duffy and William Smith O'Brien, had left the association. Fr Kenyon participated in the walk-out. Some historians argue that O'Connell had moved tactically to crush Young Ireland opposition. Others discern an attempt further to bolster O'Connell's acceptability to the Westminster Whigs. It would, however, appear that exclusively peaceful means of obtaining a political end had become a central principle for O'Connell. Frederick Lucas, editor of *The Tablet,* believed O'Connell wanted 'to crush the very life out of this hostile doctrine (physical force), put the people permanently on their guard against its advocates, and prevent it ever being seriously raised again'.[13]

Yet, the matter remains problematic. Fr Thomas O'Carroll (Cashel diocese) considered John O'Connell's behaviour 'extremely overbearing and dictatorial'. Although reprobating physical force, O'Carroll regarded the 'Peace Resolutions' as unnecessarily divisive. Nor was Daniel O'Connell always a pacifist. During the campaign for Catholic emancipation, his politics displayed studied ambiguity on the issue of force. As well, though Young Ireland constantly employed warlike images in prose and verse, it continued to disclaim revolutionary intent. In reality, no one was seriously considering force at this time. Although nationalists of every persuasion viewed repeal of the Union as the panacea for Ireland, none had argued for an insurrection.[14]

Young Irelanders tried to minimise the split, partly from loyalty to O'Connell and partly from reluctance to inflict further damage on a national movement. Hence, *The Nation* eschewed polemics. Nevertheless, O'Connell's lieutenants were bent on routing opposition. Some days after the secession, Fr Kenyon put it: '(The Young Ireland party) frequently sought to have bye-gones left for bye-gones – they abjured over and over again all idea of using physical force, while the Association held together ... but in vain. They were driven into a corner. The question was forced upon them – Do you think a nation may ever, in any circumstances other than plain self-defence, lawfully resort to arms to redress any imaginable wrong? What could these men do?' Referring to a forthcoming clergy meeting to support O'Connell, Thomas O'Carroll (Cashel diocese) corroborates the suppression of dissent: he would not attend the meeting since he would be 'put down as a black sheep and persecuted as such – merely because I dared to dissent'. Bernard Durcan, a Mayo priest, deplored O'Connell's regard for Whig favour. Fr Durcan argued there should be no support for government until it flung its 'wretched theories to the winds ... (and) open the ports, establish depots for the sale of food to the poor'.[15]

From January 1847, the Irish Confederation, headed by Wm Smith O'Brien and based at D'Olier St, provided the focus for Young Ireland secessionists. Its programme, evocative of the United Irish ideal, proclaimed: 'Whoever is for nationality; for raising Ireland to be a nation among the nations is our confederate.' Even more, 'He is an Irishman who knows his duty – that is enough. If he be a Protestant, we dare not insist that he walk by Catholic rules – if he is a Conservative, we do not pledge him to Radicalism or Whiggery. The fashioning of our constitution will lie with our Parliament and there let each battle for his own opinions as stoutly as he can.'[16] Meanwhile, *The Nation,* now edited by Gavan Duffy, and later the *United Irishman* (under John Mitchel) provided a forum through which anti-O'Connell views might be expressed.

Somewhat dismissively, Roy Foster has referred to 'Franco-philia, 1798 revivalism and separation' as typical of the Young Ireland stance.[17] Yet this does little justice to their more nuanced positions. Young Ireland's 'Francophilia' is to be seen in the context of a Europe-wide attack on the old order of established powers and a new wave of fledgling democracies. *The Nation's* '1798 revivalism' was no more than Thomas Davis's reappropriation of the country's history and culture. Young Irelanders reiterated the non-sectarian project of the 1790s for a just society, irrespective of credal allegiance. That such a project demanded separation from England was not a new tenet – it was embedded to the claims of Tone, Russell and other United Irishmen. However, the circumstances were different. With the Young Irelanders and, later, the Irish Confederation, local organisation was deficient. Aspiration tended to replace planning. Nor was the union of classes, so much desired by Davis, Smith O'Brien and Gavan Duffy, likely to follow on journalistic appeals, even though well framed.

Kenyon on Moral and Physical Force

As noted by John Martin, 'Could he write so faultlessly as he can speak.' Kenyon was a better orator than writer. His pamphlet on O'Connell's Peace Resolutions is verbose and repetitive. In addition, it is marred by offensive references to the Society of Friends. Entitled 'Physical and Moral Force', it originally appeared as a letter to the *Limerick Reporter* and was reprinted by *The Nation*. In December 1846, the Irish Confederation published it as a penny booklet.

The pamphlet addresses two positions espoused by Conciliation Hall. First, O'Connell had been insisting that physical force to attain any political right was criminal. Second, he claimed (for evidence, he appealed to the earlier campaign for Catholic emancipation) that all political rights are attainable by moral force alone. On the first of these positions, Fr Kenyon argues that the oppressed are entitled by the law of nature 'to abandon the logic of the pen for the keener logic of the sabre'. In his view, all theologians 'save Quaker divines' recognised this. With somewhat undeveloped theology he claims: '... if nine hundred lives out of a thousand, which must otherwise perish within a twelvemonth by wasting torture, could be saved by an appeal to the God of Battles, I am eccentric enough to think that humanity would be the gainer, though one hundred were sacrificed in the strife; and I believe that the God of Battles would accept the sacrifice.' Kenyon then instances early Christian soldiers in the Roman army and Crusaders of medieval times. The argument – modern theology might find it questionable – concludes: 'The first proposition then is false to reason ... injurious to the authority of the Catholic Church, and, if pushed to its legitimate consequences, subversive to government.'[18]

O'Connell had not indicated what he meant by moral force and Kenyon skilfully exploits the omission. As to the 'moral force' which gained Catholic emancipation, Kenyon shows that it was not totally pacifist: 'the abstract possibility was recognised, the imminent danger was feared, that those insulted and outraged Catholics, stung by the protracted delay ... might extort at the sword or pike point more than their pens had dared to solicit'. Thereafter, O'Connell's second axiom that all political rights can be attained by moral force alone is deemed by Kenyon 'false and visionary', a 'stupid and servile paradox'. Kenyon would grant that where men are honest and intelligent they will respect the rights of others even though these rights are claimed by moral force alone. Yet, argues Kenyon, 'it is the fatal destiny of earth that many men will be always ignorant and vicious' – in these circumstances moral force alone will be inefficacious. And so he concludes that O'Connell's policy was fatally unrealistic: it was visionary to the extent of being utterly false. If all rights could be obtained by moral force, why are there 'soldiers, marines, policemen, hangmen, catchpolls? Why jails and Bridewells and hulks?'

The point at issue was not whether physical force should be used in the immediate future. Both parties agreed that this was not feasible. The issue was rather of giving notice that force would never be used. In Kenyon's view, this was tactically ruinous since Westminster could then ignore all demands for Repeal: '... let a nation now subscribe beforehand the suicidal doctrine that in no time, or place, or circumstances shall they ever draw a sword from its sheath or even a pin from its cushion – why, then, their opinions might rate at the ragman's price of the dirty paper on which they may have been foolishly inscribed'. Although Kenyon's argument is passionately expressed, he seems reluctant directly to attack Daniel O'Connell. The edge of his contempt is reserved for John O'Connell and the officials of Conciliation Hall. It should also be noted that in July 1846 Kenyon was against quitting the Association – accurately, he foresaw that after such a split the Association might 'for two or three years drag a languishing existence into oblivion'. Similarly, at *The Nation*, Gavan Duffy adopted a moderate line: 'We rely on no other force (i.e. than moral force). We believe in no other as applicable in the smallest degree to our time and condition.'[19]

Bitter Polemics

The split led ultimately to an exhibition of sterile recrimination. As Kenyon foretold, neither group profited. Although the rhetoric of Young Ireland was more anti-government that that of the Repealers, both groups dissipated their energies in mutual recrimination.[20] Within a year, O'Connell had died at Genoa. A few years later, the repeal association was no more. On the other hand, their own rhetoric drove Young Irelanders towards ever more radical stances while failing to make the necessary preparations to attain their objectives. In the midst of famine, both sides postured on the abstract issue of force while the politics of hunger remained unaddressed. Although Kenyon accepted the confederate ideal ('a combination of classes, for the overthrow of the English legislative dominion'), he foresaw that the landlords would insist on their rights at the expense of the great majority of the people. The Confederate ideal was unlikely to be attained by the much-vaunted moral force. There were certain classes which would not tolerate the Confederates' programme – the military class, the police, the magistrates, the 'thorough-going-O'Connellite-Repealers'. These were 'part and parcel of the English interest in Ireland'. Hence, in contradistinction to Smith O'Brien, Kenyon favoured the abolition of the landlord class as a precondition for the common good.[21]

Denied access to the reading-rooms of the Repeal Association, *The Nation* initiated an anti-O'Connellite campaign to which Fr Kenyon prolifically contributed. In letters and in public speeches, he criticised 'balmy O'Connellites', bishops, priests and laypeople. To the charge that he was interested in personal advancement, he replied with accuracy: 'The vein which nature ... has allotted for my dower is generally found as unprofitable in the church as well as in the state.' This vein undoubtedly led him into precipitate actions which embarrassed even his admirers. An example is his nomination of Richard O'Gorman for the Limerick City election in 1847. Kenyon regarded this as a symbolic protest against place-hunting by Irish MPs at Westminster. Unaware of the nomination and with no organised campaign, O'Gorman (38 votes) was soundly beaten by John O'Connell (581 votes). Scenes at the nomination of candidates did little credit to anyone except, perhaps, to Richard Russell, the High Sheriff.[22]

To Gavan Duffy's dismay and Smith O'Brien's disapprobation, Kenyon wrote a strong attack on Daniel O'Connell within days of 'the Liberator's' death. *The Nation* had carried mourning columns and Smith O'Brien had submitted a resolution to the Confederation that Ireland, being in O'Connell's debt, should join in public mourning. Kenyon dissented saying that O'Connell's death had been no loss whatsoever. On the contrary, it was 'rather a gain than a loss to the country'. Even more, Ireland owed O'Connell 'nothing but forgiveness'. In the circumstances, it was unseemly that Fr Kenyon should cumulate O'Connell's deficiencies: 'He patronised liars, parasites and bullies. He brooked no greatness that grov-

elled not at his feet ... He boasted ... Above all, he was un-
steady, because he was unprincipled ... He failed in his mission, and he deserved to fail in it'. Even *The Nation* drew back
from the impolitic correspondence. Duffy refused to publish
a further letter of 7 June 1847. In this letter (published by
Mitchel's *United Irishman* in early 1848) Kenyon claimed: 'No
national benefactor ever enjoyed himself so much on the
credit of his services. He ate always heartily, drank what he
liked and slept upon feathers. His jokes were always relished,
as indeed they deserved to be; and his faults were less censured by his admirers, than was perhaps was for the good of
others.'[23]

The correspondence may well reflect Kenyon's own frustration during 1847. He himself seems to question his emotions in regard to O'Connell's place in Irish history: 'Whether
it is a wisdom I have imbibed in these mountain solitudes, or
a folly that has grown upon me or within me, or whether it is
a mere natural revulsion of enthusiasm, over-strained and dis-
appointed, I know not.' Reading the correspondence one is
reminded that these were years of famine. It is perhaps indicative of the theoretic quality of Young Ireland's concerns that,
even yet, the politics were of repeal rather than hunger, although by now James Fintan Lalor was proposing radical land
reform.

Failed Revolution

1848 has been termed 'The Year of European Revolution'.
Across the continent, from France to the eastern borders of
the Austro-Hungarian Empire, princes were dethroned and
democracies established. However, it was also the year when
Europe failed to maintain its revolution. E.J. Hobsbawm argues that the revolution throve only where the radicals were
sufficiently linked with the popular movement to drag the
moderates forward. In too many cases, would-be revolutionaries were moderate liberals whose debates became 'a by-word
of intelligent futility'.[24] To a considerable degree, this also applied to the Young Irelanders. They continued to appear more

as romantic nationalists than a serious political force. Their limited engagement in the politics of hunger manifested their distance from the mass of the people who, by and large, adhered to O'Connellism. Young Ireland's florid oratory, its citations from European romantics (Goethe, Carlyle, etc.), its hesitations on slavery, put it at far remove from the Manifesto of the Communist Party (February 1848). It can be argued that with the death of Thomas Davis Young Ireland had lost the leader who might effectively have directed its energies during the famine years.

Thus, for the Irish Confederation, 1848 opened with tensions. Several of Kenyon's fiery missives were refused publication in *The Nation*. Duffy, Smith O'Brien and Dillon felt themselves outflanked by the increasing radicalism of Mitchel, Lalor and Kenyon. Mitchel had accepted Lalor's argument for sustained opposition to rent and poor rates. The more conservative Duffy and Smith O'Brien held to the necessity of constitutional action. In February, Mitchel quit the Confederation. With John Martin and John Kenyon he formed a left-wing group pressing for armed insurrection, destruction of landlordism and, citing Lalor, 'the land for the people'. By now, the Mitchel/Martin/Kenyon group deemed Smith O'Brien's grand unity of classes as visionary and utopian.[25]

Kenyon's long contribution to the first issue of Mitchel's *United Irishman* (13 February) was a thinly veiled attack on Duffy's censorship of the priest's letters. On physical force Kenyon writes even more radically than heretofore: 'I could wish ... that all Irishmen were armed, and were able to use their arms ... I believe in the lawfulness of war ... because I have no faith in the advent of the millennium ...' Here, too, emerges his pessimism about winning over the richer classes ('part and parcel of the English interest in Ireland'). Kenyon's attack on the Poor Law system ('this law and all the laws relating to relief which preceded it since the famine') discloses a certain cynicism: 'though some partial suffering should certainly arise in consequence of the sudden obstruction of this

Poor Law, I would welcome the suffering ... as a national blessing, compared to the lingering death and perpetual misery to which we seem ... irrevocably doomed'. Clearly, he now shared Lalor's and Mitchel's view that the famine was a government/landlord plot to exterminate the Irish peasantry. Likewise, he shared their view on the necessity to prevent, by force if necessary, the export of corn from a starving country. More and more, he accepted the legitimacy of a revolution to sweep the English interest out of Ireland.[26] There remains here a problem, in view of Kenyon's wide, even rhetorical, definition of 'the English interest'.

With the outbreak of continental revolution and Chartist activities in England, even Duffy began to think seriously of rebellion. Mitchel's *United Irishman* invited government repression so that constitutional agitation would be ended and repealers of whatever allegiance be confronted with their (English) enemies.[27] At a public meeting in Templederry (April 1848), Kenyon rhetorically asked: 'Are you ready to die for Ireland?' Introducing the idea of armed struggle he declared: 'I tell you openly to be ready from day to day – to watch every opportunity, to face every obstacle, and when the moment comes we shall be found with arms in our hands – we shall not be unprepared, and then every man must arise and do battle bravely.' Certainly, it was rousing oratory. In the circumstances of popular disarray it was, arguably, irresponsible. Nonetheless, Kenyon qualified his oratory by the somewhat disingenuous rider that the Confederation advised 'no one to act imprudently or expose himself needlessly and uselessly to the harpies of the law'. From the meeting, a somewhat florid address of support was sent to the Confederation leaders. ('Onward together brothers all – Catholic, Protestant and Presbyterian ... Stand we up together for the dear old land ...').[28]

Turmoil and Defeat
The next three months were traumatic for the Young Irelanders as well as for Kenyon himself. Mitchel's radicalism alarmed the authorities sufficiently to arrest him, Smith

O'Brien and Thomas Francis Meagher. Although O'Brien and Meagher were released, Mitchel was charged with treason-felony. Kenyon rushed to Dublin and vehemently expressed his support for Mitchel in Green St courthouse. His efforts to visit Mitchel at Newgate were thwarted by officialdom. Still at Dublin, the priest urged the Confederation to adopt an emergency strategy, including Mitchel's rescue. Somewhat unrealistically, Kenyon and Martin wanted to seek French or American help. Duffy and Dillon recommended caution. Nonetheless, an emergency Council of Five was elected which Smith O'Brien refused to join although Kenyon was elected to it. It is of interest that repealers and Young Irelanders joined in a protest at Mitchel's sentence. Some 200 priests wrote to *The Nation* in support of a protest drawn up by Miley and O'Loghlen.[29]

On return to Templederry, Kenyon was confronted by an ultimatum from his bishop. Since another priest, Fr Birmingham of Borrisokane, was joined in the threatened suspension, it is likely that the episcopal move was prompted by references at Templederrry and Borrisokane to 'arming quietly', 'refraining from action until liberties were invaded' and 'rising over the whole country, not over a county or two'. For Kenyon, the alternatives were stark – immediate dismissal from his parish or unequivocal retraction of recent speeches and letters.[30] Sometime before mid-June, Kenyon reached an accommodation with Bishop Kennedy through the intermediacy of Cashel's archbishop, Dr Slattery. Although Kenyon's letter to Kennedy was laced with qualifications, it mollified the bishop. Louise Fogarty claims that Kenyon's undertaking contained a mental reservation, i.e. he would take no leading part in any rising but would have the right to take his place in the ranks should there be any uprising.[31]

A report in the *Limerick Chronicle* gave Fr Kenyon an opportunity to rebut the allegation that he had retired from politics. In a letter (10 June 1848), he declared that 'no honest Irishman who is master of his own actions should retire from it until his country is delivered from her plagues'. These plagues were 'a cruel and greedy government of foreigners and a system of trickery and treachery known ... as balmy O'Connellism'. He would fight these with all the weapons of legitimate warfare, until they were finally exterminated. One asks what is meant by 'legitimate means'? And what is the significance of his reference to a 'critical period of six to eight calendar months from this date' when, if his objectives were not attained, he would abandon politics for cynical writings and 'amassing coins'.

Meanwhile, there were further governmental moves – arrest of Gavan Duffy, suspension of *Habeas Corpus,* proscription of Confederate clubs. Mitchel was sentenced to fourteen years' deportation. According to F. S. L. Lyons, the Young Irelanders either stumbled, or were pricked into, insurrection.[32] When summoned to Dublin by the Confederates, Kenyon failed to come. Instead, he sent an ambiguous message of goodwill and pleaded inability to travel from his parish. Although one of the Confederate leaders (Devin Reilly) counselled delay until 'Fr Kenyon would be ready with a large force to act ...', the Council of Five decided to rise.[33] The insurrection was to centre on Kilkenny while assemblies in other areas would pin down army and police. Kenyon was appointed leader for the Tipperary area. The ill-prepared rising was attempted in July 1848 without organisation of any kind. Limited to south Tipperary and part of Kilkenny, it was a chaotic affair which fizzled out after a few days. Its appearance of prematurity reintroduces Kenyon's allusion to six or eight calendar months after which he might retire from politics.

Kenyon's own part remains an unresolved enigma. It is clear that he anticipated his own arrest and banishment – he made his will and sent it to Dr Kennedy. The bishop later made the claim that he had saved Kenyon from a fate similar to Mitchel's. A memoir by Fr Philip Fitzgerald gives an interesting, although not unbiased, account of events insofar as they affected Kenyon. From Slievenamon, O'Brien had dispatched a messenger to Templederry asking Fr Kenyon to lead his people in creating a diversion.[34] When the messenger reached Kenyon, the priest condemned O'Brien's action as 'fatal to the cause'. At a further meeting, this time with Thomas Francis Meagher and Maurice Leyne, he argued that the strategy faced certain disaster. It was, he said, a bootless struggle. Kenyon's further argument is cited by Fitzgerald: 'it is purely utopian to attempt revolutionising a country ... through the agencies employed by O'Brien ... you must engage the passions of the people ... seize on all the property of the country – the corn, the cattle, the very plate of the enemy should be converted into cash for the payment of foreign officers ... seize the person of every aristocrat ... and hold them as hostages ... ' Pressed to mobilise his people, Kenyon refused and O'Brien's messengers returned to Slievenamon. Meanwhile, in the parish register for 27 July 1848 Kenyon wrote: 'This evening I heard of a rebellion commenced in South Tipperary under the leadership of William Smith O'Brien – may God speed it.'[35]

Here, one has to consider Kickham's warning cited at the head of this chapter. Did Kenyon, despite all his radicalism, march to a different drum, viz. obedience to his religious superiors? In that case, all his fiery recommendations on resistance were, at best, ill-considered verbiage, the kind about which W. B. Yeats later agonised. At worst, it was hypocrisy. However, neither extreme is cogent. Men like Kenyon did take seriously their church's theology of revolution. In the famine aftermath, more than one priest – and perhaps at least one bishop – considered that the evil of the famine outweighed the perils of rebellion.[36] As news from Europe came in, many considered that what happened on the continent might with equal justification happen in Ireland. The words of Kenyon, Birmingham and others can be seen as the reaction of hard pressed pastors of a starving people.

Kenyon's involvement with Young Ireland was indeed

sincere and, for all their passion, his arguments had a certain appropriateness. One notes Fr Bermingham's justification of his own actions: '... It was only when I saw thousands consigned to famine ... that I said I would throw myself in the breach, and try to rescue them'.[37] There can be no doubt that Kenyon faced a painful dilemma resulting from his earlier stances on political matters and his desire to continue as a priest. Louise Fogarty writes: 'From this time ... the hearty, buoyant, responsive part of his nature ... was buried; the sunny enthusiasm which englamoured (his) pen was overshadowed forever.'[38] A hint of the priest's difficulty is given in John Martin's reference to his being 'a priest first and a politician afterwards'.[39] As well, Kenyon genuinely felt that O'Brien's precipitate rising could lead only to disaster for his people. In that case, he applied the criterion of many other clergy in regard to Fenianism, viz. reasonable hope of success. In all realism, Kenyon was right about O'Brien's insurrection – O'Brien himself later admitted the hopelessness of his endeavour, seeing it a matter of honour to implement his earlier recommendations. To a degree, it was a case of rhetoric outstripping reality – and when the reality confronted rhetoric, the latter was found gravely insufficient. Nevertheless, a critical question hangs over Fr Kenyon's earlier rhetoric – his question to the Templederry gathering about its readiness to 'die for Ireland' and his impassioned *apologia* for physical force. It is of interest that in subsequent years his radical friends – Mitchel, Martin, even the Fenian John O'Leary – did not censure him. Only Gavan Duffy, who in retrospect considered there was a reasonable hope for the rising's success, charged him with a *volte-face*.

Subsequent Career

An index of Kenyon's diocesan rehabilitation is his appointment as Administrator of Templederry parish in 1850. This was not quite the same as promotion to parish priest but it was an indication of episcopal confidence. The parish house continued to offer hospitality to radicals like Thomas

Clarke Luby and, in the closing months of his life, James
Fintan Lalor. During the summer of 1848, Fr Kenyon gave
protracted shelter to Mitchel's family. The priest's friendship
with John Martin continued – they visited each other at
Rostrevor and Templederry yearly. When Mitchel escaped
from Australia, Kenyon met the erstwhile convict in Paris
(October 1860 and, again, in 1866). At the latter meeting, the
mistrust between Kenyon and James Stephens commenced
which would later show itself.

When discussion of tenant right emerged, it was unlikely
that Kenyon would remain on the sidelines. Along with many
priests he debated land reform and landlord/tenant contracts.
Here again, his angled thought put him at odds with his colleagues. In Spring 1851 he engaged another Young Ireland
clergyman, Thomas Croke (later Archbishop), on the principles of the Tenant League.[40] In Kenyon's view, these were
delusive since they dealt with a desperate problem as 'a fairy
doctor may treat a devouring cancer'. Kenyon argued that
farmers should not be singled out for special treatment – 'as
eloquent a picture of woe could be wrought out of the materials
of your Limerick cellars and garrets as out of the most melan-
choly evictions'. Kenyon admits that although he was tempted
to recommend abolition of private land tenure (therefore, of
landlordism), yet he had reluctantly to conclude that ownership of land was an inevitable part of life.

Republican Leanings

The 1850s saw a decade of relative quiescence as people
tried to forget the horrors of famine years. Millions had died
or were forced into emigration. Those who survived concentrated on husbanding whatever resources they possessed.
From the middle of the decade even the tenant leagues experienced apathy. There was little mood for radical politics. Even
Young Ireland's long time supporter, Thomas Croke, believed
that armed revolution would be impossible for at least fifty
years. A Cashel priest, John Ryan, mocked the 'cabbage gar-
den, catherine dance of Ballingarry'.[41] Yet there were others,

mainly urban/small-town workers, agricultural labourers, tenant farmers and a few intellectuals such as Charles Kickham, who looked to separation from England as a panacea for Irish problems. The collapse of the Irish Independent Party led to disillusion with constitutional nationalism and provided a fruitful occasion for the rise of the Irish Republican Brotherhood both in Ireland and in America.

As is clear from his debate with Thomas Croke, John Kenyon had not retired into composition of 'cynical writings and amassing coins'. Nor was he content to become engrossed in tenant right. Perhaps his earlier reference to cellars and garrets of Limerick may evince his urban background. Yet it also hints a broader view of social reform than purely the land question. Kenyon's link with John Edward Pigot and Thomas Clarke Luby in founding the short-lived *Tribune* raises the general position of that paper, viz. a leaning towards republicanism with a secular rather than religious base.[42] This view brought Luby into the Fenian movement in the 1860s. Kenyon, too, would have tenuous but real connection with the movement through Luby and Mitchel.

In 1857-8, a miscarriage of justice occurred when two tenant farmers, Wm and Daniel McCormack, were convicted of John Ellis's murder in Dovea, Co Tipperary. A deeply unpopular man, Ellis had been murdered in late 1857. At the trial, perjured witnesses and a hostile Judge Keogh secured the conviction of the McCormacks. The campaign to secure their reprieve from execution united clergy and nationalists of diverse allegiance. In early 1858, Kenyon addressed a meeting of the campaign with all the verve of his earlier style. He made clear his reluctance to join any petition to Westminster other than demand the hanging of Judge Keogh as well as the release of the prisoners. If that composite petition were granted it would only be an infinitesimally small instalment of justice. Kenyon's speech contained an overtone of coming struggle: 'Let us treasure our wrongs ... until God inspires us with the power and opens to us a new way to right them.'[43] As of now, the people had 'no Moses to guide them'. Although the nature of the 'new way' and the identity of the 'new Moses' were left undefined, it is clear that Kenyon felt the time for petitions was already past. The Young Ireland emphasis on non-sectarianism emerges in his call to avoid 'every semblance of religious bigotry'. Despite this, the unionist press howled in outrage about his involvement in the campaign. The *Belfast Mercury* asked 'with the Fr Kenyons and Fr Scanlons and priests of such sort as instructors of Tipperary savagery, who can wonder at the murderous scenes that too frequently occur' (10 Sept 1858). A retired police magistrate, who had known Kenyon in Nenagh during 1843, raked up his leaning to ribald oratory.

At Nenagh, in his so-called '1858 Speech', Kenyon replied to a toast of the people as the source of all legitimate power. Strangely, he demurred. The people were not the true source of power. Rather, God, the true source of power, had delegated it to the people, not the privileged few. This claim was consonant even with traditional Catholic theology – although the now reactionary Pope Pius IX might not have been pleased. Kenyon indulged his inclination to satire as he reduced aristocratic pretension to farce. Having dealt with the sartorial finery of two aristocrats known to his hearers, he concluded: 'it is all feathers and stars that are used by the governing classes to keep people in awe'. The privileges of foreign rulers were 'like empty windbags – the puncture of a pin would expose their nothingness'.[44] And the Young Ireland theme was repeated as Kenyon spoke of patience, determination and preparation for the proper time to vindicate the people's rights.

Although the days of lengthy epistles were over, Fr Kenyon maintained republican connections, albeit in troubled fashion. An indication of Fenian mistrust emerges during the funeral (August 1861) of Terence Bellew MacManus. The reinterment in Glasnevin of the former Young Irelander caused acrimony between constitutional nationalists and Fenians, all of them

eager to lay claim to the dead patriot. Archbishop Cullen dir-
ected his clergy to have nothing to do with the funeral al-
though he made the pro-Cathedral available to the cortege.
The funeral committee had selected Kenyon to speak at
Glasnevin and he was more than willing to do so, despite
Cullen's stated disapproval of public display. In the days before the funeral, various factions embroiled him in a controversy not of his making. Eventually, an American, Colonel M.
D. Smith, was deputed to speak although it was Fr Patrick
Lavelle who gave the funeral tribute. Personal dislike between
Kenyon and Stephens may have played its part in the priest's
demotion. John O'Leary (as a veteran Fenian his belief is
noteworthy), believed the Fenian leadership rejected Kenyon's
proposed speech as too aspirational. Although he shared
many Fenian aims and employed much of its rhetoric,
Kenyon remained sceptical about its organisational structure.
In particular, he shared Mitchel's foreboding that there could
be no secrecy due to the ubiquity of spies. By another route,
he had come to the opinion of many clergy in their opposition to Fenianism, viz. that it led all too many people to hopeless confrontation, imprisonment and, even, execution. Within
this pattern fits his cool reception of James Stephens who
sought refuge at Templederry after the Fenian rising in 1867.
Stephens was given temporary shelter, but it was left to another
Tipperary nationalist, Peter Gill, to harbour the fugitive for
several months.[45]

The closing years of Kenyon's life bear an overtone of
seclusion. At this stage, other radical priests had moved to the
forefront. When the civil authorities considered prosecutions
in November 1862, they examined the speeches of Frs Lavelle,
Mullen, Hickey and Geraghty without reference to Kenyon.
Yet, Kenyon had not altogether retired. Occasionally, he gave
election speeches, particularly in opposition to Whig landlord
candidates. Re-echoes of Young Ireland emerged in his speech
at a banquet for The O'Donoghue, a Young Irelander now an
MP. Insisting that O'Donoghue should be supported as a na-

tionalist, he toasted 'Ireland a nation, the martyrs of Ireland, the heroes of Ireland, the artists of Ireland, the wrongs of Ireland, the rights of Ireland and the hopes of Ireland.'[46] On St Patrick's Day 1862, at Dublin's Rotunda, he addressed The Brotherhood of St Patrick which had been founded the previous year. (The Brotherhood's aims were to secure Irish independence and land reform. Although it tried to replace the failed Irish Independent Party of the 1850s, it eventually became a front for the Irish Republican Brotherhood and thus incurred Archbishop Cullen's displeasure.) In a relatively uncontroversial speech (compared, for example, with Lavelle's address 'The Catholic Doctrine on the Right To Revolt'), Kenyon emphasised the concepts of nationality and anti-sectarianism. Later in the year he spoke at Nenagh to another meeting of the Brotherhood on the same themes although his reference to the inappropriateness of force hardly endeared him to Fenians.

From the mid-1860s, Kenyon's health had begun to deteriorate. After a Paris visit to Mitchel in 1866, the latter expressed concern about the priest's appearance. From late 1868 he suffered repeated haemorrhages, the worst of these occurring in February 1869 after he had celebrated requiem Mass. For six weeks he remained in virtual isolation at Templederry presbytery, visited only by some parishioners and diocesan colleagues. On 21 March 1869 he died in the parish house.

An Ambiguous Figure?

With his esoteric learning, florid rhetoric, and readiness for controversy, John Kenyon can be seen as a tribune of the people. In the limited context of Tipperary and Limerick, he was a major figure whose remembrance is alive more than a hundred years from his death. His view of 'nationality' was that of Davis who, in introducing *The Nation*, had written:

'Nationality is our first great objective – nationality which will not only raise our people from their poverty by securing them the blessing of a domestic legislature, but inflame and purify them with a lofty and heroic love of country – a

nationality which may embrace Protestant, Catholic and
Dissenter … not a nationality which would preclude civil
war, but which would establish internal union and external independence; a nationality which would be recognised by the world, and sanctified by wisdom, virtue and
prudence'

The internal tensions of such a programme were considerable,
given an Ireland marked by religious and class conflict. Such
tensions emerge in stances which Fr Kenyon adopted in the
years after Davis's premature death. As a priest, Kenyon was a
zealous minister, careful in attention to his people. His last act
before his fatal illness was to celebrate a requiem Mass.
Tangible evidences, such as two churches and several schools,
show him to have been an energetic parish priest. In terms of
national politics, his influence is more difficult to estimate.
Certainly, he was a 'turbulent priest', especially during the
1840s. Thereafter, he had trodden a narrow line between advanced nationalism and the rigid orthodoxies imposed by
Archbishop Cullen's growing hegemony in the Irish church.
As well, his record of advanced 'nationality' put him on that
borderline where constitutional nationalists met the republi-
can/separatism of the Fenian movement.

Kenyon's incursion into the politics of his day remains
highly interesting, yet strangely flawed. His stances can be understood partly by his active, even tempestuous, personality.
Yet, for priests in nineteenth century Ireland, politics were
virtually unavoidable on issues such as land tenure and
famine. As Fr Birmingham had said, in post-famine Ireland
priests felt they had to step into the breach with their people.
Similarly, the question of repeal, following hard on the
achievement of emancipation, involved the bulk of the clergy
in secular politics to a degree virtually unknown today.
Unfortunately, circumstances of the time rendered difficult
the cross-traditions generosity of Coigly, Steel Dickson and
Porter. In the 1850s there was an increasing identification of
faith and fatherland, of religious tradition with political affili-

ation. 'Catholic' became virtually synonymous with 'nationalist'; 'Protestant' was taken to be the same as 'unionist'. Thus, the recent claim by Garret Fitzgerald is corroborated – from the mid-nineteenth century the movement for repeal of the Act of Union had become mainly a 'Catholic' affair while, again in the main, 'unionism' had been espoused by Protestants.

A welcome feature of Kenyon's engagement is his care to avoid sectarianism. Consonantly with Young Ireland thought, his rhetoric was sprinkled with anti-sectarian references. An unfortunate exception to this is his misconceived criticism of 'Quakerism' – this on the issue of pacifism. His long standing friendship with Mitchel and Martin bespoke mutual respect for religious allegiance even when there was disagreement on one issue or another. Whatever one's judgement about his advocacy of force to secure Repeal, his differences with O'Connellism shows that Catholic nationalism was by no means monolithic. Kenyon's emphasis on nationality; his interest in Irish poetry, music and dance, his intense local patriotism, were no more than the programme outlined by Thomas Davis and *The Nation* group. In pursuance of the Young Ireland ideal, Kenyon made judgements which today even his admirers must reject, e.g. his extraordinary refusal to condemn slavery in America; his rhetoric about insurrection when, clearly, there was no possibility of its success.

In regard to slavery, Kenyon appealed to a theology which still rises up to haunt Catholic history. Apart from outstanding individuals, Catholic opposition to slavery was scandalously muted. In the Irish context, it must be said that O'Connell took the better stance on the issue. Young Ireland, Mitchel and Kenyon can be praised neither for their rhetoric nor for their position on an urgent moral issue. In fairness to Kenyon, there is some evidence that by the 1860s he and Mitchel disagreed sharply on the question.[47] In regard to the use of force, perhaps his strongest argument is that used against O'Connell during the 1840s: 'If bad men could once believe that the injured and oppressed are withheld by any valid law from redressing their injuries when they are able, and shaking off their oppressors by force of arms, in the last resort, then, indeed, might violence rage uncontrolled, and the blood of the innocent be profusely shed, because that of the guilty had been iniquitously spared.'[48]

Perhaps Kenyon's weak point is the disparity between his rhetoric and practice. Despite his enthusiasm for force and talk about preparation for conflict, in the event he refused without explanation to assist his insurrectionary colleagues. Was this a theological scruple about reasonable hope of success? Had Kenyon been disillusioned by Young Ireland supinity in the days when Mitchel was on trial? Was it an example of someone who, having confused the rhetoric of revolution with its substance, baulked at the reality when it came? Or was it another verification of Kickham's reference to the unreliability of clergy in revolutionary circumstances? Here, the stance of Wm Smith O'Brien – a reluctant revolutionary who later questioned the strategy of the 1848 rising – is ostensibly more honourable. At his trial, O'Brien admitted that Young Ireland's rhetoric would incur ridicule and reproach if 'we had fled at the moment when all the contingencies which we had contemplated as justifying the use of force were realised'.[49] Kenyon's decision to stand aloof, even though costly for himself, was arguably the wiser course for his people's interests. Yet, just as the issue of slavery puts a question mark on his concept of universal justice, so his eulogies of physical force as an abstract possibility qualify, although they do not invalidate, his valuable emphases on Irish nationality and his criticism of unjust structures.

Bibliography

Davis, Richard, *The Young Ireland Movement*, Gill and MacMillan, Dublin, 1987.

Fogarty, L., *Fr John Kenyon. A Patriot Priest of '48*, Whelan and Son, Dublin, 1920.

Fitzgerald, Philip, *A Narrative of the Proceedings of the Confederates of 1848*, Duffy, Dublin, 1868.

Gleeson, John, *History of Ely O'Carroll Territory*, Gill, Dublin, 1915.

Gavan Duffy, C., *Young Ireland. A Fragment of Irish History* (2 vols), Fisher Unwin, London, 1883 & 1896.

Kerrigan, Colm, *Fr Mathew*, Cork University Press, Cork, 1992

Murphy, Ignatius, *Diocese of Killaloe 1850-1904*, Four Cours, Dublin, 1995

O'Leary, John, *Recollections of Fenians and Fenianism*, 2 vols, Downey, London, 1896.

O'Shea, James, *Priests, Politics and Society in Post-Famine Ireland*, Wolfhound, Dublin and Humanities Press, New Jersey, 1983.

Articles

Gleeson, D., 'Fr John Kenyon and Young Ireland', *Studies* (xxv), March 1946, pp 99-110.

Gwynn, D., 'Fr. Kenyon and Young Ireland' and 'The Priests and Young Ireland', *Irish Ecclesiastical Record*, 1946, vol LXXI, pp 226-46 and 508-532.

Ó Fiaich, T., 'The Clergy and Fenianism', *Irish Ecclesiastical Record* (CIX), 1968, pp 81-103.

CHAPTER SIX

THE CALLAN CURATES

Frs Thomas O'Shea (1813-1887) and Matthew O'Keeffe (1811-1887)

'When the country was in a hopeless condition in 1849 ... utterly prostrate in the midst of famine, extermination and emigrations, when despondency seized all classes and conditions of men, they in Callan did not despair of the fortunes of their country. No! It was then they unfurled the standard of Tenant Right' (Fr Thomas O'Shea, *Callan Tenant Protection Society Memorial Booklet,* p 28)[1]

'most of them are dead ...those that did not die in sheds died in the poor house ... others, and these were the most numerous, have I seen burrowing in ditches and pits of old lime-kilns ... often I crept, ankle deep in water, under these sheelings ... I will not speak of 300 adults, who, in one half year, died of starvation under my very own eyes in that parish' (Fr O Dwyer, Doon, Co Limerick describing the woes of his famine-stricken parishioners. *Limerick Reporter,* 16.4.1850)

The times were indeed horrendous when Fr Thomas O'Shea was appointed to the parish of Callan in the diocese of Ossory. It was 1848, the immediate aftermath of a famine which decimated the poorest classes in rural Irish society. Even yet, the ravages of hunger and cholera had not abated. The neighbourhood of Callan had been severely visited both by hunger and disease. A further complement to the distress was the conduct of the Earl of Desart, a major landlord in the area.

Even in 1834, a decade before the onset of famine, Callan

was beset by miserable economic conditions. In that year, Henry D. Inglis, a Scotsman who visited the town, had not yet seen in Ireland 'any town in so wretched a condition as this'. Cabins were no better than holes in the ground. On the outskirts of the town, people were either near starvation or 'barely keeping body and soul together'. Of the population (three to four thousand) one thousand had no regular employment. Six to seven hundred were entirely destitute while two hundred were in a state of beggary. Absentee landlords repudiated all duties to the poor. Yet, they persisted in the enjoyment of 'a splendid income (wrung) out of a people left to starvation or crime'.[2] Efforts towards poor relief such as enclosure of commonages and, later, payment of Poor Law rates, were resisted by these same magnates.

At Callan, Fr O'Shea joined Fr Matthew O'Keeffe who had worked there since 1843. In common with clergymen of several religious traditions, the two curates had experienced the prevalent misery at first hand. The people who died were precisely those described by Henry Inglis – landless poor and small-holders who flocked to diseased poor-houses or perished in their hovels. Not until later – when the disturbed economy affected themselves – did the more affluent take up the cause of poor relief or, for that matter, of tenant right. As in other places, the clergy of Callan had indeed stood by the poorest of their people – when Fr O'Shea arrived in the town two of his predecessors had already died of cholera. It is said that he himself witnessed eight deaths in one family after their eviction.[3]

Both priests were endowed with remarkable personal qualities. Fr O'Shea is described as 'a man of powerful intellect, large frame and big, tender heart (who) everywhere he went, was the idol of the people'.[4] Fr O'Keeffe was a scholar, an excellent orator and of determined spirit. The two men formed an effective combination in meeting the immediate distress through their priestly ministry. Yet they went even further than this in addressing the unjust economic system, so much

the root of disaster. Their response was a structured one, carefully developed. Their method was to organise the small
farmers and labourers most vulnerable to eviction.

With scant exaggeration, the *Kilkenny Journal* (30 June
1849) proclaimed the desperate situation of small tenants: 'the
Irish tenant is a mere serf on the land – at the mercy of the
landlord'. Perhaps with the exception of the north of Ireland,
where Tenant Right precariously existed, this was true of
Ireland as a whole. Even worse was the situation of landless
labourers. The area around Callan was particularly vulnerable
to economic distress. As already mentioned, many of the
landless labourers and their families had either perished or
emigrated. Among the tenants there was a predominance of
very small farmers – most had less than five acres, although
there were some strong farmers in the area.

In regard to the Desart holdings, the *Kilkenny Journal*'s,
observation on the parlous conditions of tenants was only too
accurate. Desart was prominent among landlords endeavouring to 'consolidate' their estates. The consequence was virtually indiscriminate evictions of families who could not meet
an already exorbitant rent. On Desart's lands the rent (£1-10-6
per acre) was three times higher than that sustainable by small
farmers already in desperate straits. Despite the prevalent distress, Desart refused to countenance any significant reduction
of rent. On one of his estates, tenants had been reduced from
25 families to 16. Six houses had been knocked and their occu-
pants thrown onto the road.[5]

The Callan Tenants Protection Society

In these circumstances, the Callan curates initiated the
Callan Tenants Protection Society. Similar attempts had been
made elsewhere but with little success. In October 1849, *The
Nation* called for the establishment of Tenant Societies on
wide scale. Perhaps in response to this, the Callan Society was
inaugurated in the Town Hall's Newsroom on 14 October
1849. The inaugural meeting showed every sign of detailed
planning in its resolutions and its minutes. Significantly, the

minutes show the broad range of the original committee –
clergymen, Town Commisioners, Poor Law Guardians and
tenant farmers. The lack of reference to a class perennially ab-
sent from written history – the landless people of rural society
– reflects the toll of those who by now had died or emigrated.
It may also be evidence that those able to join in resistance
were themselves in relatively secure circumstances.[6]

The seven resolutions of the inaugural meeting were emin-
ently practical. One resolution (seconded by Fr O'Shea)
warned of the destruction of the agricultural sector which
'with its fall must leave the county a howling wilderness and
leave its inhabitants to utter destruction'. Another resolution
spoke of rents 'always exorbitant ... now ... utterly intolerable'.
The sixth and seventh resolutions decided on a weekly com-
mittee-meeting (Wednesdays), a register of members and
careful record of meetings. The fourth resolution is perhaps
the most substantive as it sets forth the aims of the Society: 'to
reduce rents by every legal and constitutional means to a standard commensurate with the reduced value of agricultural
produce ... to base on this reduced value tenant right ... to foster agricultural employment'. Almost immediately, the
Kilkenny Journal gave its support by speaking of the society's
aims: to obtain fair rents, the recognition of tenant right, the
industrial employment of the labouring classes.[7]

The minute-books witness to the society's careful strategy.
Here Fr O'Keeffe showed particular acumen – his recommen-
dation that people desist from mutual competition was time-
ly. Essentially, it was a call to solidarity: 'Yourselves are your
only foes. Abandon the mischievous system of foolish competition and you lay the axe to the root of the evils of land
tenure in Ireland.' The strategy was to refuse to bid on land
from which a fellow-tenant had been evicted. Where a landlord knew that no third party would bid, he would then be
forced to accept a reasonable offer from the sitting tenant. An
inherent weakness of the plan was to leave the 'land grabber'
in an easier situation. Hence, it was crucially important that

similar tenant societies be founded throughout the region. Fr O'Keeffe recommended public petitions in two directions: to the landlords for fair rents and to Parliament for Tenant Right based upon the letting value of the land. His own work among the very poorest is reflected in his call for provision of industrial employment of labouring people 'saving them from the horrors of the poor house and yourselves from ruin in maintaining them in unprofitable idleness'.[8]

It is clear that the Callan Society had learned from O'Connell's method of democratic pressure. Both priests constantly stressed the need to avoid secret or illegal means: 'We are determined to carry out our object only by means sanctioned by law and conducive to social order and happiness.' At an immense public meeting in Callan on 11 November 1849 (the attendance had come from Tipperary and Kilkenny) Fr O'Shea reiterated the openness of the Society's operation. Referring to 'the great principles of the immortal O'Connell', he emphasised that in the Society there was nothing secret, nothing wrong, nothing illegal. Its weekly meetings, its careful minutes, its collection of information – today, this might be called 'social analysis' – gave it an unusual stability. The layout of its membership card evidences its philosophy: 'Labour, the only source of wealth' and 'Property has its duties as well as its rights'. Of note, too, is its triple call for Employment, Fair Rents and Tenant right.[9]

The Callan Society burgeoned with remarkable speed – within weeks societies existed in Mullinahone, Ballingarry, Castlecomer, Ballycallan and Danesfort. By Summer 1850, apart from Kilkenny and Tipperary, some twenty societies had been set up in Limerick, Cork, Westmeath and Wexford. As larger farmers started to join, Callan remained the exemplar for the new societies. A sign that the Callan initiative was beginning to bite is Lord Desart's attempt at what might be termed 'public relations'. Desart engineered a statement where the Callan curates were dubbed 'anti-Christian and ministers of Satan'. Pressure was applied to tenants in signing a memorial of good wishes to Desart and his 'amiable countess, who blesses your lordship's house and diffuses through a still wider circle the pleasant odour of her virtues'.[10]

Hitherto, the Callan Curates had little difficulty from church leadership although Lord Desart's mischievous gibe was clearly intended to incur such trouble. With the exception of one, Fr Salmon, all the priests in the Callan region were now active in Tenant Societies. And, even for a conservative hierarchy, the aims of these societies could hardly be a problem. Yet, there had been setbacks. For example, John O'Connell MP, warned that Tenant agitation could impede the Repeal movement. Likewise, clearances had continued – in a petition to Westminster the Callan society complained that 'within a circuit of six miles around the town ... about 280 homesteads have been levelled to the ground and the population reduced to the extent of 1,680 families'. Nevertheless, Fr O'Keeffe could justifiably say in 1853: 'no question that I know ... gained such a position in so short a period'. The curate's political acumen is discerned in his remark that the issue required more than a paragraph in the Queen's speech and the addresses of political adventurers. The required course of action was to have a Tenant Right party in the House of Commons.[11]

Meanwhile, an Ulster Tenant Right Association had been founded by William Sharman Crawford and James McKnight. A notable feature of this Association is the presence of several Presbyterian clergymen, although Henry Cooke, now dominant on the right-wing, decried common cause with Catholics or Nationalists. By spring 1850 there was talk of a conference of northern and southern tenants' protection societies. The conference, attended by more than 300 people, took place in the first week of August 1850. Fr O'Shea, already a member of the organising committee, at this stage emerged in tenant-right politics at national level.

Irish Tenant League (August 1850)

The upshot of the conference, 'The Conference of North

and South', as Gavan Duffy later termed it, was the foundation of an Irish Tenant League. Here, the prominent figures
included Fr O'Shea himself, Charles Gavan Duffy (*The
Nation*), Frederick Lucas (*The Tablet*), John Grey (*Freeman's
Journal*), William Sharman Crawford (already an M.P.), John
Rogers, a Presbyterian clergyman, and James McKnight, editor
of *The Banner of Ulster*. The committee represented a formidable coalition of journalistic expertise, political experience,
and clerical support across the religious divide. One significant decision of the League was to exact support of the
League's policies from candidates for election to Parliament.
Only those candidates would be supported who undertook to
oppose government on every issue which did not further the
cause of Irish tenants. At this stage, Dr McHale, Archbishop
of Tuam, made no secret of his support for the League. More
ambiguously, Dr Paul Cullen (Archbishop, first at Armagh
and, later, at Dublin) gave qualified indications of support.

Early in 1851, another issue obtruded itself which would
cause difficulty for the League and, in particular, for the
Callan Curates. Pope Pius IX had reestablished the English
hierarchy and instructed the English bishops to resume their
diocesan titles. An outburst of anti-Popery caused the government to introduce an Ecclesiastical Titles Bill (forbidding the
papal proposals). Irish MPs vigorously resisted the Bill. Later,
they would be dubbed the 'Irish Brigade' and 'the Pope's Brass
Band'. Along with Dr Paul Cullen, George Moore, William
Keogh and John Sadleir founded the Catholic Defence
Association, the membership of which overlapped with the
Irish Tenant League. One notices Gavan Duffy's discomfort at
the introduction of this sectarian issue lest it strain the tenant
league of north and south. Nevertheless, the alliance proceeded
and, to cite Maurice Manning, 'the agrarian and religious agit-
ations were now formed into an alliance'. While the alliance
was always an uneasy one, it nevertheless managed to prose-
cute a common electoral strategy.[12]

After the 1852 general election, forty eight MPs were re-

turned who undertook to act as an Independent Irish Party.
According to their promise, they would oppose every government unwilling to concede religious equality and agrarian reform. The fair promise was destined to disappointment.
Indeed, there is some evidence that several Irish Party MPs
were reluctant to make the promise. Yet, the Irish Party
showed cohesive opposition to the new Tory government.
Within months, the new government fell and was replaced by
a Whig-led coalition under Lord Aberdeen. To the outrage of
many, William Keogh accepted office as solicitor-general for
Ireland while John Sadleir became a Lord of the Treasury. As
has happened since, English politics wreaked havoc on Irish
alliances. The supporters of the Irish Independent Party split.
Cullen, for his own purposes, seemed determined to work
with the Aberdeen Whigs, sensing their openness to disestab-
lishing the Anglican Church. On the *volte face* of Sadleir and
Keogh, Dr Cullen expressed no public opinion. Other bishops
(Elphin; Kildare and Leighlin) refused to criticise the defect-
ing MPs and later showed readiness to vote for Keogh and
Sadleir.

In a series of bye-elections (January 1853; April 1853;
February 1854) the divisions within the clergy became evident. In each election, there was notable divergence between
bishops and priests as well as between priests themselves. At
the hustings, the Callan Curates were in much demand because of their identification with tenant right and their close
association with the founding of the Independent Party. Like
Fr Ml O'Flanagan several generations later, they lent their
considerable skills to opponents of the defaulting Irish Party
members and exposed what they deemed betrayal of the tenants' cause.

The Louth bye-election (February 1854) was a bitter contest between J. M. Cantwell (a founder of the Irish Tenant
League) and the Whig office-holder, C. S. Fortescue. Here
again, clergy took both sides. An indignant Archbishop
Cullen wrote: 'Politics are very much to the front in Louth.

The clergy are horribly divided.' Yet, Cullen also had partisan views. As to Cantwell, the Archbishop wrote that he was 'a Catholic, but does not know either the church or the clergy and charges his Protestant wife with raising his *(sic)* children as Protestants'. Cullen's judgement was: 'it is not worth the trouble in returning such Catholics in Parliament'. On the other hand, he deemed Fortescue 'a good young man of liberal ideas, an enemy of the Established Church'. With this reference to the Established Church, Cullen's own long-term objectives may well be adumbrated. In regard to the Louth election, the Archbishop did not address the socio-political issues involved. Instead he lamented that the priests were divided among themselves 'and publicly abused each other'. O'Shea's involvement in the Louth election incurred episcopal hostility both at Armagh and Dublin. On the pretext that religion would suffer because of clerical divisions, Archbishop Cullen urged an amenable Bishop Walsh to recall O'Shea and forbid him to take part in further public meetings. A rigid episcopal style is disclosed in Walsh's threat to suspend O'Shea from his priestly functions. It should also be noted that Fr O'Shea claimed his involvement in the Louth election had the sanction of his own parish priest and the tacit support of three bishops.[13]

Further Moves against the Callan Curates

While the pro-tenant motivation of O'Shea and O'Keeffe is clear, the agenda of Cullen and, indeed, of members of the Independent Irish Party is by no means so. Larger battles of ecclesiastical politics and, in some cases, of political opportunism were being fought. The Irish Party had its share of adventurers, e.g. Sadleir and Keogh. For Archbishop Cullen, clerical discipline was paramount, almost an obsession. Alongside this, other questions were at work: disestablishment of the Anglican Church, university education, ecclesiastical titles legislation, proselytism. In local context, factionalism among the clergy and bitter public discourse were causing dissension in many dioceses. Again, in a situation where bishops had quasi-absolute power in their dioceses, the temperament of the Bishop of Ossory also played its part. To a considerable degree, Frs O'Shea and O'Keeffe became the victims of this hierarchical and political interplay. One can argue that their treatment evinces scant justice either to the Callan Society or to priests who had worked selflessly for their people.[14]

Fr O'Keeffe, although a scholar and dedicated pastor, was also a man of forthright ways. From his pulpit he proved the scourge of evicting landlords – somewhat mischievously Cullen later adduced this as a complaint against him. There is some evidence that his criticisms of Sir William Cuffe (doubtless, a scion of the Desart family) almost incurred a civil prosecution against the priest. Then, in September 1854, Sergeant William Shee, MP for County Kilkenny since 1852, broke ranks with the Independent Irish Party to propose his own tenant right bill, a more 'moderate' one than that of W. Sharman Crawford. Although hitherto a supporter of Shee, Fr O'Keeffe remonstrated by letter. Shee promptly gave the *Kilkenny Journal* both O'Keeffe's letter and his own reply. The priest's letter was strongly critical – the *Banner of Ulster*, itself favourable to tenant right, thought O'Keeffe displayed 'more bitterness than we could have expected from his general character'.[15] Yet it was not a major issue and, doubtless, could have been easily resolved. Inexplicably, except perhaps through hostility to O'Keeffe and an undoubtedly close friendship with Shee, Bishop Walsh imposed silence on O'Keeffe as he had earlier done in regard to O'Shea. (In the 1857 general election, the Ossory clergy threw their weight against Shee. Here again, it is noticeable that Bishop Walsh supported Sergeant Shee. In the outcome, Shee finished at the bottom of the poll. Eventually, he returned to England and became the first Catholic since the Reformation to be a justice of the Queen's Bench).

Thus, by late 1854 the Callan Curates had both incurred episcopal discipline. A train of hierarchical thought would argue that they should have accepted the discipline without comment. Certainly, for Cullen's rigid mind that is what should have happened. Yet, given the high profile of both priests, such obfuscation was impossible. Frederick Lucas, Charles Gavan Duffy and George Moore learned of the moves against the curates. They convened a public meeting in Callan on 29 October 1854. Here, Fr O'Shea addressed a large crowd in spirited defence of his colleague. The meeting decided on a threefold appeal to Rome. The first, to be handled by the curates themselves, was an appeal against Dr Walsh's behaviour. The second would be a general complaint, signed by the clergy, against Dr Cullen's ecclesiastical policies. The third appeal would be from Irish MPs to protest Cullen's political policies.

The personal appeal by the Callan Curates did not go ahead. One feature – an apparently abusive one – is that Dr Walsh forbade Fr O'Keeffe to travel to Rome with a memorial. On the general clerical appeal there was little more success. Although many priests were outraged by Cullen's procedures, it proved difficult to get them to agree a formulation and, then, to sign the memorial. Only a minority of priests – notably Fr O'Dwyer of Doon (Co Limerick) with whose description of famine distress this chapter opened – were sufficiently intrepid to espouse the project in public fashion. It is noteworthy that Fr O'Shea circulated the memorial in Wexford while Fr O'Keeffe accepted nomination as one to whom subscriptions might be sent. In regard to the M.P's appeal, Frederick Lucas did go to Rome, was courteously received, but made no progress in the labyrinth of Vatican procedures. In fact, the downturn of the Independent Irish Party had already commenced. Gavan Duffy, despondent at episcopal opportunism and the increasingly sectarian note in Cullen's policies, quit Ireland for Australia. Lucas, discouraged and in poor health, returned to his native England where he died shortly afterwards.

The procedure of appeals and memorials, while amply justified, was not well managed.[16] And in the course of the litigation Paul Cullen deployed his thorough knowledge of Vatican politics, by working on the Pope's conservatism. Behind the emotive arguments, Cullen's larger strategy was at work. It did not include the concerns of the Irish Tenant League but rather of the institutional church as discerned by the Archbishop. Paramount in his strategy was the formation of a rigidly disciplined clergy and a unified Irish hierarchy. In his memorandum to the Vatican, Cullen inserted a thinly veiled criticism of the Archbishop of Tuam, John McHale, while lamenting that Fr O'Shea could claim the support of more than one Irish bishop. A skilful reference to Mazzini and Kossuth was calculated to rouse the emotions of a now rabidly conservative Pope Pius ix. A note of bitterness is evident when Cullen refers to the curates having 'continually praised themselves in the newspapers of the Irish Tenant League as men of great merit, notable for charity and full of ardent patriotism'. The barb, characteristic of the Archbishop, then follows: 'Their conduct however did not seem to their bishop to merit such eulogies'.

Rome's bland courtesy to Lucas was accompanied by an instruction that the Callan Curates abide by their bishop's ruling. Priests were to avoid politics and confine themselves to their specific ministry. In this decision Cullen had achieved a remarkable although predictable victory. Now, even at the expense of movements like Tenant Right, he had secured the silence of priests on issues of which he did not approve. And, he was freer to pursue his own designs. A presage of a new religio-political involvement is given by Cullen's own 'exceptions' where priests could speak 'politically'. For example, priests could tell people not to vote for an election candidate who was avowedly hostile to the church. The problem here is definition of 'hostility' and of who should frame the definition. A model closer to our own day was emerging – priests were being ordered out of party politics 'so that they could be all the more effective on moral issues in politics whenever they arose'. Even here, the question remains of what constitutes a moral issue.

Although accepted by the Callan curates, the Vatican's decision created a legacy of bitterness. Years later, Charles Kickham discouraged the leadership of priests in radical movements – 'Every priest believes himself bound to bow humbly to the decrees of his superiors. And the censure might come at some critical moment ... and then the people (are) left disheartened.'[17] Kickham cites Fr O'Shea ('one of the best and ablest priests of the League') as remarking on a controversial occasion: "Tis not the people who are rotten. 'Tis the priests are rotten, aye, and the bishops are rotten.' It is probable that the society founded by the Callan Curates had done its best work in the immediate aftermath of the famine. Towards the mid-fifties, distress had been mitigated although the question of Tenant Right remained unresolved. Throughout the country tenant protection societies continued their work. Yet, until the 1870s they suffered from apathy and, at times, dissension. As to the Callan Curates, their bishop was unable to show much generosity. During 1855, both men were moved from Callan. Fr O'Keeffe was appointed curate in Dunnamaggan. Fr O'Shea was sent to Cullohill. Before his removal, Fr O'Shea expressed gratitude to the secretary of the Callan Society, Thomas Shelly, for its consistent support of the tenant cause and of the Callan Curates.[18]

Doubtless, present day residents of Cullohill would not agree with Frederick Lucas's reference to O'Shea's banishment: 'to a miserable locality, where there (is) absolutely no society for a man of his mental capacity'.[19] Archdeacon Fitzgerald, who knew a good deal about episcopal sanctions, discloses the true ecclesiastical situation in a letter to Gavan Duffy: 'O'Shea and Doyle and Keeffe (*sic*) are in penal exile.'[20] The enthusiastic but uncontroversial memoir of Canon W. Carrigan hints at the displeasure felt in Callan at the priests' removal: 'If affectionate and sympathetic hearts could have any claim in preventing it, the Callan people would have prevented his departure.'[21] About the time of his original move against the curates, Dr Walsh was hooted in the streets of

Kilkenny. Popular displeasure at the transfer of Frs O'Shea and O'Keeffe is reflected in the bishop's tight-lipped claim that he had not lorded it over 'his' clergy – he had, he claimed, 'interdicted only the abuse of rights and that to two priests solely' (*Limerick Reporter*, 21 Dec 1855). Years later, in the notorious case of another Callan priest, Fr Robert O'Keeffe, supporters vowed he would not be transferred by episcopal *fiat* in the manner of the Callan Curates.

In a new context at Dunnamaggan and Cullohill, the former Callan Curates did not cease their friendship. Fr O'Keeffe continued his association with the local Tenants Defence Association and, through his efforts 'many a poor homestead was preserved from destruction'.[22] Matthew O'Keeffe is also remembered for his work in education of the area's poor. As parish priest at Aghaboe, he again associated himself with tenant right in the Independent Club. It is, perhaps, an indication of his colleagues' recognition of earlier injustice that, in 1871, they recommended him to become co-adjutor bishop to Dr Walsh. However, it was another – Archbishop Cullen's nephew – who was appointed by Dr Walsh.

As to Fr O'Shea, he became parish priest of Camross in 1863. Nor had his spirit of independence deserted him. When Charles Gavan Duffy returned from Australia in 1865, O'Shea arranged a reunion. From Mountrath the priest wrote: 'Give me some days notice that I may try to have some of our surviving friends to meet you.' Perhaps with a touch of irony, he adds: 'I'm preparing the children for the visitation of my amiable and patriotic bishop and this alone prevents me running up to shake your ... hand.'[23] In the general election of 1868, he helped to oppose Charles R. Barry, a crown prosecutor in the Fenian trials, in the latter's campaign for Dungarvan Borough. Alongside O'Shea in this endeavour were Fr Anderson (an Augustinian who had already been victimised by Dr Cullen), Fr Jack Vaughan and Fr Patrick Lavelle.[24] A popular slogan of this campaign referred to Barry's part in the Fenian trials: '(Even) A Tory before a Traitor.'

From the appointment of a new bishop in Ossory, Dr Moran, the situation of Frs O'Shea and O'Keeffe seems to have changed. Both priests spoke in a long debate of the Laois Independent Club which pledged support to the emerging Home Rule movement.[25] In 1873, Fr O'Shea became Canon Theologian of Ossory diocese. As to Fr O'Keeffe, he was appointed Canon in 1873, awarded a doctorate of divinity in 1880, and in 1883 precentor of the diocesan chapter. During 1874 and again in 1875 the former Callan Curates lent their weight towards continued support by tenants for Isaac Butt and Charles Stewart Parnell. However, their most significant work was during the time of greatest need, viz. the immediate aftermath of the Great Famine.

Fr O'Keeffe died on 29 November 1887 while earlier in the same year (30 March) Fr O'Shea died of pneumonia. Of Fr O'Keeffe, Carrigan justly wrote: 'By his death, one of the men who contributed much to the making of New Ireland has passed away, and in the day of Ireland's prosperity his memory will be fresh ...'[26] Carrigan's enthusiasm is unbounded yet scarcely excessive. As to the public perception in Callan, the curates' memory remained long undimmed. At the height of another Callan dispute – the case of Fr Robert O'Keeffe – a protest meeting held in 1871 outside 'the Big Chapel' heard that the Callan Curates were 'the only ones to speak for the poor people and ... they had been put out of the parish'.[27] In broader canvas, the Callan Curates occupy a notable place. Tribute is due to their energy, dedication and efficiency in organising protection for the poorest of the poor. It has been said that they 'assailed the fabric of landlordism, buttressed as it then was ... and seemingly unshakeable'.[28] Their bishop's move against them and Cullen's part therein presaged a new kind of church. Under Cullen's leadership there was small room for tenant agitation or other radical causes. This new model prized clerical discipline, and was far too interested in organisational concerns to rest easy with the independent activity of men like the Callan Curates.

It would be inexact to present the Callan Curates as perennial dissidents. From all evidence, they were unremitting in their priestly work – attention to the sick, concern for education of children, resistance to opportunistic proselytism which was part of the Protestant 'Second Reformation'. In their later days, as they became exemplars of a selfless radicalism, both men earned reputations as wise consultors not only in their diocese but also in the nascent Land League. In this, too, they represent a kind of clerical radicalism too frequently overlooked.

Bibliography

Carrigan, W., *History and Antiquities of the Diocese of Ossory,*
Dossier on Appeal to Rome by Frederick Lucas, National Library of Ireland P 5524.
Duffy, Charles Gavan, *The League of North and South,* London, 1886
Duffy, Charles Gavan, *My Life in Two Hemispheres* (2 Vols), Fisher Unwin, London, 1898.
Lucas, Edward V., *Life of Frederick Lucas, M.P.,* London, 1886.
Moore, M.G., *An Irish Gentleman – George Henry Moore,* London 1913.
Norman, E.R., *The Catholic Church and Ireland in the Age of Rebellion. 1859-1873,* London 1965.
O'Dwyer Ml., *Callan Tenant Protection Society,* Callan Heritage Society, 1994.
O'Shea, James, *Priest, Politics and Society in Post-famine Ireland,* Wolfhound Press, Dublin, 1983.
O'Broin, Leon, *Charles Gavan Duffy,* 1967.
Whyte, J.H., *The Independent Irish Party 1850-59,* O U P, Oxford, 1958.

Articles
Delaney, James J., 'Sir William Shee, the Queen's Sergeant', *Old Kilkenny Review,* 1964, pp 52-7.
Kennedy, J., 'Thomas Shelly of Callan', *Old Kilkenny Review,* 1988, pp 492-502.
Phelan Margaret, 'Father Thomas O'Shea and the Callan Tenants Protection Society', *Old Kilkenny Review,* 1980, pp 44-58.
Whyte, J.H. 'Fresh Light on Archbishop Cullen and the Tenant League', *Irish Ecclesiastical Record* (Jan-June 1963) XCIX, pp 170-6.
Unsigned (but clearly from Carrigan's *History and Antiquities of the Diocese of Ossory*), 'Father Matt Keeffe', *Old Kilkenny Review,* 1960, pp 25-9.

CHAPTER SEVEN

AN ISHMAEL OF THE CHURCH IN IRELAND

Isaac Nelson (1812-1888)

'We are labouring for the common good, not as members of churches, but as Irishmen' (Nelson's letter to the *Northern Whig*, 18 Nov 1880).

Isaac Nelson, Presbyterian minister and member of parliament, belies the assumption that unyielding unionism or Orangeism speak for all Ulster Protestants. When he died at Sugarfield House on the Shankill Road, the location of his residence at a confluence of loyalist and nationalist enclaves symbolised his challenge to sectarian bitterness. For many years, he had opposed the slide into religious bigotry which marked the decades 1850-1880. With extraordinary courage he had questioned the mix of religious fervour and political conservatism. Casting himself in the mould of radical clergymen of the 1790s he had called for inclusiveness rather than the bigotry which he discerned in revivalist church leadership. As a result, he was deemed 'the Ishmael of the Church in Ireland'.[1]

During sectarian riots in August 1864 Nelson repeatedly exposed himself to danger by protecting Catholic women and children whose homes were under attack. Later, in a brief political career, he spoke for social reform throughout the whole country without regard to sectarian interests. After his death, the *Irish Times* noted with some delicacy that his attitudes 'had not the effect of increasing his popularity with his brethren in the church' (9 March 1888). And yet, more than a century after his death, one historian could rank him among Shankill's 'most famous sons'.[2]

A Belfastman, Nelson was educated at the city's Academical Institution. After distinguishing himself in classical studies, he worked at the Institute for several years as assistant to Dr E. Hincks, the professor of classics. Meanwhile, he followed courses for church ministry and in November 1837 was licensed to preach by the Belfast presbytery. Ironically, his later theological opponent, William Gibson, was licensed on the same day. In August 1838 he was ordained to serve as assistant minister to the Presbyterian congregation at Comber, Co Down. In March 1842 he was nominated minister of the Presbyterian congregation at Belfast's Donegall St, where he served for nearly forty years. Given his critical stances, it is perhaps unsurprising that his congregation remained a small one, although his trenchant sermons attracted many passing hearers.

By any standard, Isaac Nelson was an impressive man. A somewhat eulogistic reference credits him with the mind of a specialist and the face of a philosopher. His resoluteness can be guaged from a repeated claim that he had the hide of a rhinoceros![3] A student who remembered him in old age at Donegall St describes 'a stout and burly physique, a strong deep chested man who might be expected to amble or trot into his eighties by reason of inherent vigour; and the face, to the eyes of youth, was that of a man beyond 65, gray or white-haired ... a strong face, rather hard in expression ...' Yet there were consistently warm tributes to Nelson's pastoral solicitude from men and women who benefitted by his ministry.[4]

Isaac Nelson came to Donegall St 'with a very high reputation as a scholar, a theologian and a man of popular gifts'. Temperamentally, he may have been unsuited to his new context. Any hint of 'conventional majority' seemed to evoke his immediate opposition. At Belfast, the mid-century Presbyterian leadership showed little sympathy for the radicalism of the 1790s. In response to the perceived threat of Catholic advances under Daniel O'Connell, the dominance of Henry Cooke and Hugh Hanna had brought the ecclesias-

tical temper towards political conservatism. Cooke's denunciation of 'fierce democracy on the on hand and the more terri-
ble Popery on the other' made it difficult for those who
favoured a less sectarian organisation of church and country.

Initially, Nelson's ministry had been unexceptional. Still at
Comber, he was part of an Ulster delegation to Scotland
where his 'clever and brusque exhibitions' charmed his hearers. His difficulties seem to have emerged from the more sub-
tle politics of the Belfast presbytery. Yet even here, his work
showed energy and foresight. Apart from vigorous preaching
at Donegall St, there was involvement with the Belfast Town
Mission and its intensive house visitation. Nelson's popularity
outside more affluent ecclesiastical groupings is suggested in
his enthusiastic reception by the Belfast Working Classes
Association. There is a hint of impatience with leading eccles-
iastics when he recommends the same association to disregard
'the hard words with which the Schoolmen have surrounded
knowledge'.[5]

Dispute on Queen's Colleges

A background to this impatience is the strategy employed
by General Assembly on the proposed Queen's Colleges.
Assembly had withdrawn its theological students from the
Belfast Academical Institute alleging heresy on the part of
some professors. In mirror image of Catholic bishops, it demanded control over theological professorships. Even sympathisers with Presbyterian claims disagreed with the strategy.
The *Northern Whig* wondered if an independent College and
the demands of General Assembly could be reconciled. In
some exasperation, the *Whig* recommended endowing 'up to
twelve professors of Assembly but let us have Queen's College
free' (*Whig* 29.8.46). Yet, Cooke and his party persevered.
Eventually they secured endowment of church-controlled
professorships under Assembly's control.

It appears that Nelson, described by the *Northern Whig* as
the first classical scholar in the Assembly, expected to be appointed to the professorship of Greek. He had had a splendid

record at Belfast Academical Institution and in his earlier years taught classical Greek. On the other hand, his determined anti-slavery activities would not have endeared him to the powerful Henry Cooke faction. Likewise, he incurred hostility by public opposition to Cooke on the importance of teaching classical Greek The *Northern Whig,* no friend of Cooke's, declared it fortunate that Nelson was still able to defend the place of classical Greek (4.12.47). There is considerable truth in George Gilfinnan's remark that 'The doctors, deserted by the man of the desert, deserted him in their turn.'[6]

In any case, it was a minister of the Free Church of Scotland who was appointed to Assembly's College. Masson, the new professor, gave his inaugural lecture in November 1847. Some reports deemed it excessively informal and redolent of sectarianism. Almost immediately, a series of letters attacked Masson for superficiality, for incorrect method and, even, for misleading claims in regard to authorship of a well-received book. The critic, subsigning himself 'Aristarchus', was taken by the *Banner of Ulster* to be Isaac Nelson. Nelson's letters over his own name were not printed by the *Banner* but were published by the *Northern Whig* in a lengthy series through December. They show hostility to Gibson and Masson, both of whom now held chairs at Assembly's College. Nelson's blunt style also reveals his detestation of ministers who sought academic distinctions for their own advancement. He concluded a lengthy critique of Masson by remarking that 'professorial honours are often in inverse ratio of Ministerial success and the best qualification for a chair is the strangulation of a congregation'.[7]

The somewhat bitter correspondence remained one-sided insofar as Masson refused 'to come down' into the arena of public discussion in regard either to his credentials or his methods. Nonetheless, it uncovered a cynicism on the part of Assembly's leadership about double-jobbing. At least two professors – none other than Dr Cooke and Dr Gibson – also re-

tained their congregational ministry. A correspondent to the
Northern Whig argued that the professorships were created to
draw down government money and, in the case of Masson, to
sweeten relations with the Free Church of Scotland. Isaac
Nelson himself would later declare in General Assembly that
if he had been seeking 'situations or honours and such DDs as
the world bestowed he might have pursued a different course'.[8]
Progressively, he came to believe that political and religious
hypocrisy was rife, even in his own community. He became
virtually obsessed with a mission to unmask such hypocrisy,
whether ecclesiastical or political. Very quickly, through pamphlets and extended sermons at Donegall St, he became a dissident figure in the Belfast presbytery. Although he remained
within General Assembly's remit, he 'cared not a farthing for
standing, as he usually stood alone against the world' (obituary in *Witness,* 9 March 1888).[9]

Like many of our 'Unusual Suspects', Nelson's care for sick
or suffering people was outstanding. So, too, was his liturgical
devotion. Even Henry Cooke would say: 'I could fight with
Mr Nelson when necessary, and I could walk ten miles to hear
him pray.' Another opponent remembered the earnestness of
Nelson's prayers even when he was 'the pulpit Ishmaelite of
Belfast'. Although his habitual congregation was small and his
church somewhat gloomy, his preaching attracted students
and inhabitants of the town. A common thread is their appreciation of his sermons along with unease at his denunciations
of contemporary movements and persons. Thirty years after
his death, Dr Samuel Prenter admitted that although the
Donegall St sermons were 'generally a tirade of abuse against
someone or some movement ... (yet) ... the man's genius
would break out and corruscate even in spite of himself'.
Another tribute to Nelson's preaching is given by J. B. Armour,
a courageous voice at a later time. While a student at Belfast,
Armour frequented Donegall St church, believing 'I can learn
more from him (Nelson) than any other man'.[10]

Anti-Slavery Positions

Just as Nelson's dissidence within Presbyterianism can be exaggerated, so too can his critical stances be mistaken for reaction to disappointment. On many issues, his critique of injustice is deeply felt and well considered. This is clear in his opposition not only to slavery but also to association with slave-holders. The question had proved divisive in many quarters. Daniel O'Connell's attitude and its ethical superiority to the pragmatism of 'Young Ireland' have been noted in an earlier chapter of this study. For the Presbyterian General Assembly, the question was no less difficult since many Irish Presbyterians had already settled in America. Likewise, Assembly's relationship to the newly established Free Church of Scotland proved an important factor in the controversy.

For Isaac Nelson, there was no ambiguity. In April 1845, he called for dissociation from churches tolerant of 'man-steal-ing'.[11] Refuting a theologian (Dr Cunningham, of the Free Church of Scotland) who had defended some Presbyterian stances in America, he called on the Belfast presbytery to clarify its own attitude. Already a member of the British and Foreign Anti-Slavery Society, he provided hospitality to Frederick Douglass, a former slave, who in late 1845 addressed meetings throughout Ireland and England. (In fairness, it should be said that other Presbyterian divines such as Wm Gibson and the politically liberal Henry Montgomery shared platforms with Frederick Douglass.) After one such meeting, Nelson was strongly critical of Presbyterian clergymen. In the *Belfast Newsletter,* he also attacked the newly constituted Free Church of Scotland which had accepted support from American Presbyterians although some of these were slave-holders.[12]

The resulting dispute tells much about Nelson and General Assembly. Nelson's collaboration with Dr Montgomery (a member of the 'New Light' or Remonstrant Synod) was criticised as disloyal, although Cooke and Montgomery had joined a delegation to the Viceroy on the proposed Queen's Colleges. Another criticism was that Montgomery and

O'Connell held the same view on communication with slave-holders. In reply, Nelson defended practical collaboration in a good cause, viz. 'to break the manacles from the poor slave'. If O'Connell and Montgomery were united thus far, was it not all the more challenge to General Assembly to do its ethical duty? In a typical flourish he argues: 'Save me from the propositions of the Orthodox ... in this work (should not) all parties unite till freedom is given to the bodies; then let each party direct the soul to Christ as they conscientiously believe best.'[13] At the instance of unnamed clerics, the *Banner of Ulster* (Nelson called it the *Wasp of Ulster*) refused all letters from Donegall St. However, the *Northern Whig* enabled Nelson to obviate the censorship.

Neither the *Banner* nor the generality of Ulster Presbyterians should be taken as pro-slavery. Rather, it was a pragmatic matter. Just as 'Young Ireland' would take help from wherever it came, evangelical Protestants did not want a break with their Scottish Free Church brethren. Again, there were many Irish Presbyterians in the southern states of America whom the General Assembly was reluctant to castigate. Nor should it be forgotten how far Dr Cooke had influenced the clerical leadership in a politically conservative direction. An outstanding example of lay Presbyterian stances is the work of Mary Ann McCracken who until her death distributed anti-slavery tracts at Belfast docks. For Isaac Nelson, it was a question of principle, not of pragmatics. It was a case of good against evil.

Nelson's argument persistently developed the horrors of slavery at the humane and religious levels. Theologically, his opposition grew out of 'the holy feeling of brotherhood that links man to man in ... the family of the Lord Jesus, however scattered ...' At General Assembly (July 1846), he stressed that the ideals of his own ministry were invested in the rejection of slavery. Again, at the 1847 General Assembly, he and Dr Cooke clashed on American Presbyterians' countenance of slavery 'with great warmth, for some time'. Nelson believed that re-

jection of slavery engaged the very core of Presbyterian witness. Hence, in frequent public meetings he incurred hostility,
not least by suggesting that highly-placed Irish clergymen did
not want the question pressed too far. By August 1847, he was
a constant presence at anti-slavery gatherings where he trenchantly criticised church practice in that regard.[14] These appearances were not limited to Belfast – during 1847, Nelson
also addressed an Edinburgh meeting of the Free Church of
Scotland anti-slavery society. Sixteen years later, during the
American civil war, he would publish another attack on the
iniquities of slavery subsequent to his lecture to the
Presbyterian Young Men's Society.[15]

Evangelical 'Revival' of 1859

Here was another example of Isaac Nelson's resolution in
going 'against the tide'. The 'revival' stemmed from Dr William
Gibson's visit to the United States where he had been impressed
by a similar 'revival'. In Ireland, the 'revival' was marked by
open air preaching, mass rallies and hugely attended prayer
meetings. There were claims of miraculous occurrences and
dramatic conversions. The *Banner of Ulster,* the chronicler of
the 'revival', hailed an enthusiasm which had ' swept over almost all churches in Antrim, Down, Tyrone, Derry and
Armagh' (*Banner of Ulster,* 31.12.59). The *Banner* claimed that
tens of thousands had joined the church: 'the very reprobates
of society have been brought within the Christian pale; the
common vices have disappeared ... Church accommodation
has fallen short of the demand ...' Yet, the index of reform was
limited: diminution of drunkenness, swearing and petty
theft. Socio-political criticism was discouraged as distracting
from personal devotion. Although its more lasting effects are
disputed, the revival did increase church membership. As to
its longer influence, it was not a catalyst for change but rather
articulated values deemed central to Presbyterian well-being.[16]

While the 'revival' has several roots, it can be linked to insecurity about communal identity. Presbyterians had endured
decades of social change. Many believed their self-identity

was threatened by a newly confident Roman Catholic Church. While some Presbyterians resented the privileges of Anglicanism, many accepted Henry Cooke's endorsement of pan-Protestant evangelism. A notable feature of Cooke's work was its linkage of Presbyterian interests to political conservatism (even if this meant alliance with landlords and Tory magnates). From the 1830s, the so-called 'nuptials of Hillsborough' sealed a Protestant unity cast in essentially anti-Catholic terms. As J. B. Armour noted many decades later, an unobserved cost of these 'nuptials' was the reduction of Presbyterians to being 'circus riders in the tory hippodrome'.[17]

In fairness, it should be said that there were sober proponents of the revival. The sympathetic Dr James McCosh warned that its 'physiological accidents' were not as spectacular as pretended. Nor were these manifestations irrefutable evidence of divine intervention.[18] By far the most influential figure of the revival was Dr Wm Gibson, professor of ethics and moderator of General Assembly. Through *The Banner of Ulster* and his book *The Year of Grace: A History of the Ulster Revival of 1859,* Gibson ensured widespread publicity for the 'revival'.[19] His church at Rosemary St hosted enthusiastic religious services. Across Ulster, lay preaching, conversions, guest lectures, all contributed to an atmosphere of renewal and rejuvenation.

Hence, it required unusual courage to question what so many considered a new visitation of God. Yet, the revival had its critics although they faced charges of narrowness and, in Nelson's case, of harbouring personal rancour. From the start, Dr Montgomery warned about dangers of delusion. Also in 1859, the Reverend T. McNeece published *Words of Caution and Counsel on the Present Religious Revival.* Some years later (1866), another minister, W. Hamilton, published *An Inquiry into the Scriptural Character of the Revival.* Their works, along with that of Dr Hincks (one wonders if this was Nelson's old principal at Belfast Academical Institute), were regarded as unhelpful if not disloyal.

Without doubt, the most acerbic critic of the revival was Isaac Nelson. Even before the appearance of his *Year of Delusion,* he had indicted the methods used by revivalists, as 'imposture, pretence and falsehood'. The Donegall St pulpit became a focus for critical questioning of what was afoot. In October 1859, two of Nelson's sermons were published as a pamphlet, *A Notice of the late Revival and some of the attempted Explanations of that Phenomenon.* Here, Nelson's priorities are evident: rejection of sectarianism practised 'under the sacred name of Revival'; criticism of the 'natural propensity of denominations to enlarge their numbers', and attack on 'a necromantic formula of the blood of Christ'. On the burgeoning of new, independent congregations Nelson put it: 'In proportion as the truth is received among men, Christ increases and sects decrease' (letter in *The Banner of Ulster,* 6.12.59). Reviewing Nelson's pamphlet, *The Banner* criticised its pretentious scholarship and the grammatical construction of some passages. Here, *The Banner* may have been subtly referring to the old dispute about the Assembly's chair of classics.

Nelson's *Year of Delusion* became the best-known of the dissident analyses. It was a succession of pamphlets or tracts on 'miracles', 'lay preaching', 'the place of the Holy spirit', etc. On all of these, Nelson believed the 'revival' had falsified Presbyterian theology. Nelson's suspicions were aroused by the 'revival's' failure to address urgent social issues such as sectarian hatred and the poverty which affected so many people around Belfast. Thus, he claimed the revival was 'a huge juggle, a giant imposture, having no more to do with Christianity than the phenomena of electro-biology'. Although the criticism was extremely harsh it was ably presented and, in religious circles, the book became a minor classic.

It would be unsafe to suggest that Nelson's opposition to 'the year of grace' was motivated by personal animosity. Doubtless, Nelson was temperamentally driven to question received opinions. Years later, a not unsympathetic obituary in *The Witness* suggests that 'the conventional view on any subject had from its very conventionality a repellent effect upon his mind' (9 March 1888). Nonetheless, his arguments about distraction from the gospel's social content are of great interest. In attacking the sectarian divisions heightened by the 'year of grace', he used terminology redolent of Porter and Steel Dickson. Disconsonant with the Evangelical Alliance spearheaded by Cooke was his rejection of what he called the natural propensity of denominations to enlarge their numbers. Nelson's argument that 'in proportion as the truth is received among men, Christ increases and sects decrease' (*The Banner of Ulster*, 6.12.1859) was not fashionable in revivalist circles. As a result, he became an isolated figure whose arguments were ascribed to personal disappointment or even dissent for its own sake. An instance of his isolation – or perhaps of his effectiveness, since there were others who remained muted critics of the 'year of grace' – is *The Banner*'s claim that he was the solitary objector among Belfast Presbyterian ministers (20.5.1860). Despite such criticisms, he persevered in his attack on revivalism even into the late 1860s when he published a substantial reply to Reverend John Macnaughtan on the question.[20]

Nelson's stances were not restricted to attacks on the Ulster Revival and work for the anti-slavery cause. With scant regard for diplomacy, he criticised a prevalent lack of study among ministers and the resultant effect, viz. that church doctrines were merely 'spoken of' rather than 'thought through'. Other issues on which he dissented from his colleagues were the royal grant to ministers *(regium donum)* and the narrower question of 'assurance of salvation'. Unlike the majority of the Belfast presbytery, he resisted the compromises necessary to consolidate the *regium donum* for Presbyterian ministers – here again he feared for the independence of his church.

Anti-Sectarianism

Perhaps the issue on which he approached most closely to his radical predecessors is the necessity for co-existence of

Protestants, Catholics and Dissenters. In Nelson's case, his attitude was formed by experience of riots near his home on the Shankill where house burnings, woundings and even fatalities episodically occurred.

Such practical experience is evident in his letters to the *Banner of Ulster* during 1864. In one, he calls for effective Christianity rather than 'the ruinous spirit of ignorant boasting and fanatical arrogance'. An excessive preoccupation with the emoluments of state *(regium donum)* had turned Presbyterianism into a mercantile religion. Its popular tracts were about money, its doctrines were verbal rather than reflective, its concerns were about legacies, wills, and leases. Nelson argued that Belfast was dominated by 'something called orthodox Christianity, paraded by place hunters ... utterly without practical power to influence society, except for evil'. Sunday liturgies had become exhortations to give money, accounts of the conversion of Roman Catholics, incitements to regard neighbours as sinful, and legitimations to frighten them as enemies of religion. Anyone who emphasised that true religion started with love of neighbour 'would be torn to pieces by sensation piety ... or ... pronounced an infidel'. Thus he concluded that the prevalent theology was corrupt and erroneous.

Even more, he argued that Presbyterian ministers should 'like their fathers, espouse the cause of civil liberty and social progress'. Here, he criticised even the Protestant Reformation as 'a combination of statecraft and ecclesiastical concordats'. In view of long standing misrule there was a duty 'to break every yoke and undo the heavy burdens'. There is re-echo of Tone's *Letter in Favour of the Catholics* when Nelson reprobates the treatment of Irish Catholics as aliens in race, language and culture. A further hostage was given in his call that Presbyterians be 'opponents of the monarchical element in church government ... and ... supporters of republicanism in the worship of our Creator'. This led him to praise O'Connell's anti-slavery positions and pay fulsome tribute to the Irish Catholic priesthood.[21]

Defence of Riot Victims

For many years, Nelson lived at Sugarfield House close to sugar refineries in the western foothills of Belfast. Nearby, at Wilton Square, he owned premises which he leased to tenants irrespective of their religion. In August 1864 the area was affected by rioting which elicited Nelson's personal courage and anti-sectarianism. In a *Banner* contribution, he wrote of 'guarding during a long night of August last, affrighted Roman Catholics over whom we watched to save their lives from Presbyterian violence'. Among the rioters were several people who had been active in the 1859 Revival. The riot had resulted in at least one fatality and several injuries. In its pattern there is a distressing similarity to subsequent history – blackmail, protection money, hidden arms and allegations of official partiality. The allegations caused a Police Commission to investigate future disposition of police and military.

In December, at the request of Catholic residents, Nelson gave evidence to the commission. He spoke of three nights terror when families were intimidated by gangs of Orangemen. In reply to questions, he agreed he had put his life in danger and said he would do so again, if necessary. Minutely, he described the sufferings of children terrified by threats and the danger to sixteen people whom he had protected under his roof. To no avail, he had requested the Orange institution to discipline named members. Commenting on the Commission's terms of reference, he said that 'a healthier tone of moral and religious feeling must exist before any civil or military arrangements would be of much avail'. A leader in the *Northern Whig* made noises about sectarianism on both sides, about people 'hating each other for love of God'. Of the 'lower classes' the *Whig* put it: 'we all know what they are'.[22]

Politics and Social Action

Mention has already been made of Isaac Nelson's favourable reference to Daniel O'Connell. From the 1830s, O'Connell's object had been revocation of the Act of Union and institution of an Irish parliament. The Repeal movement had prospered until the split with 'Young Ireland'. After O'Connell's death the movement gradually disintegrated. The issue of repeal had been overtaken by other questions, notably the separatist Fenian movement. Alongside Fenianism was another political thrust, viz. the Home Government Association founded in 1870 by a former Trinity don and barrister, Isaac Butt. A conservative Protestant, Butt was popular in nationalist circles for his defence of Young Ireland and, later, of Fenian prisoners. The Association was an unwieldy coalition of Protestant interests, constitutional nationalists and others who saw a native parliament as leading to full separation. In Butt's association, Protestant landlords, Fenian sympathisers and an assortment of Gladstone Liberals came together under the banner of 'Home Rule'. As new issues came to the fore, e.g. land reform and church disestablishment, Butt's organisation came under internal pressure. Some feared that Home Rule would become a stalking horse of the dreaded Rome Rule. Nevertheless, there were many Protestants who were prepared to support the establishment of an Irish parliament.

At the end of 1873 Butt transformed his Association into a national movement called the Home Rule League. Shortly afterwards, a general election (the first under secret ballot) returned fifty-nine MPs committed in one way or other to the ideal of Home Rule. According to F. S. L. Lyons it was a significant change in Irish politics – the old polarisation of Liberals and Conservatives was replaced by a new thrust which would become more powerful through the coming decades.[23] As the ideal of Home Rule was clarified, Protestants (and particularly Ulster Protestants) showed alarm. Even liberal Protestants drew back from what they considered a threat to Protestant interests, more especially as the all-Ireland and Catholic dimensions emerged. However, there were others, particularly in the Protestant Home Rule Association, who did not share this alarm. Isaac Nelson was one such Protestant. When John O'Connor Power (Home Rule MP for Mayo) spoke at the Ulster Hall in February 1874,

Nelson was the only Protestant clergyman to sit on the platform.[24] Some years later, J. D. Houston defined the position
of Protestant Home Rulers: 'if by the term ... is simply meant
a liberal-minded politician – one who is willing to acquiesce
in a fairly reasonable legislative scheme for the better government of Ireland ... who is disposed to give the scheme a fair
trial ... then there is a large number of such people in Ulster,
far more than anti home-rule writers and speakers are prepared to admit'.[25]

Clearly, Nelson had been involved with the League for
some time – he was among six Ulster representatives on its
council for 1874.[26] In April of the same year he argued for
Home Rule through his *Present Importance of Irish History*,
originally a lecture at Donegall St.[27] Not unexpectedly, the
Belfast presbytery was displeased with activities at Donegall
St and particularly those of its minister. A visitation of 1873
criticised lack of a Sabbath School there as well as looseness in
financial accounting. One can infer that for Nelson the socio-
political dimension of his work was taking precedence over
attention to administrative niceties.

As to the Home Rule League, it continued to have internal
troubles. These stemmed not only from restive MPs but also
from discontent with Butt's leadership. The land question
had presented itself with increasing urgency and C. S. Parnell's
so-called New Departure spelled trouble for Butt's erratic
leadership. Parnell's star was in the ascendant due to his skilful
incorporation of land and constitutional questions. At a
Dublin meeting (October 1879) Parnell instituted the Irish
National Land League. He had invited ninety persons
favourable to land reform. Nearly all were Catholics with the
exception of Nelson and a Glaswegian, John Ferguson. From
the meeting, 'An Appeal to the Irish Race' was issued by a
committee of fifty-four people.[28]

Election to Westminster

At the general election of 1880 Nelson was nominated by
Parnell to stand for Leitrim. The election, although now by

secret ballot, amply illustrates the difficulties of late nineteenth century campaigns. Four candidates stood for Leitrim
– two Parnellites (Thomas Quinn and Isaac Nelson); a conservative (A. Loftus Tottenham); a local landlord (Major
O'Beirne). The Leitrim clergy supported Quinn as a bishop's
man who had done good service to Belfast Catholics. With
little regard for personal gallantries, *The Freeman's Journal* declared itself mystified why the voters should select 'a Presbyterian clergyman of rather crazy political proclivities' (*Freeman's
Journal*, 30.3.1880). After disturbances in Mohill and strong
remarks by Dr Langan (the Catholic dean of the area), a split
vote elected Loftus Tottenham. Nelson had creditable support although he finished last in the poll. Nationally, it was a
triumph for Parnell who was elected in Cork city, Mayo and
Meath, while Gladstone's Liberals swept into power.

However, Isaac Nelson did reach Westminster. In May
1880 he was elected for Mayo, facilitated by Parnell's option
for the Cork City seat. His acceptance speech evinces non-
sectarian and politically radical views.[29] Nelson thanked the
Mayo electors for allowing him to represent Irish interests in
'an alien Parliament' and for the confidence shown him by
'my Catholic fellow-countrymen'. Sectarian differences were
softened in his reference to having defended the Catholic
Church against all detractors. An historical allusion is made
in his desire to shake hands 'across the Boyne'. Nelson avowed
his purpose at Westminster would be to ensure that the situation in Ireland, the situation in Mayo, with its hunger and
evictions, should not be 'allowed to continue for one moment'.
In referring to the land question, he emphasised that money
would have to be found 'to save our starving population in
their homes'. Meanwhile, the Belfast presbytery held an official visitation at Donegall St but it was not attended by
Nelson. Nor was any communication received from him.

On the Sunday following his election, Nelson's congregation was vastly more numerous than usual. Clearly, he knew
people expected dramatic words and he did not disappoint

them. He argued that Christian faith could not be different in
Ulster to what it was in Connacht. The very simple devotions
in the West of Ireland could leave people closer to Christ than
if they had been 'babbling to the British Association about
molecules and protoplasm'. Attacking hierarchical pretensions in the churches, he declared that prelacy led inevitably
to papacy. Although the Christian faith was the same in the
west of Ireland as in Ulster, the churches had become associa-
tions for the furtherance of party interests. In Westminster he
would defend truth in the same way as he did in pulpit or
platform. He would continue to proclaim 'the Republican
platform of Presbyterianism and liberty of action under
Christ Jesus'. In the circumstances, he invited trouble with his
forthright dictum: 'No bishop, No King!' Reports of the service disclose that he was aware that he would have to resign
his ministry and that he had not attended Belfast presbytery
meetings because 'we have all gone into party grooves'. When
another official 'visitation' took place, Nelson reiterated that
practical Christianity would prevent 'evictions in Connaught
as well as the burning of villages in India'. In the event, the
presbytery accepted Nelson's resignation from active ministry
and, without more than the usual politeness, bade goodbye to
one of its most inconvenient members.[30]

Westminster

At Westminster, Nelson articulated his own and his party's
concerns. As member of Parliament for Mayo, he embarked
on a new way of life. Yet, his disjointed manner of speech and
impatience with parliamentary customs did not promise well
for a career in parliament. Altogether, his attendance spanned
little more than two years. On one occasion, his persistent in-
terruptions led to removal from the House. In his maiden
speech, Nelson instanced the poorly attended debate on the
Relief of Distress (Ireland) Bill as disinterest in Irish affairs.
He called for a just settlement to the unsatisfactory relations
between landlords and tenants.[31] In other words, justice
rather than charity! Some weeks later, he returned to land

tenure. Landlordism was, he said, 'the Shylock of Irish industry'. The greater part of Ulster had been plundered from the Irish by monarchs who spoke about God while ruining the people. Declaring his confidence in Gladstone's good intent, he asked the prime minister to 'resume those lands once more and turn them to the support of the families living on them'. Later again, he asked the Chief Secretary for Ireland to address the problems of small farmers and labourers in his (Nelson's) constituency. To the accompaniment of calls for order, he claimed that 'Ireland never had a constitution but the will of Englishmen'.[32]

Debating an Arrears of Rent (Ireland) Bill, he deemed these arrears as not of fair rent but of robbery, dishonesty and extortion. Rather than speak of 'arrears', the land should be 'resumed' by government and small compensation paid. Since the land was given by the Creator for the people's support, peace in Ireland would not come until the people became masters of their own industry. Short of that, Westminster could not govern Ireland. They might rule Ireland with 60,000 men: lacking the consent and assent of the people, they would have neither peace nor stability in the country.[33]

In two other debates Nelson disclosed his view on the role of the churches in Irish society. In neither case were his remarks likely to please the more conservative of his church leaders. The debate on University Tests, occurring a month after his parliamentary debut, shows his inexperience as a parliamentarian and his abiding resentment of the old dispute on Assembly's College. With clear reference to Henry Cooke, he recalled that Presbyterians had endeavoured to distinguish sacred from secular education. The result was sacred rhetoric (Cooke had been professor of sacred rhetoric), which had become merely 'a sacred sham'.[34] With somewhat heavy irony – although the old battles had long since receded – Nelson pointed out: 'There is no sacred mode of determining an angle in trigonometry ... no heresy lurking in the middle voice of a Greek verb'. Hence, he argued for higher education to be left free of 'ligatures' tied by clerics who cared little for the elevation of the human mind if they could succeed in their purpose. Just as psychology should be based on philosophical truths, Christianity should live by its own inherent power. Almost two years later, when speaking to the Belfast Harbour Bill, he rejoiced in anything which would help the prosperity of the city. Nonetheless, he did not rejoice 'in the fanaticism and party spirit and tyranny by which the best emotions of the people were poisoned and by which the people themselves were in a constant state of hostility to one another'.[35]

Nelson's stances incurred more than resentment. Late in 1880 when rioters besieged his house, his request for police protection was refused. In a letter to the *Northern Whig* he claimed that no one had more cause than he to complain of police tactics (*N. Whig,* 18.11.80). In addition, there were difficulties even with his new political allies. A fellow Belfastman, F. J. Bigger, complained about his absence from a Commons debate on police estimates. Nelson's excuse was that he was at Irish meetings in Leeds and Newcastle.[36] Bigger, a Catholic convert, had also taken issue with some of his remarks in the universities debate. According to Bigger, he had assailed the claims of the Catholic hierarchy 'to a fair distribution of public funds for ecclesiastical purposes'. With considerable justice, Nelson replied that he had in mind 'my former struggles against the so-called sacred Presbyterian Chairs now endowed by public funds' (*N. Whig,* 18.11.80). Bigger also charged him with an insult to the Catholic clergy through Nelson's use of the biblical text, 'Render to Caesar the things that are Caesar's and to God the things that are God's'. Nelson replied that he had merely taken issue with a Catholic priest who had so interpreted the text as to favour the exorbitant demands of Irish landlords.

It is unclear why tensions so rapidly arose between Nelson and his Parnellite colleagues. Certainly, his interchange with Bigger hints at irregular attendance in the Commons. It is also possible that since he believed fully in Gladstone's integrity he was uneasy about Parnellite expediencies adopted by during 1881-2 . This would show a certain lack of political hardihood on his part and a naïvete in his belief that the principles of church, pulpit and parliament were exactly the same. For whatever reason, from 1882 Nelson had ceased to attend Westminster.

Thereafter, he lived in virtual seclusion at Sugarfield House. A life-long bachelor, he retired to his classical studies just as he had commenced adult life as a classics teacher. He had long since ceased to attend General Assembly where once he had been troublesome 'as a thorn is to the side and the fly-blister to the flesh' (Geo Gilfinnan in *Remoter Stars*). In these last years, the former minister of Donegall St and short-term member of parliament was cared for by his sister, Mary Nelson. When he died on 6 March 1886 a general election was in the offing and a new era in Irish politics was promised by the return of Gladstone. As to Isaac Nelson, once the church Ishmael of Belfast, his funeral went unnoticed. By request of his sister, it was conducted in utter privacy. The obituaries gave their meed of faint praise, speaking of talent put to negative use, of rankling disappointment, of sincerity despite brusqueness, etc. They did not capture the essential aspects of this fascinating character.

It is all too easy to misjudge Nelson's protest. To exaggerate it would ignore his constant loyalty to Presbyterian tenets. His opposition to the leadership, even in the 1840s and 50s, showed concern for the church of which he was a member. In essence, despite his brusqueness, he called on Presbyterianism to be true to its inheritance as 'republican in worship of God, anti-monarchical in ecclesiastical structure'. In this sense, perhaps, his supposed admiration for Oliver Cromwell is to be understood. On the other hand, it is a mistake to reduce Nelson's non-conformity to eccentric disposition or, worse, disappointment in his personal life. The reminiscences of those who knew him are indeed instructive, especially on his prejudice against fellow-clergymen who vaunted academic titles. Yet most of these commentators viewed his work from a conservative standpoint and, given Nelson's brusqueness, it was all too easy to speak of personal embitterment. Whatever about personal motivations, Nelson – like his predecessors and successors – forcefully reminds us of the critical dimension within Irish Presbyterianism. As Wm Steel Dickson and James Porter knew, as J. B. Armour constantly asserted, Presbyterianism is at its best when standing for justice and truth. In his tough-minded opposition to religious pretensions and to the monstrosities of slavery, in his defence of free academic enquiry, in his provocative although cerebral pulpitry, Nelson represents for those outside his tradition a beacon of Protestantism in its best sense.

Further Reading

Holmes, J. Finlay, *Henry Cooke,* Belfast Christian Journals 1981.
Holmes, Janice E., 'Ignorant, Ill-Mannered and Exciteable. Clerical Attitudes towards the laity in the Ulster Revival of 1859' in *Ulster Local Studies,* vol 13, No 1, Summer 1991.
Moore, S.J., *The Great Revival In Ireland 1859,* Belfast 1859.

PART THREE

The Old Order Changeth?

The Old Order Changeth?

If the previous chapters in this study contain a lesson it is that modern Ireland is composed of many strands. From the 1790s, the complex weave includes 'colonial patriots' such as Henry Grattan, Lord Moira and Lord Charlemont. Then there were the United Irishmen, constituted in 1791 by radical Volunteer elements such as Wm Drennan, James Napper Tandy and Archibald Hamilton Rowan. Of importance, too, is Defenderism which in association with the United Irishmen moved towards organised politics during the 1790s. For a time, it looked as if a confluence of progressive thought would achieve parliamentary reform and religious emancipation for Catholics and Protestant dissenters.

From its foundation in 1795, a reactionary Orange Order was used by hard-line loyalism to oppose democratic reform and religious emancipation. Despite the promise of reform politics a repressive backlash to the rising of 1798 seemed to dash all hopes for a 'cordial union of Irishmen'. From 1799, proposals for legislative union of Britain and Ireland created unexpected alignments. Many Orangemen rejected the proposed union. So did College Green loyalists who did not want 'their' parliament abolished. On the other hand, many Catholics – believing that things could not be worse than under the status quo – cautiously accepted the Act of Union. The brief moment of 'uniting' in a radical cause splintered as Catholics and Protestants reverted to seeking narrow sectarian advantage. Gradually, they were polarised by fears of absorption each by the other. 'Zero-sum' politics ensured that advance on any one side was seen as a threatening regression by the other. Many factors operated here – in particular, a prevalent distrust fostered by opponents of all reform.

Thereafter, a series of events were to change the face of Irish society and would shape the lineaments of our contemporary Irish society, north and south. Broadly they can be listed: the Reform Act of 1829 announcing religious emancipation of excluded groups; the growth of Catholic self confidence under Daniel O'Connell; the 'second Protestant reformation' from the 1820s; the famines of the 1840s; the Young Ireland cultural political movement; the emergence of 'Catholic nationalism' (an unsatisfactorily loose term); the disestablishment of the Church of Ireland; the consolidation of Irish Catholicism effected by Paul Cardinal Cullen; the land question. Pivotal to subsequent events is Gladstone's attempt to address the Irish question and his proposals for Irish 'Home Government'. In the 1880s, the land question briefly united Catholics and a substantial proportion of Presbyterian tenant farmers behind Gladstone's Liberal party. Some of the events of this period are reminiscent of the 1790s. Yet, as the question of Home Rule emerged, Presbyterians in the west and south of Ulster took fright at what they perceived to be Catholic nationalist advance. The proposition that 'Home Rule was Home Rule' began to gain currency. The securely Protestant north-east (where memories of 1798 persisted) remained loyal to Gladstone much longer. When Gladstone's Home Rule Bill was introduced in 1886, Ulster Presbyterians turned in the main to conservative candidates even though many retained doubts about supporting what they felt was an Anglican-dominated establishment.[1]

Hence one also considers the emergence of an organised separatist movement, notably the Fenian society and the Irish Republican Brotherhood. Here, the Australian and American 'diaspora' provided a well-spring of sympathy for Irish resistance movements. By the 1870s, all the above mentioned factors had intermingled in a troubled pattern of conflict, mutual exclusion and, sometimes, temporary resolution. The 'Irish

Question' remained unsolved despite several attempts to achieve a 'settlement'. The nuances of nineteenth-century Irish politics cannot be followed here. Rather, it is hoped to present some further 'Unusual Suspects' who tried within their own communities to address festering issues in ways sufficiently imaginative to incur opprobrium from entrenched interests. Yet, they have bequeathed a legacy which is not only historically interesting but socially valuable.

Introducing these 'Unusual Suspects' it may be well to focus on Gladstone's attempts to solve the 'Irish Question'. His address of the constitutional and agrarian issues exposed once more the 'fault lines' in Ireland between Catholics and Protestants, between landlords and tenants. The exceptions to these fault lines, the 'suspects' who refused to be constrained by long-standing divisions, are of interest although events all too frequently cast them to one side. There were Irish Protestants who did not oppose Home Rule, since their self confidence and generosity to their fellow countrymen made them ready to give the proposal a fair chance. There was a radical Protestantism which criticised official Unionism for ignoring the interests of its working class supporters and endorsing an aristocratic leadership simply because it was Unionist and anti-Catholic. For this reason, Maurice Goldring has remarked that Northern Ireland is heir to 'the liveliest legacy of religious dissent that once dominated politics throughout the British Isles'.[2]

Again, on the land question, there were landlords who envisaged a just solution, e.g. Wm Sharman Crawford, a northern Protestant landlord who championed tenant right. Particularly apposite to this study is the readiness of Presbyterian clergymen to support the call for justice to tenants. J. B. Armour was outstanding among these, yet he was by no means the only one. Repeatedly, he called for justice to tenants and agricultural labourers. In doing so, he criticised the confessional selfishness which made some Presbyterian leaders endorse Tory politics, even when such endorsement worked against tenants' interests.

F. S. L. Lyons makes the fascinating point that the reversal of the Act of Union commenced in Belfast during the early 1900s.[3] The rejuvenation of the Irish Republican Brotherhood by Denis McCullogh, Bulmer Hobson and, later, Sean McDermott and the foundation of Dungannon Clubs, (1905), influenced Sinn Féin (also founded in 1905) towards separatist republicanism. Along with other movements such as the Wolfe Tone Society, the Gaelic League, the Gaelic Athletic Association, and some years later, the Irish Volunteers, they would create an impetus which led to the foundation of an independent Irish state. Many Protestants (some of them Unionists) played a leading role in the Gaelic League and the Yeatsean cultural revival. As to the strengthening of the separatist demand whether of the 'dual monarchy' kind (Arthur Griffith) or of the republican kind, advocated pre-eminently by the Fenian legacy, a thrust had been under way from the 1890s.

For many reasons, some of these recently articulated by Desmond Fennell, the liberationist project was rarely expressed in socialist terms. It is the singular merit of James Larkin and James Connolly to have done this, each in his own way.[4] Likewise, there were Catholics who did not aspire to confessional victory but criticised the ideology and practices of 'muscular Catholicism'. As a result, when the partial sundering of the Union was effected in 1922, many problems remained outstanding. The imposition of partition had destroyed what the project of 1798 attempted to build – a cordial union of Irishmen. One of our 'Unusual Suspects', J. B. Armour (by conviction a liberal Unionist), saw this solution as something 'out of Hell'. To those who had earlier opposed Home Rule he declared: 'We are all Home Rulers now – but in a way no one ever desired'. In regard to social justice, two deeply conservative states had been set up. Alongside another Presbyterian colleague, Rev J. A. H. Irwin (Killead, Co Antrim), Armour had signally contributed through his insistence on a secular politics where Protestants and Catholics would participate for the benefit of all.[5] For decades, his radical questioning of clerical hegemonies would be ignored.

Another 'Unusual Suspect', Fr Ml O'Flanagan, had started from a different point, viz. the Fenian and Land League traditions. Where Armour was a liberal Unionist, O'Flanagan was an advanced nationalist. He brought enormous personal skills to a criticism of British policies in Ireland, advocated republican separatism, limitation of clerical influence in politics and an openness to radical social reform in both agrarian and urban contexts. His attempts to open dialogue with the Unionist tradition is highly interesting even today. When, eventually, an independent Irish state was constituted he broke the consensus of the Catholic leadership in mounting a sustained critique of the new administrations – Cumann na nGael and Fianna Fáil. Even today, O'Flanagan is a reminder that the constitutional issue has to be accompanied by the social issue, that poverty and exclusion are not addressed simply by changing the symbolic constructs of sovereignty.

One can argue, as does John McGahern, that the two states of partitioned Ireland became inward-looking, pedantic theocracies. Whatever the validity of this judgement, many energetic and generous spirits contested the prevalent conservatism. In the south, during the 1930s and 1940s, the indomitable Peadar O'Donnell probed the innate conservatism of the establishments, civil and ecclesiastical. Others like George Gilmore and Lil Nic Dhonchadha (headmistress of the Church of Ireland teachers training college) held to the old republican ideal along with radical social reform. In the context of this study, two Church of Ireland clergymen – R.M. Hilliard and his nephew, Stephen Hilliard – are extremely interesting for their contributions on socio-political questions in Ireland and elsewhere.

CHAPTER EIGHT

Armour of Ballymoney

'Today, the name of J. B. Armour lives on in Ballymoney with the Armour Day Centre just across the road from the church, a street in one of the nearby housing estates being called Armour Avenue, and in Armour House in Dalriada School'. (Len Snodgrass, *Armour's Meeting House 1885-1985*, p 59).

James Brown Armour is, perhaps, an unlikely member of the 'suspects' here mentioned. In religion he was uncompromisingly Presbyterian. As minister at Ballymoney, he viewed his task with undeviating scrupulousness. On education, on temperance and on social responsibility, he worked indefatigably through seven decades. His commitment to Calvinist principles was rock-like, even to considering Oliver Cromwell 'the greatest moral force seen in English history'. In politics, Armour supported union with Britain, viewing its empire as a force for good. For him, justice in Ireland did not require separation from Britain. He supported the 'great war' of 1914-18 in terms evocative of Patrick Pearse's 'bloody sacrifice for a glorious thing'. Even after his declaration for Home Rule he also supported the Union – 'not the Union of the ascendancy of a clique and the domination of a faction, but a Union where every class and every creed should have its place, and where all, not as now, shall have liberty to live and thrive'. Nevertheless, as Robert Lynd has pointed out, he was 'for a time public enemy number one in his own church'. A great part of Armour's significance is his challenge not only to his church 'but (to) the whole northern community in which his lot was cast'. For church and state, Armour's challenge is still apposite since many issues he addressed remain unresolved.[1]

In the bitter years from 1969, Douglas Gageby, a distinguished editor of the *Irish Times,* recurrently alluded to Armour's views on social justice, political generosity and inter-church relations. In a remarkable editorial on the centenary of Armour's ordination, Gageby wrote of his 'passionate opposition to the landlords and brewers, the machine politicians of the Tory party. To them, J. B. Armour was as barbed in speech as a young Bogsider' (editorial, 8 Sept 1969). Although it would be a mistake to cast him as a prototype republican, or even as a nationalist, his astringent realism and political generosity liken him to his predecessors, James Porter, Wm Steel Dickson and Isaac Nelson. His persistence in going 'against the tide' in matters civil and ecclesiastical renders him of enduring interest.

Early Years

J. B. Armour was born on 31 Jan 1841 at Lisboy, near Ballymoney in Co Antrim. Here, his parents farmed a moderate holding of sixty acres. By background, therefore, Armour had cognisance of tenant conditions and problems. In the north Antrim Route district, a tradition of agrarian radicalism survived from earlier times. The activities of the Hearts of Steel were still remembered. As well, memories of political liberalism from the United Irish activity in the 1790s had not been excised. A field memoir for the Ordnance survey in 1835 noticed that Ballymoney district was 'in great measure free from those party dissensions and bickerings which prevail in most of the neighbouring parishes'. Even more, according to the note: 'Whatever may be the religious or political creed of any man it is not suffered to affect social intercourse with his neighbours.' Such liberal disposition is well attested in Armour's own work of a later time.[2]

Amour's higher education commenced at the Belfast Academical Institute (inaugurated in 1813 by the former

United Irishman, Wm Drennan). In 1860 he entered Queen's University, Belfast to read classics with the intention of sitting for the Indian Civil Service. He interrupted his undergraduate work for at least a year to attend Queen's University, Cork (1863). From there he somewhat pompously reported on an atmosphere of dissipation, very different from the sober ethos of Belfast. He referred to the Cork students' indolence and their concern with external appearances. Later he remembered 'there was an atmosphere there ... but it was an atmosphere of smoke'. More significant is his remark to John Megaw that in Cork city 'there seems to be none of that bigotry with regard to religious principles which ... is too evident in Belfast'. Armour's student letters from Cork (mainly to his friend, Megaw) disclose an earnest, even prim, disposition. Even at this early stage his interest in Presbyterianism is clear and, perhaps, unusually earnest for a man of his age. On the other hand, he had a distinctly sceptical attitude to the excesses of an evangelical 'Year of Grace' promoted from 1859 by conservative preachers and their publication *The Banner of Ulster*.[3]

His sojourn in Cork brought the young northerner into contact with a sector of Irish life very different from Belfast or, for that matter, around Ballymoney – middle class, mainly Catholic, mainly (although by no means overwhelmingly) sympathetic to Irish nationalism. On at least one occasion he visited a home where Fenian politics were evident. Armour's observation of nationalist views at Cork was relaxed. It did not imbue him with that fear of southern Catholicism, later a feature of the communities with whom he worked. Perhaps this experience helped him to adopt positions which were truly 'against the tide' in their openness to a magnanimous settlement in Irish politics. After return to Belfast, he took his Master's degree (1866) and in the same year entered Assembly's College to study for the Presbyterian ministry. In July 1869 he was ordained as assistant and successor to J. L. Rentoul at Trinity Church, Ballymoney. There he would remain until his death in 1929.

Early Ministry At Ballymoney

J. B. McMinn considers the possibility that Armour entered the ministry unwillingly and thereafter was frustrated by confinement to a small town far from the centre of secular and ecclesiastical politics . However, no such frustration is evident as the new minister energetically approached his task. With sensitive generosity he deferred entry to the Manse until his predecessor's family had secured a home. Thereafter, his work evinces the strengths of Presbyterian ministry, viz. preaching the gospel and close involvement in the affairs of the congregation. Apart from his sermons, the church's General Assembly, normally in early Summer, and speeches for parliamentary candidates (Liberal Unionists and, later, Liberals) form the context of those positions which would plunge him into controversy. Armour was an outstanding preacher – learned, mordantly humorous and invariably topical. His nick-name, 'The Black Wolf', reflects his appearance: tall, somewhat gaunt, black-bearded, bespectacled.

Close pastoral involvement in the affairs of Ballymoney is reflected in the tradition that when difficulties arose in the town it was frequently said: 'all we can do is send for J. B.' As his political involvement grew, Armour scrupulously maintained the distinction between liturgy and politics. During severe turmoil, sometimes with members of his own congregation, he took care never to oppress their consciences. Testimonies to his concern for all his congregation are many – those who criticised his politics lauded his attention to the sick and troubled, to fostering temperance, and ensuring that young people gained access to higher education.[4] His insistence on separating politics from preaching is worthy of note, given his involvement in political questions throughout his long life. On this, Armour's reasoning is similar to Fr Michael O'Flanagan, from whom he differed in many ways on Irish politics: 'God sent me to preach the gospel as well as I could, but I claim the right of every citizen, outside of my pulpit, to express my opinion on any social question ... and anyone who

denies that right to me is denying the right of private judgement and of free speech. If you deny the right of private
judgement and of free speech, how much do you have of
Protestantism worth keeping? Nothing at all.'[5]

At Ballymoney, Armour's relations with clergy of other
traditions were consistently warm. Nonetheless, he held that
'Romanism, or for that matter, high Churchism could not
possibly be squared with Christianity as revealed ... in the
teaching of the founder of our faith.' Although he believed
'Romanism' as a system was inherently flawed, yet throughout
his ministry he ceaselessly argued for recognition of Catholics'
political and educational rights. In an obituary tribute, the
Catholic parish priest of Ballymoney avowed that the towns-
people saw him as 'a great friend and father to all without distinction'.[6] In regard to the Anglican system, he had a critical
approach, especially at the institutional level. Until 1869,
Presbyterians as well as Catholics had been disadvantaged by
Anglican establishment. Armour traced a close link between
Anglicanism and the Tory/landowning ascendancy. This
forms the background of his assertion (June 1900) that
Trinity College, Dublin had educated nine-tenths of the
country's oppressors. When Anthony Traill, the Provost of
Trinity, protested, Armour replied that the oppressors he had
in mind were the landlords, the anglican clergy and the legal
establishment. While making it clear that – after Disestablishment of the churches – Anglicanism might no longer be oppressive, he insisted that the Anglican clergy had resisted
Catholic emancipation, the legalising of marriages by Presbyterian ministers, the land acts and 'many other measures which
were passed in spite of their opposition'.[7]

While actively engaged at Trinity church, Armour became
principal (and for a time the only teacher) at Ballymoney
Intermediate School. Although his assistance to poor students
is well documented, this work may have augmented his ministerial stipend of £65 per annum. In education he favoured
what a later time would call 'equality of opportunity'. With

characteristically brusque language he defended the Intermediate Education Act from its critics: it brought 'educational advantage within the reach of hundreds who would never have had the chance without it ... let the Jeremiahs in kid gloves, like Matthew Arnold, and the damaged Solomons, like Mr Mahaffy, say what they will ...'[8] He saw the intermediate system as especially helpful to poorer children in getting the education they might otherwise be denied. At General Assembly he argued that secular education could never be the foe of religion: rather, it would 'one day slay the dragon of denominationalism'. Thus, Armour opposed the prophets of doom – the well-established endowed schools and the dogmatists within Presbyterianism – who predicted ruin for children exposed to the newer system.[9] At the Ballymoney Intermediate School, even at his own expense, he ensured that fees were never a problem for poorer children. After his marriage (1883) to Jennie Staveley Hamilton, (descendant of Wm Staveley, the radical minister at Knockbracken, Co Down) he took an appointment as classics master at Magee College, Derry. This necessitated a long rail journey on three or four days weekly. After some time, the possibility of his appointment to the chair of history and pastoral theology arose but seems to have been blocked on account of his alleged radicalism in education, in politics and, perhaps, in land policy.

The Land Question

Three months after Armour's ordination, the Route Tenants Defence association was founded at Ballymoney. In the years which followed, he attended its meetings and sometimes spoke from its platforms. Although his views were shared by many in the Route district, yet his forthright espousal of tenant right marked his opposition to landlords and magnates. Throughout his life he was critical of the landed classes and what he saw as their easy bedfellows, the Anglican church and the Tory establishment. In this context, Armour's 'Dervock speech' – to protest the eviction of three people, including Alexander Field, a Presbyterian minister – is of considerable note. Here Armour criticised the ecclesiastical tendency to evade controverted social issues: '... what great social problem for protection either of the labourer in the factory or the tenant farmer (has) the church ... ever helped to solve? Not one!' While supporting Field, he drew attention to the worse plight of tenants who 'have to pay not only for the value of their land, but hand over their work and toil to make their landlord's speculation pay five per cent'.[10] In this Dervock speech, Armour discloses his sensitivity to the socio-economic issues affecting the poorer members of the community.

From this early date one notices the anti-Tory drift of Armour's speeches. Despite such antipathy, he could support T. W. Russell – initially a Tory – who showed genuine interest in land reform. Although J. R. B. McMinn has questioned how far the Route tenants envisaged co-operation with farmers throughout Ireland, in Armour's case the land question was island-wide. Justice was requisite for all parts of the country. Addressing a meeting of tenant farmers (a hail of stones rained on the windows and he later had to run a gauntlet of missiles), he insisted: '... the inhabitants of the (other) provinces are not necessarily blood-thirsty savages, animated by ... passions for robbing and massacring Ulster folks ... there are wrongs to be redressed and rights to be established, as well beyond as on this side of the Boyne'. Speaking for land reform, he demanded 'the principles of even handed justice in the North, South, East and West of Ireland'. And, somewhat untypically for the day, he was careful to include the cause of the day labourers, calling more than once for reform of their conditions.[11]

Throughout the 1870s the land question perdured. At all times Armour criticised 'a system which consults for the luxury of the few at the expense of the many'.[12] The word 'system' should be noted, as it was systems, not persons, which evoked his wrath. Behind the striking images which pepper Armour's speeches is a dignified restraint in regard to the individuals he opposed. As to the landlords, he was willing to let bygones be bygones 'provided they became bygones themselves'. In this much-cited address at Ballymoney Town Hall (Jan 1880), he emphasised: 'We want no violent retaliation for the despotism of years ... only that rents be fair, that the terms of tenure be such as ... Irishmen shall not be weighed by feudal restrictions...'.[13] In response to J. A. Froude's aphorism that landlordism was despotism tempered by assassination, Armour proposed the constitutional way of reform: 'a revolution in the land laws which will prevent agents from vexing tenants and tenants from wishing their landlords in uncomfortable quarters'.[14] By 1889 he supported the demand that tenants own the soil they tilled. Even after the passage of several land reforms, he criticised the bias of courts towards landlordism: 'They have made the Land Commission a landlords' courthouse, and they have weeded out of the Sub-Commissioners the greater part of those in sympathy with the tenants. Now the landlord party is to administer the Acts passed in favour of the tenants'.[15] This was another factor which fuelled his anti-Tory positions.

One gleans something of Armour's sense of justice in his long-standing memory of a farmer's humiliation by a landlord. The landlord, 'a haughty little man', seemed more attentive to his cigar than to the tenant in danger of eviction. Armour had then vowed: 'if God ever gave me an opportunity, I would use what little strength was mine to drive a nail into the coffin of that system ...' Such a memory was behind his claim: 'the first duty of every tenant farmer is to turn out the government now in office (Disraeli's), which is simply the most immoral and incapable government that ever frittered away the force of a great nation'.[16] The anti-Tory barbs which Armour used so frequently, and his reminders to Presbyterians of their deference to the 'prancing colonels' and landlords, caused resentment. Even his activity on tenant right was noted by the upper councils of his church – in 1913 he asked rhetorically: 'Did any Presbyteriam minister who ever stood on a tenant platform get a call to Belfast ...?'[17] Nonetheless, it

should be remarked that in the work for tenant-right several
Presbyterian clergymen were determined allies, notably Samuel
Finlay (Kilraughts), J. S. Mairs (Dunloy), Archibald
Robinson (Broughshane). If Armour of Ballymoney was to
prove a severe trial to his brethren, it was for reasons addition-
al to his commitment to tenant right.

Presbyterian Conservatism

Why, then, did Armour's frankness engender such hostility
within his church? It is necessary to observe the altered temper of Presbyterianism since the time of Porter, Steel Dickson
and Sinclair Kelbourne. Between the late eighteenth and late
nineteenth century a change had occurred in the social attitudes of the Presbyterian communion. After the Act of
Union, Presbyterians felt their interests better protected by
Westminster than by the Dublin parliament of the 1790s. The
grant of the *Regium Donum* to Presbyterian clergymen, the
decline of the Reverend Henry Montgomey's more liberal influence, and some favourable amendments to the civil law,
opened the way to a stance very different from the 1790s.
Under Dr Henry Cooke, a leading advocate of conservative
evangelism, a practical alliance between Episcopalianism,
Presbyterianism, Orangeism, landlords and tenants had
emerged by the 1850s. Catholicism and any form of political
radicalism were defined as enemies. Although he disavowed
political objectives, Cooke had in fact allied with the Tories
and the landlords. Lest there should be co-operation with
Catholics he opposed agitation for tenant right although this
would have benefitted Presbyterian smallholders. Men such
as Dr Alexander Goudy (minister of Strabane and nephew of
Dr James Porter) were sidelined. Presbyterianism, at least in
Armour's view, had become a branch of the Unionist party.[18]
He would later speak of the 'Upaz tree' of ascendancy, viz.
Toryism, landlordism and Anglican establishment.

And so, the political context of Armour's decades had altered since the 1780s, when Presbyterians and Catholics were
virtually disenfranchised. By the 1860s, electoral franchise had

been extended and would be further widened in the Ballot Act of 1872. Sectarian divisions had been nourished by an assortment of propagandists and unfortunately by not a few ministers of the churches. From the 1850s the Catholic vote returned largely nationalist MPs (not always Catholics themselves). Presbyterians – mainly farmers, smaller business people, and workers in the trades spawned by the industrial revolution – on the whole voted for Unionist or Tory candidates. As a result, northern MPs and major office-holders were Anglicans from landed or big-business families. Some historians such as Lyons and, later, McMinn, argue that the liberal Presbyterian voice was stifled after Gladstone's proposal for Home Rule in 1886. William Armour, son of the minister of Ballymoney, suggests that after the Franchise Act of 1884 the new vote – mainly Orange labourers – was captured by a party machinery which had been dominant for some decades . In this hypothesis, by 1885 'Liberalism was swept out of Ulster as an effective power'.[19] Armour (although not only he) argued that Presbyterians were being used by groups which did not wholeheartedly represent their interests. At General Assembly he referred to 'The prancing colonels, the blustering captains, the squirming majors, the sons of old manufacturers (and) ... landlords ... (who) turned out to be the enemies of our church, the weakness of the union, the silent foes of our educational policy'.[20]

The old mistrust of Dissenters for the Anglican establishment emerges in Armour's reminder that 'Fair play and even-handed justice in the making of appointments ... have never been the marks of the episcopal mind or ... of any government that has borne sway in our island'. The minister of Ballymoney charged that 'we have been so stupid to think that (Anglican churchmen) in matters political were the only heaven-sent guides to save us from the errors of the Pope'. This compliance with upper class dictation, in Armour's view, had 'deprived our church of its due share in politics and ... tended to rouse the millions of our countrymen against an official caucus which (had) always claimed the chief seats in every synagogue' (*Witness* 18.6.86).

From 1870, the year after Armour's appointment to Ballymoney, Irish politics began to face questions articulated by Gladstone – disestablishment of the Anglican church, the land issue, the provision of a Catholic University. Finally, the question of Home Rule came to the fore, propelled by Gladstone's successive Home Rule Bills (1886 and 1893). As all too often in Ireland, the issues overspilled from national politics to exacerbate long-standing tensions between the churches. Armour's later stances on events such as the war of 1914-18 and the rise of Sinn Féin disclose that, although a trenchant critic of Tory unionism, he was neither a separatist nor a republican. Under a Liberal government he was ready to accept a chaplaincy to Lord Aberdeen at the vice-regal lodge. In so far as he can be categorised, he was a liberal in the Gladstonian sense typified by F. S. L. Lyons as 'that medley of Whigs and radicals, churchmen and non-conformists, bourgeoisie and working-men'.[21] He had an unbounded admiration for Gladstone, sharing the latter's views on the 'Irish Question' and the problem of Papal infallibility (defined at Rome in 1870). When criticism of Gladstone was at its height in 1893, he organised a memorial that official Presbyterian criticism of the prime minister did not in fact represent all Presbyterians. During this decade Armour spoke for Liberal candidates and, at least on one occasion, defined his own view of Liberalism. Speaking at Kilraughts for W. P. Sinclair, he spoke of Liberalism as 'a belief in progress and the dignity of human life, an abhorrence of class legislation and selfish interests and a desire that justice should run through all laws'.

It was not automatic that Armour should have been involved in such questions. Nevertheless, they preoccupied him throughout the coming decades as matters of principle. At General Assembly, he opposed what he saw as an unnatural cohesion of Presbyterians and Anglicans under the Tory banner. This was, he argued, a political Protestantism, identified with and dependent upon landlordism.[22] Time after time, he insisted that Presbyterians were getting the worst of such an alliance. Under Tory leadership was created 'a stalking horse to cover a multitude of political hypocrisies'. For Armour, Presbyterianism was at its best when supporting 'free institutions and civil and religious liberty'.[23] This perception made him insist that liberty was indivisible – it had to be for all citizens, no matter their religious or political views. In education, on the land question, in political representation, his thought was inclusive – even as he argued from the perspective of his own community and for the interests of his own church. Thus Wm Armour can claim that, for his father, the chief obstacle to justice in Ireland was the supremacy of a local caste with a conception of empire 'which ended at Yorktown'.[24]

Regarded from several generations later, Armour's generosity towards those outside the Protestant tradition is both striking and exemplary. Such generosity has to be seen against the background of a strand within northern Protestantism which was open to all fair reforms. This liberal strand was at its weakest when Gladstone proposed Home Rule for Ireland and it almost disappeared after 1886. Yet it did exist after that date, even in the form of a Protestant Home Rule Association (and was articulated by J. C. D. Houston: 'if by the term is simply meant a liberal-minded politician – one who is willing to acquiesce in a fairly reasonable legislative scheme for the better government of Ireland ... then there is a large number of such people in Ulster, far more, I believe, than anti-Home Rule writers and speakers are prepared to admit'.[25] When he became an ardent supporter of Home Rule in the 1890s, Armour was confident that Presbyterianism could more than hold its own in a fair scheme of home government. At a time when many in his own church saw Catholicism as the chief enemy, he insisted that Catholics were fellow countrymen with whom it was a duty to live in harmony. Courageously, he reiterated that something wrong south of the Boyne could not be right in the north. According to Wm. Armour, he 'understood completely and fully the Catholic case without divesting himself of one particle of his own views'.[26] For him, just as free institutions were the great Presbyterian legacy, toleration was the essence of Christianity. Such tolerance is all the more remarkable since Armour held Catholicism was 'the one form of religion that never appealed to me on any side'. The idea of Papal infallibility meant the end of free judgement in secular as well as religious matters – this his spirit of independence could not accept.[27]

Despite this, to the end of his life, Armour spoke for equality in religious and political rights. In a remarkable speech on elementary education, he offset 'true Christianity against pagan sectarianism; civil liberty against ecclesiastical tyranny'. Instead, he asked for a broader spirit in the matter of education: 'If you treat it simply as a question of the well-being of Presbytery alone you will secretly betray the cause of Presbytery which is equal rights to all ...'[28] Debating the Universities Bill he called for all-round generosity. When the General Assembly protested against the endowment of a Roman Catholic University in Dublin, Armour dissented vigorously: 'You are hostile to the grant of anything to three-fourths of your countrymen who only ask for a modicum of fair play. Is it a wise policy for an eighth of the population to set itself to irritate and annoy the seven eighths? Is a policy which they will regard as hatred, in accordance with Christian principles?' At the end of his life he confided that he had fought his own people for the right of free opinion and had argued in that spirit the rights of Catholics. In the mid 1920s and after partition he still argued that Protestants and Catholics alike must show the spirit of brotherliness, must hear what the other had to say. Although the context was different, the problem remained the same – to grant each other the right of investigation, to practice fairmindedness and to exercise creative leadership.[30]

In the context of the time, it is unsurprising that Armour's repeated argument that Presbyterians were being used as

'mere circus riders in the Tory hippodrome', evoked hostility
and even ostracism. While his theological orthodoxy was
never in question, his readiness to break ranks on social issues
caused great difficulty. In March 1893, his dramatic speech on
Home Rule to the General Assembly resulted in bitter criticism and boycott from a few colleagues. Thereafter, in some
districts, he was banned from pulpits because of congregations' hostility. This he termed 'a new Presbyterian doctrine of
obedience to Unionism'.[31] Many years later, an obituary notice
remarked that he frequently had to fight the General
Assembly with 'the whole house against him'. It is, nonetheless, a favourable index of relations within Presbyterianism
that recognition of Armour's sincerity and, perhaps, a type-
cast of him as the perennial objector, deterred real anger from
becoming irreparable hatred. Thus, even people who on occasion experienced his biting sarcasm could honour him in notable ways towards the end of his life. In 1909, the *Northern
Whig* put it: 'Mr. Armour is a hard hitter, but he cherishes no
bitterness towards those with whom he is brought into conflict. The General Assembly always hears him gladly, not because it agrees with him, for it seldom does that, but he has
the gift of epigrammatic speech and the saving grace of humour.'[32]

A Measure of Official Acceptance

After the election of a Liberal government in 1906, Armour
was appointed a personal chaplain to the Viceroy, Lord
Aberdeen. As such he had to visit Dublin with some regularity
and had considerable influence at the vice-regal residence. J.
B. Dougherty (a friend and distant relative of Armour) was
appointed Under Secretary for Ireland in 1908. Armour's
long-standing complaint about the exclusion of Presbyterians
was to some extent addressed. Dougherty consulted him on
appointments to educational boards, on county lieutenancies
and, at least once, on a judgeship. J. B. McMinn adverts to
the irony that Armour, who had long complained about the
use of influence in appointments, was now part of the process

himself. Certainly, he spoke for people he considered meritor-
ious, even when they had opposed him on political or religious matters. Likewise, he used his 'channel of influence' to
safeguard the interests of Magee College, Derry. Yet McMinn's
point should not be overlooked: Armour desired 'to secure
posts for Liberals after so many years of Unionist domination'. It is hardly accidental that after the passage of Lloyd
George's Insurance Act (1911) Armour was himself appointed
an insurance commissioner for Antrim.[33]

Nor is it surprising that in 1910 Armour should be appointed to the newly created Queen's University senate. For
many years he had shrewdly, although not always popularly,
contributed to educational questions at General Assembly of
his own church. On the university question he was both incis-
ively critical and generously liberal. From 1900 he had spoken
for a state-aided Catholic university. Personally. he favoured
united secular education with religious formation devolving
on the several churches. Thus he repeatedly argued for non-
denominationalism at Queen's University despite opposition
from Protestants and a very different strategy by the Catholic
bishops. At the General Assembly of 1908 he had to acknowledge that his own views were shared by few others, even
among Catholics. Yet he recommended that a message be sent
to Catholics from the Assembly: 'You and we differ in our
idea of education. We cannot pursue it together, but we give
you your claim and we send you the word: though we dis-
agree, may God's blessing be with you now and forever'.[34]

When appointed to the university senate, Armour worked
vigorously on the college regulations for matriculation in
view of a huge failure rate in the examination. Believing this
was due to mismatch of the Intermediate syllabus and the
matriculation subjects, he argued that students from poorer
families were being disadvantaged. Likewise, he strove to as-
sure Catholics of respect for their traditions. Here he showed
particular generosity and attracted odium to the point of
being termed a pawn of the Catholic bishops. Although not

an Irish language enthusiast, he nonetheless argued for a chair in Celtic studies. When General Assembly attacked the lectureship in scholastic philosophy (then held by a Dublin priest, Dr Denis O'Keeffe), he argued against the implication that nobody be admitted to the university 'unless they signed the thirty nine articles of Scotch philosophy'. The college was not an exclusively Protestant institution: 'the University was for Ulster and practically one half of Ulster was Catholic'. Only 'a tribe of reactionaries' under the leadership of 'mad Mullahs' could wish thus to constrict the idea of a university.[35] Due perhaps to his own outspokenness, Armour was not re-elected to the university senate in 1914. Nor did Augustine Birrell re-appoint him, since the Chief Secretary was advised to nominate a Catholic. Wm Armour remarks: 'This episode reflects the caste-ridden state of Ireland at the time. Mr Armour's name was everywhere venerated among Catholics and he would have fought tooth and nail for them on the Senate. But he was not a member of their faith ... Nor would Protestant organisations nominate a friend of Catholics'.[36]

About 1910 a note of disspiritment appears in Armour's personal letters – as if he felt on the margin of political and ecclesiastical affairs. Although warned about a heart condition, he did not slacken his ministry at Ballymoney. He wrote to his sister-in-law: 'It is a severe trial to be in the backwater of life, and only to view the fight from a canoe among the reeds and rushes.'[37] Nevertheless, Armour's work was far from complete and several campaigns lay before him. In all of these – as during the turbulence of his whole ministry – a secure familial base enabled him to withstand difficulties courageously and even with mischievous humour. During a public tribute to him in early 1909, Armour avowed his debt to Jennie Armour's support – had he the choice of reincarnation, it would be as husband 'of my present wife'.[38] Due to the collaboration of this remarkable couple, the manse at Ballymoney remained a centre of unstinted hospitality, a base for pastoral activity and, at times, the location where unpopular socio-political issues could be discussed and promoted.

Home Rule

To understand the particular significance of Armour's work from 1910 to 1929, it will be useful to return to the development of his views on the Home Rule question. In 1886, when the first Home Rule Bill was mooted, he feared it might strengthen demands for separation from Britain. As well, if Irish MPs left Westminster, a safeguard against religious persecution on the part of the majority would have been withdrawn.[39] And so, perhaps with some misgivings, he went along with the General Assembly's stated opposition to the Bill. However, by 1891 he had come to a different opinion. Now he regretted that 'The prancing colonels, the blustering captains, the squirming majors, the sons of old manufacturers ... landlords professing conversion' had been allowed to sway the Assembly's vote in 1886. Some have argued this *volte face* arose from chagrin at Unionist/Tory mismanagement of land reform. On the other hand, J. B. McMinn sees the conversion as a protest at Conservative/Anglican monopoly of parliamentary seats and public offices. In any event, by 1893 Armour was ready to support whatever reform would give Ireland 'such a measure of self-government as is consistent with the unity of the empire, the supremacy of parliament and the protection of minorities ...'[40]

Now an open supporter of Home Rule, he spoke for the Liberals in Britain and took part in a by-election campaign at South Hackney, London. About the same time – in Ballynure, Co Antrim – he declared to a meeting of tenant farmers that: '... a race of Presbyterians and Protestants worthy of the best traditions of our faith will arise ... with their minds cleared of Unionist cant and blood purified from the rust of serfdom (who) will claim to dwell in the land, not under the protection of the Saxon, not by permission of the Celt, but in virtue of the services they will render to a country which we love'. Clearly he had broken with hard-line Unionism: 'If Unionism means ... the ascendancy of a sect, I cease to respect it and to attempt to buttress up what has no right to exist'.[41]

In a remarkable speech to the special Assembly at May Street, Belfast (March 1893) Armour braved a meeting determinedly hostile to the second Home Rule Bill. He claimed that the principle of Home Rule was a Presbyterian one and that Gladstone's proposal, with due modification, should be given fair trial. In opposing Home Rule the Assembly was saving the landlord class – 'the curse and scourge of Ireland'. In addition, it was saddling the tenants with impossible rents. Over loud heckling he insisted that if tenants refused to pay a penny of purchase money or withheld their rent, they were breaking no divine law. Through 'a senseless fear of Romanism' and out of dislike for Gladstone, the Assembly (would) sacrifice the progress of true Presbyterianism in Ireland for generations'.[42] The official resolution, not Armour's amendment, was unanimously carried. Three months later, when the General Assembly reiterated its opposition to Home Rule, Armour wrote of Belfast as 'the temple of the rankest Toryism' and the centre of Presbyterian Unionism. Prophetically he further wrote that Home Rule would come but too late 'and in a form which will be revolutionary'.[43]

Home Rule did not come at this point. As F. S. L. Lyons puts it: Home Rule 'was quickly knocked on the head by the house of Lords and with Gladstone's retirement from politics a few months later it was evident that Home Rule was dead and buried without hope of any speedy resurrection'.[44] The liberalism represented by J. B. Armour, J. B. Dougherty, J. D. Houston and many Irish Protestants was defeated in a general election which introduced a decade of Unionist hegemony. Writing to Armour, Dougherty reflected on the lack of support for the liberal programme by the tenant farmers: 'those fellows will come and listen to you and then go and vote against their own interests from fear of the Pope'.[45] Dougherty may well have been right: subsequent historians argue that those who attended Liberal meetings in 1894 and 1895 had greater interest in land reform than in Home Rule.

During 1910, when Armour was approaching seventy, a

new proposal for Irish Home Rule was mooted. The Irish party under John Redmond had been able to extract from H. H. Asquith a commitment to introduce the measure in return for their budgetary support. Asquith, albeit reluctantly, spoke of a policy which 'while safeguarding the supremacy ... of the Imperial Parliament will set up in Ireland a system of full self-government in regard to purely Irish affairs'.[46] Almost immediately, conservative unionism mounted a backlash led by Edward Carson, an erstwhile MP for Dublin University. Threats of violent resistance were made. A declaration of independence in Ulster was mooted and, eventually, there was talk of an invitation to the German Kaiser. In fiery words Carson warned: 'We must be prepared ... the morning Home Rule passes, ourselves to become responsible for the government of the Protestant province of Ulster.'[47] Once again, Presbyterian support was sought by the Tories and once again this drew Armour's scorn. Under the somewhat provocative heading, 'The Ulster Comedy. God's Silly People', the *Daily News* published an interview with Armour. He dismissed the widespread threats of violent reaction as 'a bad attack of delirium tremens'. If there were a parliament in Dublin, Protestants would have at least a quarter of the seats. As to Presbyterians, they had no need to fear they would be thrown to devils and wolves: 'under no conceivable circumstances could they have less recognition than they had during all the days of Tory rule in Ireland'. The alarmist cries about Home Rule being Rome Rule were created by the Ascendancy party in Dublin – once again, the Tory party was using Ulster for its own ends. For Presbyterians to support the party of the brewers would prove they were 'God's silly people'.[48]

While respecting Carson's abilities, Armour thought his garrison mentality was the same as the landlord theory. Admiring John Redmond, he endorsed the call for 'settlement, peace and goodwill between all Irishmen'.[49] He rejected both Carsonism and Sinn Féin on the grounds that, as he put it, one cannot found a state that will last on hate. Well before the Larne gun-running (which Joseph Lee has deemed the first introduction of the gun in twentieth century Irish politics) he believed Carson was recommending Fenian methods in face of unpalatable legislation. In the run-up to the Presbyterian Convention (February, 1912), Armour discountenanced support of Carsonism: it would tie the Presbyterian church to the Tory party. He continued to argue that the church should do as he did at Ballymoney, viz. leave people free to be Unionist or Liberal or Home Ruler and to keep politics from the pulpit. With several other ministers he refused to attend the Presbyterian Convention or to sign the Covenant of 1 Sept 1912. When preparations were made for 'Ulster Day' he declared it ought to be called 'the Protestant Fool's Day'. He asked: '... with the right of free speech tabooed and the right of private judgement declared of the Devil – is what remains of Protestantism worth keeping? If one hamstrings one's religion is it a religion worth preserving?'[50]

Roger Casement

In September 1913, Ballymoney hosted a meeting to oppose Carson's policy. One of the principal speakers was Sir Roger Casement, then acclaimed for his work in the Putomayo. Another speaker was Captain Jack White, later a founder of the Irish Citizen Army. Although Armour did not speak, he had helped to organise the meeting and received Casement at the Manse. The significance of this meeting should not be over-emphasised as, despite the hopes of Armour and Casement, it did not lead to similar meetings elsewhere. It is noteworthy that the speeches most approved of by Armour were those of Alec Wilson, an Anglican, and John Dinsmore, a Presbyterian. Wilson had stressed that many Ulster Protestants desired the welfare of Ireland no matter what the form of government, that Carsonism headed only to a cul-de-sac, and that anti-Catholic propaganda was to be deplored. Dinsmore rehearsed many of Armour's own views: the baneful effect of a clique at Belfast, their dilution of support for the land campaign, the manipulation by the linen magnates of working people and tenants – when the latter 'asked for bread they were given *The Boyne Water*'. Armour would also have agreed with Dinsmore that 'The Pope is worth at least a half a million per annum to the linen lords of Ulster. It is not loyalty these men are out for, it is loot; and the true protagonists in the struggle are not the puppet Carsons and Londonderrys, but the great linen magnates of Belfast'.[51]

Hostile observers mocked the Ballymoney gathering as 'a little handful of cranks', 'a small isolated pocket of dissident Protestants', 'the last few survivors of the Ulster Liberals of the old type'. With a logic none too clear, the *Times* correspondent inferred that since there were many radicals around Ballymoney who were 'substantial people', the four or five hundred who attended at the town hall 'dislike the methods of the covenanters more than they like Home Rule ...'[52] Armour's opposition to Carson persisted during these months. The minister of Ballymoney was now clearly identified with acceptance of Home Rule as both a challenge and an opportunity for Irish people. In so far as the term is relevant to historical understanding, Armour was unambiguously a Protestant Home Ruler. Whatever about the claim of the *Times* correspondent, there was a marked lack of enthusiasm for Carsonite agitation in the Route district. According to William Armour, prominent Tories ascribed the shortfall to 'wickedness inspired from Trinity Manse'.[53]

The campaign against Home Rule did, however, continue. As well as somewhat paradoxical talk of secession from the United Kingdom, as well as importation of guns at Larne, there was under the so-called exclusion demand, viz. that certain Ulster counties be excluded from the remit of Home Rule proposals. Armour's opposition to the exclusion demand was implacable since he favoured Irish unity just as much as he favoured union with Great Britain. Thus he called for persistence by government in its Home Rule proposals: 'if the bill was on the statute book, the excitement in Ulster would die down in a few weeks, as no sane person wants exclusion in any shape'.[53] Exclusion would benefit neither Catholics not Protestants: Tory hegemony 'would give Catholic and Protestant Home Rulers no quarter and therefore ... would stir up the Catholics in the south and west to harass ... the scattered Protestants'.[55] This argument against 'exclusion' will be considered later in the context of partition (from 1921). Yet, in August 1914, the outbreak of war with Germany seemed to put in suspension the Home Rule question. As well, it provided yet another theatre for Armour's remarkably energetic activities.

The 1914-18 War

J. B. Armour's enthusiasm for the allied cause was immediate and, it can be argued, excessive. Like Pearse on Irish independence, he spoke in heightened terms of the ethical issues: 'the very flower of our race is offering the supreme sacrifice it is given to men to make'. The same hyperbole is evident in another claim: 'From the fields of Flanders and France light is arising – the streaks of victory'. At this distance, such romantic enthusiasm calls for the same critique as all references to 'blood sacrifice' whether in Irish nationalist or British imperialist rhetoric. Practically, Trinity Manse became a focal point where Armour and his wife supported those who had gone to the war. Although the Irish question remained important, he viewed the allied cause as paramount. Strongly approving of Redmond's stance he repeatedly praised those Irish Volunteers who had responded to Redmond's Woodenbridge speech. Even here, Armour's call for fair play was insistent. He deprecated favouritism at the War Office towards the Ulster Volunteers and against Redmondites who had joined the British Army. Such continuation of ascendancy spirit was, he wrote, both unjust and self-defeating. In the closing months of 1914 he spotted Asquith's betrayal of Redmond through capitulation to Unionist pressure: '... I would not be surprised if Redmond had his nails pared as they will whittle down the Home Rule Bill in the vain hope of oiling the hair of Ulster Unionists'.[56]

In 1915 Armour repeated that the Tories had no vision and, he wrote, 'where there is no vision the people perish'. When Asquith brayed that Ulster would not be coerced and tried to justify dismemberment of Ireland, Armour remarked: 'He might as well say that the brewers, distillers and publicans cannot be coerced to submit to legislation they oppose.'[57] By 1917 Armour decried Lloyd George's cynicism: ' (he) has bungled the Irish question ... Being ultra-Tory he will not coerce Ulster. Will he be able to coerce the three fourths of the Irish people backed up by the Irish in America and the colonies. He is prepared to coerce all the Protestants in the South and the West who have rights similar to those in Ulster'.[58] Towards the end of the war Armour began to hope for a radical change, in particular, the banishment of hatred and cruelty in public affairs. To achieve this, as he put it, both church and state would have to apply themselves more honourably. On the Sunday before Armistice Day he preached at Ballymoney on 'A new Heavens and a new Earth'; the sermon was typically practical, calling for justice to all the demobilised soldiers. Nor did Armour omit to mention the problems still unresolved in Ireland – a new attitude to all those who lived on the same island and, more generally, to law and morality was essential. Even a year after the war, in July 1919, he could speak of the peace as introducing the dawn of a new day for the world.[59]

Attitudes to Sinn Féin

Although J. B. Armour sympathised with nationalist leaders such as Redmond and Dillon, at no point was he either a separatist or a republican. He remained a Unionist in the most liberal sense – favourable both to the unity of Ireland and union within the United Kingdom. More exactly, he believed a self-governing united Ireland within the broader empire would foster democratic politics. It would also encourage practical tolerance between the religious traditions. In such a context, he believed, Presbyterianism could hold its own and social justice could be fostered. Thus, Armour's enthusiasm for Home Rule should be placed in the context of non-sectarian, democratic politics where the power of hitherto dominant interests would be reduced to just proportion. Although he disagreed with Unionist attitudes to Catholic aspirations, he criticised Sinn Féin for the same reasons as he had opposed the activities of Edward Carson.[60] Having opposed the Larne gun-running, he saw the importation of arms by the Irish Volunteers as equally dangerous. With some courage, just a month after the rising in Dublin, he argued that Carson's lesson had been learned only too well: 'It is dawning on many that the real mistake of the government was in not coming down hard on the gun-runners of Ulster ... it is becoming evident that they were committing suicide as well as endangering the security of the Empire'. Once again, he risked opprobrium by criticising those who saw the 1916 insurgents as 'sinners above all the Galileans' while the same people regarded Carson's gun-runners as saints and heroes. In his view, both groups had flouted the law dangerously and both were wrong.[61]

It will be remembered that in September 1913 Sir Roger Casement had been Armour's guest at Ballymoney. When it emerged that Casement had undertaken a trip to Germany in 1914, hostile voices were raised more against Armour than against Casement. While the *Belfast Telegraph* trumpeted 'From Ballymoney to Berlin', Armour remarked on the irony: 'We are all traitors like Sir Roger ... Certain, in Ulster before the war coquetted with the Kaiser and brought on the war sooner than it would have come. But that was patriotism'.[62] After Casement's arrest and the subsequent capital sentence, Armour refused to pontificate but, like Arthur Conan Doyle, spoke of insanity. And with his usual magnanimity he wrote in July 1916: '... it is impossible to question on the evidence the justice of the sentence ... We remember him in his sanity and found him a very charming guest ... A worthy man who in a crisis lost his mental balance is the verdict on Sir Roger. I am really sorry for the fate of the man.'[63] As republican demands clarified during 1917 Armour pinned his hopes on the

national politics of Redmond and the Irish party. He lamented the victory of Sinn Féin at the North Roscommon by-election of February 1917. Here, he differs greatly from another
figure in our collection of 'Unusual Suspects', Father Michael
O' Flanagan, one of the chief architects of that electoral victory.
With this election, constitutional republicanism appeared on
the Irish political stage for the first time. It can be said that
Armour may not have understood the emotional forces gathering behind Sinn Féin from late 1917 and, even in mid-1919
could argue that 'The idea of an Irish republic is rather fantas-
tic.'[64]

Armour's approach to Irish politics is singularly consistent.
His chief questions were of morality rather than expediency:
what is right? what is just? what will favour the well-being of
all Irish people? His answers came not from dogmatism, not
from sectional interest, but from 'free investigation' (this he
saw as both a Presbyterian imperative and a cherished right).
According to Wm Armour, he differed from dominant sections in Ireland by his insistence on 'an absolute standard of
morality at which to aim'. Perhaps misunderstanding its de-
rivation, he disliked the title Sinn Féin: 'For ourselves alone is
in the teeth of all Christian principles hitherto accepted.'[65]
Since Armour regarded the War effort as of primary importance, he utterly disapproved of the rising in Easter 1916. He
also disagreed with the use of force by either unionist or nationalist to oppose laws they did not like. Yet, once again, his
generosity appears in his view that leniency should be shown
to the rank and file of the insurgents and his opposition to execution of their leaders.

Attitudes to Partition

Quite simply, Armour viewed this as unnatural and un-
workable. In 1914 and again in 1916, there was talk of excluding northern counties from the remit of Home Rule. Armour
dissented vehemently on practical as well as moral grounds.
By definition, the proposal was divisive of Irish people: it was
also a betrayal of Protestants. To accept partition would be to

acquiesce in another version of Sinn Féin, ourselves alone. In June 1916, he wrote: 'Now we will only defend the Six Counties and let the other Protestants stew in the Home Rule juice.'[66] From 1920, as the 'exclusion' measure loomed ever nearer, Armour opposed it at every opportunity. In his view, the defeat of Redmond had destroyed possibilities for national reconciliation. Now, even Unionists were compelled to accept 'a form of Home Rule that the Devil himself could never have imagined'. Whereas they could have had major influence in earlier versions of Home Rule, now they were confronted with a 'bastard Parliament' in Belfast and the probability of a separate Republic centred in Dublin.[67]

Armour's speech to the General Assembly of 1920 deserves close attention. The Committee on the State of the Country had forwarded an anodyne motion on the Bill for the Better Government of Ireland (later Government of Ireland Act, 1920). Armour proposed an amendment diagnosing the ills of partition. Partition was 'divisive, anti-Unionist, tending to accentuate racial and religious hatreds, and ruinous to the commercial and moral prosperity of Ireland'. With characteristic irony he told the Assembly they were all Home Rulers now, while he remained a Unionist who wanted the union of Ireland. The Bill envisaged an unnatural division whereby two Irelands would be created. As well, it meant abandonment of southern Protestants to their own devices. In 1921, Armour returned to the issue. He wished the six-county parliament well but argued it could never be a permanent legislative body. As to the unionist leader Sir James Craig, he deserved better than to be 'the wet nurse to a kind of bastard Parliament'. And, in a resume of his old antagonism to engrained privilege, Armour lamented that Presbyterians had surrendered their destinies 'to what I shall call the Landlord and the Church of Ireland party'.[68]

Closing Years

Aged more than eighty years, and despite earlier warnings on ill-health, Armour continued his work with extraordinary

energy. After the Anglo-Irish treaty, he co-operated with the
northern administration by serving on the Insurance Committee for Antrim. Even yet he was ready to criticise shortcomings. In his view, since there was an identity of interest
throughout Ireland, the tariff barriers between north and
south were a matter for regret. He still discerned a bias against
Presbyterians in the matter of official appointments – on one
occasion, he called on General Assembly not to allow their
church to be trampled on, even by a Belfast government.[69]
Although neither the southern nor the northern administration welcomed criticism, opposition to his views in the mid-
1920s lacked the virulence and the ill-temper of former years.
Armour's remarks, if not welcomed, seemed to be recognised
as patently sincere and, in the last analysis, as from a critic *ab
intra*. Thus, the conclusion of his biography by Wm Armour
fittingly ends with a chapter 'Sundown, Splendid and Serene'.
On a couple of visits to Dublin he was received cordially by
the Free State authorities. His own church authorities honoured him more than once at Ballymoney and even political
opponents saluted his turbulent interventions through almost
sixty years.

On Armour's retirement from the active ministry (September 1925) his congregation at Ballymoney along with the
Presbyterian Moderator signalled the outstanding merit of his
service. Regrettably, the choice of his successor occasioned ill-
feeling from which he remained aloof. A verse in 'The War in
the Roddenfoot' summates the difficulty:

'The Christians in the Roddenfoot are sore perplexed they say
For Mr Armour has resigned and thus began the fray.'[70]
There is some suggestion, impossible to quantify, that Armour's
radicalism impeded the candidacy of his son, J. B. M. (Max)
Armour. Max Armour was, indeed, 'called' but only by the
barest majority and he did not accept appointment. It was
typical of J. B. Armour that he gave fullest co-operation to his
eventual successor, H. C. Waddell. It is also typical of Armour's
generosity that his outstanding memorial at Ballymoney

should be dedicated to another – the Rentoul clock on Trinity church-tower which he had erected to honour his predecessor. Some time remained to savour an active retirement. Armour's enthusiasms remained undimmed – on the Insurance Board, in educational matters, in pastoral work alongside his successor.

At a public function in Ballymoney (Jan 1928) Armour caught a heavy chill. Late in the evening of 25 January he died of pneumonia, at the Manse.

Conclusion

J. B. McMinn rightly warns that there is danger of presenting Armour in colours which misrepresent him. Armour the radical foe of Toryism, the defender of Home Rule, the opponent of partition, the protagonist of a united Ireland is a reality. Nonetheless, years after his death and with the bitter legacy of partition still unresolved, there is a temptation to present him in terms which would not do justice to his complexity. It must again be stressed that Armour was a unionist in two directions – north/south of Ireland and east/west from Ireland to Britain. He was neither a separatist nor a republican as we understand the terms. Indeed, on occasion he regarded the moderate nationalist, John Dillon, as leaning excessively in the direction of Sinn Féin. Although his generosity impelled him to safeguard the rights of Celtic scholars as well as of Catholics at Queen's University, Belfast, there is no evidence that he was personally attracted to 'Irish-Ireland' or what some might term 'Fenianism'. Nor can it be said that rhetoric about 1798 would have met his approval. He was deeply opposed to the rising of 1916 and, as his son has acknowledged, probably underestimated the emotional appeal Sinn Féin for many of his fellow-countrymen. It has also been mentioned that 'Romanism' as a system repelled him both at the emotional and rational levels. One or two remarks on the general changes after the 1914-18 war hint at an inconsistency in his radical thinking. For example, one notes with some surprise that the author of the 'Devrock speech' can also write in August 1919: 'thousands ... will not work – why should they, when they get for loafing about as much as they could get as workers'. About the same time, he can regret that Lloyd George was losing his earlier radicalism.[71]

For all that, Armour's life-work is of great significance many decades after his death. Deeply attached to Presbyterianism, he perceived that an ungenerous or intolerant religion was hardly worth possessing. A principle uttered (by an Orange politician) during the land campaign remained with him throughout his life: 'This is no question of Protestantism or party allegiance but of justice and fair play.'[72] For Armour, Presbyterianism as a Christian profession stood or fell with its ability to defend 'institutions of liberty'. Indeed, precisely in doing this it was at its best and most likely to thrive. Selfish group-interest led only to division and suffering. And so, at major cost to himself, he spoke for the rights of others – the Catholics, the tenant farmers, the students without money or powerful family background. Such generous principle is a challenge to all Christian churches and to all political traditions in an Ireland many decades after Armour's death. Dean Victor Griffin's reminder is apt: 'Too often in Northern Ireland Protestantism in general is perceived as the religious dimension of unionism and Roman Catholicism as the religious dimension of nationalism ... The only winners are cynicism and disillusionment with all religion and politics ... '[73]

Hence, Douglas Gageby was right persistently to cite the minister of Ballymoney to a southern readership – and perhaps also to northern people who had not heard of him. Intolerance of the 'other', whether in constitutional, cultural or social justice issues, is fatal to any conception of a 'new Ireland'. Armour's honesty, no matter how acerbic, is both a valuable legacy and an enduring inspiration. It was said of him that on nationality, education, land or church, 'he left nothing unattacked which he ought to attack and ... there were few things which he attacked which he did not improve'.[74]

This is a generous epitaph. In his ability to open a vista of toleration accompanied by needed reforms, J. B. Armour merits an honoured place among our 'Unusual Suspects'.

Further Reading

Armour William B., *Armour of Ballymoney,* Duckworth, London, 1934.
McMinn, J.B., *Against the Tide*, Public Records Office, Northern Ireland, 1985.
Snodgrass, L., *Armour's Meeting House*, Ballymoney, 1985.

CHAPTER NINE

'THEY HAVE FOOLED YOU AGAIN'

Fr Michael O'Flanagan (1876-1942)

Superficially, there are major contrasts between Ml O'Flanagan and the redoubtable J. B. Armour. In speech, in cultural roots, in personal sensibilities, they seem utterly diverse. O'Flanagan exemplifies a recognisable strain in southern Catholicism while Armour remains quintessentially a northern Protestant. The traditional Catholicism of one can be contrasted with the orthodox Presbyterianism of the other. Again, whereas Armour lauded the British empire as an embodiment of moral purpose, O'Flanagan denounced it as an instrument of repression. In regard to the war of 1914-18 they differed fundamentally. Armour's enthusiasm contrasts with O'Flanagan's view that the war was about money and colonial interests – it was 'a manufactured hatred ... built up by lying newspapers and ministers who sit in their offices ... and play with the lives of men by the million'.[1] On the question of Sinn Féin, they differed widely – Armour had deep respect for John Redmond while O'Flanagan played a signal role in the defeat of Redmond's party. Yet, both men exemplify a courageous radicalism on important socio-religious questions. They also incurred hostility from establishments which, despite all differences, they each contested.

Michael Flanagan (only later did he assume the traditional Gaelic 'O') was born in August 1876 near Castlerea, Co Roscommon. In his formative years he was surrounded by a fenian tradition compounded by the land struggle of the decades from 1870. His early schooling was at 'the Don school', founded by the O'Conor Don. For higher education he was sent to the diocesan college at Summerhill, Sligo. The few records of this period disclose his incipient interest in the national politics of C. S. Parnell and, more narrowly, in the progress of the church then under construction at Castlerea.

In late 1894 Michael Flanagan entered Maynooth College, the national seminary for the Catholic priesthood. Here he encountered professors who subsequently influenced the politico-cultural scene of early twentieth-century Ireland. Daniel Mannix (later Archbishop of Melbourne), Walter McDonnell (author of the controversial *Reminiscences of a Maynooth Professor*) and Ml O'Hickey (professor of Irish whose conflict with the bishops incurred his dismissal from Maynooth) were among his teachers. Student colleagues were Peter Coffey (in subsequent years a distinguished Professor of Social Theory), Robert Fullerton and Thomas Burbage. Later, Ml Flanagan would remember the turgid system at Maynooth which encouraged conformity rather than originality, compliance rather than enquiry. Nevertheless, he performed more than creditably in a wide range of disciplines and in 1900 was ordained for Elphin diocese by Bishop Clancy.[3]

Early Public Involvements

A shared characteristic of 'unusual suspects' is their energetic readiness for change. Such energy is apparent from the outset of Ml O'Flanagan's appointment as 'professor' at Summerhill. Almost immediately he took part in the Irish language revival. In 1903 and again in 1904, he was secretary to the Sligo Feis. At this stage he became acquainted with Douglas Hyde and Patrick Pearse, both of whom adjudicated competitions in 1903 and 1904. Also in 1904, he published a short monograph on the Irish language. This was a contribution to the current debate on variations in script and pronunciation which continued for decades. Somewhat awkwardly, Fr O'Flanagan's introduction defines his purpose: 'to explain the rules of aspiration and eclipsis in terms of the anatomy of the vocal organs'. The monograph can be set in the context of Patrick Pearse's editorship of the Gaelic League's *Claíomh Solais* with its endeavour to standardise grammar, spelling and style of the Irish language.[4] During these years, O' Flanagan proposed that an emblem – the fáinne or gold ring – be worn as a sign of readiness to converse in Irish.

After 1904, Fr O'Flanagan undertook projects in the United States to promote Irish lace-making and garner funds for the Franciscan Missionaries, newly installed at Loughglynn, Co Roscommon. Thus commenced his particular under-standing of the Irish 'diaspora'. As he travelled the United States, O'Flanagan made widespread contacts, lay and cleri-cal. Later he drew on these experiences to enlist American support for Irish independence. Returning in 1910 he reported 'the existence in every part of the States of an Irish population that is ever anxious to hear of home progress and to meet rep-resentatives of any Irish movement'. Elected to the standing committee of the Gaelic League in August 1910 he obtained leave of absence from Elphin to raise money in America for the League. From a campaign office on Madison Avenue (New York), he set up an exhibition of Irish goods at Philadelphia. The energetic imagination applied to this task is a forerunner of O'Flanagan's later career. His readiness for trenchant criticism is instanced by his remarks on the League's somewhat complacent policies. When he recom-mended that Conradh na Gaeilge's finances should become more business-like, many of the standing committee took of-fence. The offence was compounded when he deemed it iron-ic that there was no Irish language journal for Irish speakers in America. Tensions arose within the League even on these pro-posals and, perhaps with relief, O'Flanagan returned to his diocese in 1912.

At this stage, O'Flanagan had good relations with his diocesan authorities. He was appointed by Bishop Clancy as curate in Roscommon town where his reputation as a preacher grew rapidly. An invitation to preach Lenten sermons at San

Silvestro, Rome, marks this distinction. At home, his work for the Irish language continued. To date, as he approached his thirty-sixth year, he had not been in any way singular as a Catholic clergyman. His energy was indeed remarkable, his bluntness was perhaps an irritant to more settled people, his commitment to Irish-Ireland culture was noticeable but not in any way unique.

Yet, in May 1913 an incident occurred which indicates that Fr O'Flanagan was not overly concerned with a safe ecclesiastical career.[5] A strike at Sligo docks had dragged on from March when workers for Sligo Steam Navigation had demanded more wages. 'Scab' labour was brought from England and there were confrontations with the police. When trade union leader Jim Larkin visited the strikers, the County Council denounced his 'foul anti-Christian, socialist doctrines'. When, said one councillor, 'Larkin attacked the church it was the duty of every public body to condemn him'. It is of interest that Ml O'Flanagan, now ministering at Roscommon, visited the strikers and advised them to continue insisting on their rights.

Cliffoney and Beyond

In global terms, the year 1914 was momentous. August saw the outbreak of 'the Great War'. More locally, the year also saw the death of Bishop Clancy and the installation of a new bishop, Dr Bernard Coyne. In August, Ml O'Flanagan was transferred from Roscommon to the remote, although very beautiful, parish of Cliffoney. It would be unfair to assert that O'Flanagan's removal to Cliffoney was a punishment for his visit to the strikers. And it should also be said that, once there, O'Flanagan showed wholehearted commitment to a people with whom he developed a lasting bond of mutual respect. Nonetheless, for whatever reason, relations between Coyne and O'Flanagan seem less than friendly.

At a time when income varied considerably from parish to parish, diocesan assignments were a lever to keep more than one imaginative priest within the bounds of acceptable 'docility'. Whatever the intentions of Dr Coyne, Fr O'Flanagan was not interested in docility, acceptable or otherwise. In fact, his brief period at Cliffoney thrust him further along the path of social criticism and almost centre-stage of Irish politics. Several episodes occurred, notably the funeral of Diarmuid O'Donovan Rossa and a dispute with the Congested Districts Board on the question of turbary rights. As a sub-text to these is the world war, the involvement of Irishmen therein and a sustained criticism of public bodies which had become remote from the concerns 'the rank and file' of the people.[6]

A Fenian Funeral

In mid-summer 1915, O'Donovan Rossa died in the United States after a long illness. For a generation of nationalists he epitomised the spirit of resistance to British rule in Ireland. At the request of O'Donovan's family, Tom Clarke – an old Fenian – remitted the organisation of the funeral to the Wolfe Tone Memorial Committee. Ml O'Flanagan had met O'Donovan in the United States and the family had requested his participation in the funeral. According to Tom Clarke's son, the selection of a speaker to give an address at Glasnevin lay between Patrick Pearse and Ml O'Flanagan. In the event, O'Flanagan was deputed to speak at City Hall while Pearse was invited to give an oration at Glasnevin. The lives of both men would be significantly affected by their role in the final tribute to O'Donovan Rossa.[7]

Pearse's Glasnevin address was indeed the more skillfully crafted of the two. Its stylistic balance, its emotional concentration, its restrained yet powerful denunciation of colonial rule, places it among the best of revolutionary oratory. O'Flanagan's words may lack the precision Pearse's address. Nevertheless, one can understand why the priest's speech evoked so enthusiastic response that, to cite the *Funeral Souvenir Booklet*, 'for some minutes the walls of Dublin's city hall resounded to such applause as would have gladdened the heart of Rossa'. O'Flanagan paid full tribute to O'Donovan's place in Irish history and rebutted the hostile whisper that his views on Irish separatism had changed. Emergent resistance is hinted at by both Pearse and O'Flanagan. Said Pearse: 'They think they have conquered one half and intimidated the other half.' Said O'Flanagan: 'The old catch-cries and platitudes are not going down the throats of Irish people today as they were a few months ago.' In O'Flanagan's view the return of O'Donovan Rossa presaged 'a new epoch in the history of Ireland'.[8]

The organising committee had shown political acumen as well as organisational ability. It involved advanced nationalist personnel of the Irish Republican Brotherhood, the Irish Volunteers, the Irish Citizen Army (including James Connolly) and Cumann na mBan (the women's republican organisation). Nevertheless, ample room was made for others such as John Redmond's National Volunteers as well as elected representatives and cultural bodies. At the City Hall, and in clear reference to the split in the Volunteers, O'Flanagan called for a new unity: 'We have received O'Donovan Rossa into Ireland in the ... spirit of unity and brotherhood. Many who have been estranged by the extraordinary occurrences of the past year or two will be brought together again over the body of our hero'.

Were these days in August 1915 a turning point in contemporary Irish history? the commencement of a new epoch? P. H. Pearse may have expressed the mood of the IRB as that organisation moved closer to endorsing an armed rising. Fr O'Flanagan on the other hand did not trust secret societies and was, perhaps, too committed to 'the will of the people' to rest happy with arcane decisions by a small group. The deep feeling of the crowds which honoured O'Donovan Rossa should not be confused with any formulated commitment to armed revolution. And there is no evidence that Ml O'Flanagan was party to that decision when it was made. Nonetheless, his participation in O'Donovan Rossa's funeral brought him to national prominence, just as his words showed his adherence to the Fenian spirit.

Dispute on Turbary Rights

In itself, the dispute was a small matter – public allotments of bog on the Hippesley and Ashley estates at Cloonkeen, Co Sligo. Yet, it was also a test case in regard to the procedures of the Congested Districts Board which, despite good work, had become embroiled in government policy on war recruitment. In its land redistribution practices, the board seemed to favour people who had close relatives in the British army. Fr O'Flanagan later accused the Board of acting 'as the masters instead of the servants of the people'. When the Board refused local access to bog at Cloonkeen O'Flanagan asked whether his parishioners could be expected 'to allow their children shiver in the cold next winter'. After Mass on 29 June 1915, he advised everyone 'who wants a turfbank and can work a turf spade' to go to the waste bog on the following day. Fr O'Flanagan led two hundred people who cut twelve hundred cubic feet of turf and banked it close to the RIC barracks. The case received wide publicity. Eventually it reached the High Court where an injunction was granted. After some months the matter was resolved by a partial allotment of the disputed bog without prejudice to other needy people.[9]

Such public action seems to have displeased Bishop Coyne. The breaking point may have been reached in October 1915 when O'Flanagan publicly contested government policy on food production for the war effort. The venue was a meeting in Sligo addressed by T. W. Russell of the Board of Agriculture. Fr O'Flanagan's stormy intervention may well have been meant as a criticism of the 'war effort'. In regard to the purpose of the meeting, viz increase in agricultural output, he argued: 'The famine of 1847 would never have been written across the pages of Irish history if the men of that day ... risked death rather than part with their oat crop'. Using vivid images from the Famine period,

O'Flanagan called on each farmer to retain enough oats for his family until the next harvest. For decades, the call 'Stick to the Oats' would be associated with the priest of Cliffoney.[10]

There were more immediate consequences, however. In a matter of days O'Flanagan was transferred from his parish. The move discloses unease of both church and state at social criticism made in public. Although Ml O'Flanagan accepted the move to Crossna, Co Roscommon, his parishioners barred the church to his successor, Fr McHugh. Despite repeated demands for O'Flanagan's restoration, Dr Coyne stood firm. The church remained closed until Christmas Day 1915.

Crossna

Fr O'Flanagan's new appointment brought him to the remote but very beautiful district of Cootehall, near Boyle. If the move was intended to silence a turbulent priest it did not succeed. There is ample evidence that Ml O'Flanagan's interests ran more widely than the parochial. Already he had served as an executive member of Conradh na Gaeilge. Likewise, for several years he was on the non-resident executive of the Sinn Féin party led by Arthur Griffith.

During Jan 1916, a meeting in Cork protested against 'economic conscription' by local employers who forced their employees to enlist in the British Army. O'Flanagan's address received wide publicity as disrespectful of the 'war effort'. Cooler analysis shows that it went no further than advanced nationalist opinion of the day. Mildly pro-German overtones can be discerned in some of his remarks, e.g. that talk about a German invasion was scaremongering and that 'the Germans would be no worse than the English'. The *Cork Constitution* editorialised on insult to Protestants and humiliation of 'the better-educated members of the Roman Catholic community'. One such Catholic wrote of 'the scurrilous attitude and speech of Fr Michael O'Flanagan and those priests who supported him'. (The platform was occupied also by several Capuchin fathers.) Police memoranda detailed 'a very disloyal

speech by Rev Ml O'Flanagan' while Lord Midleton complained to Dublin Castle about his remarks on the war effort.
Approaches were made to Cardinal Logue (Armagh) to discipline the refractory priest. Within days of his return to
Crossna, O'Flanagan was ordered by his bishop not to attend
meetings outside his own parish without his (Bishop Coyne's)
written permission.[11]

Articles on the Land Question

Whatever his attitude to Dr Coyne's order, Fr O'Flanagan
did not regard himself as forbidden to use his pen. In April
1916, a private letter to the rector of the Irish College, Rome,
(Monsignor O'Hagan) discloses some impatience with the
clerical leadership as based on routine and conformity – the
very opposite of 'breadth of vision and capacity to get out of a
rut'. Through 1916 O'Flanagan wrote prolifically on social
and political issues, especially in D. P. Moran's *Leader*. Several
articles (March-April 1916), ostensibly on the Congested
Districts Board, disclose his sympathy with agrarian radicalism. Appropriation of ranches, redistribution of large farms
and resettlement of landless people become his dominant
theme. In 'The Congested Districts Board and the Ranches'
(*Leader*, 1 April 1916), O'Flanagan argues that since ranches
were against the interests of landless people and small farmers,
it was government's duty to 'clear them out of the people's
way'. Failing that, cattle driving and occupation of fallow
land (which had occurred in some places) did not 'constitute
agrarian outrage'. Rather, they vindicated 'that elemental
sense of justice, springing from the unspoiled conscience of
the people'. A few years later, the conservative economic policy of the first Dáil rejected O'Flanagan's agrarian views as excessively radical. In the meantime, he argued for rural self-suf-
ficiency through reliance on staple foods such as potatoes and
oats. ('Wheat or Oats', *Leader* 25 March). Again, there is an
interesting subversiveness to O'Flanagan's exposure of patronage, local and national. Instead of seeking favours people

should look for their rights: '(those) who are kept busy looking for favours ... will never give much trouble looking for
rights ... as soon as the Irish people learn to despise favours
... they will have some chance of getting rights' ('The CDB
and Patronage', *Leader*, 22 April). On 8 April ('The Pace of
the Congested Districts Board'), he derided the pace of the
board, calling for someone to 'hustle the business of land redistribution along'.

The Easter Rising and Its Aftermath

A glorious protest? A disgraceful stab in the back'? So it
was for the *Irish Independent* and the *Irish Times*. Excoriation
of the participants was followed by calls for punishment of
the leaders. What were the views of Ml O'Flanagan? Writing
to the *Freeman's Journal* in June 1916, he raised the issue of interned prisoners. Because of censorship he was unable to ar-
ticulate his views on the rising itself: these would come later.
There is no evidence that O'Flanagan knew of the rising beforehand. Since it was a small group who decided to initiate
the rising we can conclude that O'Flanagan did not have early
notice of it. That is not to say he remained unaffected – he
knew P. H. Pearse and Thomas Clarke personally and, very
likely, other signatories of the Easter manifesto. Given his
speech at O'Donovan's funeral, it can be assumed that he
shared their aspirations.

Republicanism Resurgent

Even by April 1916, Irish nationalists had not yet articulated
an agreed republican programme. Many remained optimistic
about Home Rule as a means for progress in education, culture, and national economy. Liberal Protestants, (for example, Isaac Nelson and J. B. Armour) had believed that Home
Rule could facilitate democratic politics with people of all traditions working for an equitable society. During 1916,
Armour (an enthusiastic supporter of John Redmond) criticised Asquith's proposals for the exclusion of northern counties

from Home Rule. In Armour's view, Redmond had worked honourably for this solution to the 'Irish Question' but had been cynically betrayed by capitulation to unionist pressure.

At this stage, the context of O'Flanagan's thought is indeed the Easter rising. Perhaps even more he engages with Asquith's revival of the idea of Home Rule with six northern counties excluded. How firm was Asquith's proposal it is difficult to gauge – it may have been a ploy to mitigate American criticism on the executions of the 1916 leaders. On 23 June, a conference of nationalist politicians at Omagh reluctantly accepted Asquith's proposals. D. P. Moran's *Leader* also toyed with the idea: the prospect of freedom for four fifths of Ireland was preferable to all Ireland under martial law with a vague promise of Home Rule after the war. On the other hand, people like Armour saw it as the worst of all prospects emphasising that nobody wanted the dismemberment of the country. Meanwhile, a group of northern lawyers headed by George Gavan Duffy, George Murnaghan and Fergus O'Connor, founded the Irish Nation League to counteract the danger of partition. They received considerable support from liberal Protestants and, indeed, from a number of Catholic bishops.

O'Flanagan's subsequent history shows him to be a separatist/republican in sentiment and conviction. Nevertheless, two of his stances at this time were considerably nuanced on Home Rule and relations with Protestants who opposed it. As evinced in his *Freeman's Journal* letter (20 June), his sympathies are with Irish political prisoners. Yet, the letter recommends acceptance of Asquith's proposals and defends northern unionists' rights to opt out of an all-Ireland parliament. Years later, political opponents of O'Flanagan would cite the letter as an instance of his 'weather cock' political instincts. Others, most recently John Biggs-Davison, used the letter to support a 'two-nations' theory.[12]

Hence, O'Flanagan's arguments require some examination even though he later moved beyond them. Part of his argu-

ment is from political consequences: rejection of Home Rule
would lose support for Ireland's case in in America and elsewhere. Later, in debate with Louis Walsh (a spokesman for
the Irish Nation League), he claimed that his position arose
also from recognition of 'the great advantage of getting control of our education so that we might be able to proceed
rapidly with the revival of the Irish language which (is the)
bulwark of our nationality' (*Leader*, 20 Oct 1916).

Relations with Northern Unionists

In view of recent developments in the Irish 'peace process'
and, in particular, a search for accommodation between
Unionist and Nationalist traditions, Ml O'Flanagan's contributions on that subject are worthy of closer attention.
Through Summer/Autumn 1916, his *Freeman's* letter and subsequent articles in the *Leader* addressed the question of double minorities in Ireland with an approach both novel and
provocative. With some understatement he put it: 'the Ulster
difficulty is a real difficulty'. Yet he welcomed the difficulty
since it was also an opportunity: 'When we solve the Ulster
difficulty we shall realise the dream of past generations of
Irishmen' (*Leader*, 2 Sept 1916). He proposed removing the
question of Irish unity from 'supra-rational mysticism' to 'entirely profane and secular' democratic politics. The primary
fact was that 'the Orangeman has as much right to live as a
Greenman'. If, as nationalists claimed, the principle of nationality entailed government in accordance with the will of
the people, then it was wrong to govern the people of Antrim
and Down against the will of the majority in these counties.
And, argued O'Flanagan, if anyone wished to know the nationality of another, the best test was 'Ask him'. Another dis-
turbing claim was made in the *Freeman's* letter. The argument
for national unity could not be made on geography alone. In
Ireland, geographical unity and national unity were not iden-
tical: 'Geography has worked hard to make one nation out of
Ireland; history has worked against it'. Nor could the Ulster

Unionists be coerced to transfer their allegiances. In an often-cited passage, Fr O'Flanagan asked: 'After three hundred years England has begun to despair of compelling us to love her by force. Are we … to start where England left off and … compel Antrim and Down to love us by force?' Predictably, the letter and the *Leader* articles caused a furore, especially among nationalists. Louis Walsh suggested that O'Flanagan should now burn references to his O'Donovan speech of 1915. John Dillon (Irish Party) regarded the letter as partitionist. In face of criticism, O'Flanagan retained his nerve: 'since I began to write about the Ulster question, I have been told that I have lost the confidence of many of my friends. I knew before I began to write that that would be one of the consequences. But what was I to do? Guess first what would please my friends and then write? We have too many men in Ireland engaged in that game'.[13]

The extensive *Leader* debate carried on through the summer and autumn. Taken as a whole, it outlines the political values which would emerge as Sinn Féin became a resurgent political force. It discloses Ml O'Flanagan's own respect for both the unionist and nationalist traditions. It evinces his view that the 'Irish Question' was soluble only by Irish people themselves (ironically, this is another version of Sinn Féin!). As he put it: 'We have to come to an agreement with the Ulster Covenanters even though it be only an agreement to differ. We have begun to treat them as fellow men. If we go a little further along the road, we may find after a time that they will be willing to treat us as fellow countrymen' (*Leader* 2 Sept 1916). With particular insistence he argues: if we reject the Unionist claim to a homogeneous Ulster, we cannot also claim that Ireland is homogeneous. Although holding firmly to the view that Ireland had a right to political autonomy, he also re-echoes James Connolly in declaring that 'the principal thing about a nation is not the land but the people' (*Leader*, 30 Sept 1916). At no stage did O'Flanagan deride the non-nationalist tradition. Rather, he argued that both traditions have equal right to respect. Twenty years later, during the Spanish Civil War, he paid special tribute to northern Protestants who opposed Franco in Spain.

The *Leader* correspondence shows that Fr O'Flanagan believed coercion of Ulster unionists was both wrong and unfeasible. An independent Ireland could no more subdue Ulster than could England hold Ireland as a peaceful colony. What, then, was the way forward? In an article of 23 Sept he discussed three options, viz. leave things as they are; 'educate or win' Ulster (as recommended by Louis Walsh); address the real seat of the trouble. Discussing these options he has in mind a reformed Ireland with legal, educational and social change. To Louis Walsh's proposal of 'educating Ulster' by cultivation of open-minded Unionists, O'Flanagan posed a counter question – was it not a question of educating Ireland as a whole? It is clear, even in summer 1916, that he regarded the seat of the trouble as the abuse of religion and politics. It was wrong to gather people under the banner of religion and devote the resultant organisation to purely political ends. Doubtless, he had in mind the Ancient Order of Hibernians, the Orange Order and, probably, involvement of churchmen in keeping orange and nationalist politics 'under ecclesiastical influence. This eroded the 'taproot' of democratic freedoms. Religion was abused for unworthy ends while politics was debased by ecclesiastical sanctions where these had no right to operate. In a challenge directed to his own community he argued: 'when we are in a position to assert that such double interference has not merely ceased but that we have provided against its recrudescence then we shall stand upon that clear and solid ground ... for us to educate and win Ulster'.[14]

O'Flanagan's essays are courageously imaginative. For all their weak points, they explore political options while addressing opponents with delicacy and sensitivity. They are all the more remarkable in that their author was not deeply conversant with the northern situation of division and bigotry. As a result of such limited experience, there are discernible weaknesses in his arguments. One of these may be a naïvete about Orange readiness for a friendly approach. Over a year later, in an address at Omagh, he proposed 'to look beneath the ugly husk of Orangeism for the precise kernel that Ireland needs in her future development'. In response to a sceptical comment about this openness, he admitted that the weak point in his argument was Orange hostility. Nationalists could not expect to convert Orangemen. The task was to build 'an Irish democracy broad, tolerant and reasonably (sic) democratic – a democracy that would make no distinction between Protestant and Catholic'. Perhaps over-optimistically, he opined that when this was achieved 'all that was best in the orange movement would join their (nationalist) movement'.[15] Such weaknesses were deftly but courteously exposed by Louis Walsh in the *Leader* correspondence. For example, O'Flanagan had not taken up the question of guarantees to Ulster nationalists. After 1922, this issue would considerably develop O'Flanagan's own thinking. Another weakness is that although he constantly referred to Antrim and Down, where there were Unionist majorities, such was not the case in the other Ulster counties. Certainly, the logic of his case did not fit the demographics of the six north eastern counties of Ireland.

Democratic Politics

Throughout the *Leader* correspondence one notices O'Flanagan's emphasis on a secular, democratic model of politics. In essence, he was proposing a new model where 'the rank and file of the people' exercised their own political judgement. Such judgement was to be motivated not by direction from above and for confessional interests but rather by the objective of justice for all. Decrying clerical influence, his view was that it fostered institutional advantage and sectarian division rather than genuine democracy. Collusion between church and state degraded politics and religion. At Omagh, O'Flanagan hoped that Irish politics would be genuinely republican or, at least, 'be decided upon under a free, independent Ireland by vote of the Irish people'. As he put it, the task of bishops and priests was not to teach people politics – 'they had just one man's right to Irish citizenship … it was the man who counted, not the collar'. In another reference, he gave a hostage to the future: 'if the secular life of the Irish people is to be held in the grip of an ecclesiastical organisation imposing its will upon the people, I will go to Belfast to sign the covenant'.[16]

The Election of the Snows (Feb 1917)

By August 1916 a regrouping of advanced nationalists was afoot. The Irish National Aid and Volunteer Dependents' Fund became a unitary body. With Michael Collins as organising secretary, it soon became an ideal base on which to rebuild the Irish Republican Brotherhood. Also in August, the Gaelic League's annual convention paid tribute to 'the heroes who died in the rising'. Meanwhile, a reconstituted council of the Irish Republican Brotherhood established contact with Irish nationalists in the United States. In October, the Irish Nation League called for release of prisoners, resistance to conscription and implementation of national self-government. When J. J. O'Kelly, Stephen O'Mara and Laurence Ginnell joined the League, it moved closer to the politics of the executed leaders. Sinn Féin oscillated, badly served by Herbert Pim (a convert from Unionism) who was in secret conversations with Dublin Castle. As yet, there was no concerted strategy among the diverse groups and a by-election (West Cork) was easily won by a Redmondite.

The aftermath of the Easter rising was felt in Roscommon, particularly as news of imprisonments and executions filtered through the country. During a radio broadcast (January 1938), O'Flanagan spoke of people's despair in the months after the rising. A wave of state terrorism was unleashed. The army raided homes and parish halls. Arrests continued. Above all were the executions in Dublin. Though posed in 1938, Fr

O'Flanagan's question gives a clue to his thought while still at Crossna: 'would the example of the inspiration of the men of 1916 or the terror caused by their defeat have the greater effect?' On 22 December 1916, the MP for North Roscommon (James J O'Kelly) died. O'Kelly's popularity gave reason to believe that John Redmond's Irish Party would retain the seat. Viewed in hindsight, the North Roscommon poll (Feb 1917) reveals the unobserved changes at work in the months following the rebellion. At the election, George Plunkett (father of Joseph Mary Plunkett) sought endorsement of the Easter rising. After the count of votes, Michael O'Flanagan interpreted the victory as such an endorsement. In a triple claim he argued that Plunkett's election showed the feelings of the people were 'those of the men who had kept alight the torch of freedom handed down from Wolfe Tone and Robert Emmet'; that the people now rejected Redmond's party for its oscillation about the rising; that the time had come to reject 'the present policy of corruption and job seeking'. Meanwhile, the press deemed Plunkett's election 'an act of defiant treason at the polls'. Perceptively, the *Irish Times* foresaw that Redmond's party could be swept out of three quarters of their seats 'by the same forces that carried Count Plunkett to victory (in a constituency) believed to be so peaceful and so free from Sinn Féin and the rebellion taint'.[17]

The electoral campaign was truly remarkable. Years later, Peadar O'Donnell spoke of young men and women, who despite a standstill caused by the weather 'swept the county in a mass canvas'.[18] These included Michael Collins, Arthur Griffith, Rory O'Connor, Kevin O'Shiel and many others who would later come to prominence in national politics. As initiator of Plunkett's candidacy, as organiser and speaker throughout the campaign, Fr Michael O'Flanagan was central to this 'election of the snows'. He influenced small farmers by emphasising land reform. His repudiation of conscription found resonance with families throughout the constituency. Countless others listened sympathetically to his evocation of the Easter rising. His critique of the Irish Party was effective in its focus on John Redmond's trust in London's *bona fides*.

Particularly noticeable was O'Flanagan's organisational flair. To facilitate the campaign, he directed a mass clearing of snow-bound roads. Likewise, he ensured a maximal turn-out on polling day – it was better that young men 'carry their fathers on their backs ... than have to serve as conscripts in the trenches in Flanders'. Louis Walsh, O'Flanagan's erstwhile critic and now a helper in the campaign, wrote: 'Fr O'Flanagan would carry any nationalist constituency ... his wonderful influence creates rather a puzzle for me ... because so much of the victory was due to his marvellous personality I am wondering if the results of the election really represent an awakening of the country as we would fain believe it to be.'[19] Again in hindsight, several positions can be argued. With Plunkett's election for North Roscommon a new chapter in modern Irish history was opening and to that change Ml O'Flanagan had contributed hugely.

Sinn Féin

The North Roscommon outcome and Plunkett's declaration that he would not attend a 'usurper Westminster parliament' prompted Kilkenny Corporation to make him a freeman of the city. At the civic event, Fr O'Flanagan declared that Redmond's party was leading Ireland into a political quagmire, that it was now time to raise Ireland's case at the mooted Peace Conference and to stop 'bargaining for crumbs in a foreign Parliament at Westminster'. This strongly political address incurred a rebuke from Bishop Coyne. The bishop threatened suspension from his ministry if O'Flanagan continued to address public meetings. Thus, in June 1917, when a South Longford election was fought by the interned Joseph McGuinness (the slogan was 'Put him in to get him out'), Fr O'Flanagan could not address the hustings. Instead, he *wrote* for a pre-election meeting in Longford's Market Square. Referring to clerical support of the Irish Party candidate, he criticised an abuse of power which was damaging Irish politics. In evident allusion to Bishop Coyne's prohibition he regretted that religion was being used 'as a weapon in party political struggles'.[20]

At Crossna, Fr O'Flanagan continued his ministry. Although he has not documented personal difficulties, it was for him a time of strain. Certainly he believed that a new social-cultural-political revolution was afoot and that he should contribute in whatever manner his talents allowed. A year later, his Omagh speech (August 1917) with its criticism of ecclesiastical politics, led to a protracted absence from his parish. In a welter of rumour (for example, that Cardinal Logue was insisting on his suspension), his immediate superior, Fr Tom Flanagan, described him as 'a wonderful priest, popular with all, as well as with Protestant neighbours and their clergy'. Yet, there was a dilemma of conscience – ecclesiastical obedience or quitting a process in which he was now deeply involved. One discerns the dilemma in his letter to Sinn Féin's Castlerea branch regretting inability to attend their convention 'except on conditions that would make my presence injurious to the movement rather than beneficial'.[21]

Vice-President of Sinn Féin (1917)

The primary task of the Sinn Féin convention (26-27 Oct) was to agree a new constitution. Preparatory work had been done by sub-committees. The Plunkett Convention (April), the Mansion House Committee (it met several times through the summer), the drafting group itself, disclosed varying aspirations. Compromises were made which appear in the constitution itself. Sinn Féin's objective was recognition of an independent Irish republic. However, this was qualified by the proviso that when an independent Ireland was achieved 'the Irish people may by referendum freely choose their own form of government'. The formulation held together at least two strands. Arthur Griffith had long explored the idea of 'dual monarchy'; Cathal Brugha insisted on the call for a full Irish republic. According to some historians (notably Brian Murphy) Eamon de Valera supplied the compromise – the complete republican demand could be mitigated if circumstances required it. Thus, the Convention avoided disunity and, in the words of Michael Laffan, 'the Sinn Féin movement previously a vague sentiment, like nationalism or separatism, had become an organised and united party'.[22]

There was also the question of office-holders. On the prior withdrawal of Arthur Griffith and Count Plunkett, Eamon de Valera was appointed President of Sinn Féin. With hindsight, one notices in the executive an exact balance of those who would later accept the Anglo-Irish treaty and those who would reject it. Ml O'Flanagan and Arthur Griffith were elected joint Vice-Presidents. Laurence Ginnell and William Cosgrave became treasurers while Austin Stack and Darrel Figgis were elected joint secretaries. Knowing the compromises behind this line-up, O'Flanagan claimed in 1934 that 'the split was there from the start'.[23]

Suspension From Ministry

Returning to Crossna, Fr O'Flanagan realised the difficulties of his situation. As Vice-President of Sinn Féin, he now had national prominence. A round of duties would demand involvement in quasi-political matters. One asks was there not a tension between his criticisms of clergymen in politics and the activities now demanded of him? His own answer was that he acted as a citizen rather than a clergyman exercising religious sanction. Nonetheless, his problems would multiply. In 1918 the majority of the Sinn Féin executive were arrested under the Defense of the Realm Act. With De Valera and Griffith imprisoned, O'Flanagan was acting head of Sinn Féin. Through April and May 1918, he chaired Sinn Féin meetings in Dublin on land reform, economic rejuvenation and reform of political life.

When a by-election in East Cavan was set for May 1918 the tension between parish work and socio-political activity reached a climax. Arthur Griffith was nominated to stand for Sinn Féin. With a threat of conscription still in the air, it was felt that a defeat would embolden the government to enact the rumoured measure. For O'Flanagan, there was also the matter of Dr Coyne's repeated threat of suspension from ministry. Yet, he decided to take part in the campaign deeming the overall good of the people 'more fundamental than the commands of an individual bishop'.[24] In the campaign, the conscription threat and Ireland's right to self-government became the focus of his addresses. His analysis of the war runs exactly counter to that of J. B. Armour. While Armour saw it as a great moral endeavour O'Flanagan viewed the war more cynically. The hostilities had been manufactured by 'lying newspapers and lying ministers … sitting in their offices … who play with the lives of men by the millions'. Furthermore, when the war ended 'those royal cousins who rule England and Germany will come together and drink their champagne glasses over the graves of millions of the flower of manhood of both Germany and England'.[25]

Arthur Griffith was indeed elected. Before the end of the month Fr O'Flanagan was suspended from active ministry. Although it cannot have been a surprise, it was a personal blow. To a parishioner he wrote that although 'torn from the altar' he was not 'torn from the hearts of the people'. Years afterwards he revealed that the most valuable support was his mother's recognition of his conscientious decision. When the suspension became known, there were local protests. Parishioners declared that 'from the spiritual point of view no better priest ever set foot in our midst'. The parish priest added high praise for his curate. On the other hand, the *Irish Catholic* termed the parishioners' action 'religious Bolshevism'. The tory press also lauded Bishop Coyne's firmness. Meanwhile, Fr O'Flanagan's successor, Fr Clyne, was prevented from entering Crossna church. The matter was resolved only when O'Flanagan wrote to the parishioners that his difficulties with the bishop should not become an occasion for division or bitterness.[26]

General Election (Dec 1918)

With brief intermissions, Fr O'Flanagan would spend the rest of his life outside parish ministry, a 'silenced' priest. After his suspension he resided in Dublin where, as Vice-President of Sinn Féin, he took part in events now gathering pace. The anticipated general election was moving to the centre of attention. Relations with the Labour Party, ratification of Sinn Féin candidates from the national constituencies, advance publicity etc. were co-ordinated by the executive. Noticing that candidates from the constituencies did not include women, Cumann na mBan (the women's branch of the movement) requested that an electoral strategy, if contested in the spirit of Easter 1916, should include women candidates. Unfortunately, the executive temporised and when it proposed a list of twenty suitable candidates no woman figured amongst these.

Ironically, the campaign which drastically changed Anglo-Irish relations opened on Armistice Day, 1918. In the campaign, Ml O'Flanagan's role was acknowledged for decades by his fellow workers. In essence, his activity recreated on national scale his earlier work during the 'election of the snows'. The Sinn Féin Manifesto becomes the theme of his electoral addresses: withdrawal from Westminster; institution of an Irish parliament; development of Irish resources for the benefit of the people; recourse to any peace conference. Likewise, he emphasised the Irish Party's decline from its earlier radicalism. The party, he claimed, habituated to Westminster's corridors, found it 'second nature' to subordinate Irish interests to those of empire. Pro-war attitudes of Irish Party leaders were an easy target as O'Flanagan stressed that young men were sent to fight for the freedom of every small nation but their own.

O'Flanagan's earlier difficulties at Crossna are recalled by a remark in Longford (Dec 1918). Now, he refers to an earlier time when 'I did not think the time had come to break the muzzle and had to stay away from Longford'.[27] The opportunity had come to bring freedom and prosperity to Ireland.

With Czars and Kaisers gone, it was possible to 'topple the little tin pot Kaisers in this country'.

On the eve of poll, he could report that 'the day of freedom (was) at hand'. The actual count disclosed a landslide victory for Sinn Féin – Sinn Féin (73), Irish Party (6), Unionists (26).

Dáil Éireann

Sinn Féin's victory was both opportunity and challenge. Much remained to do. P S O'Hegarty reports Fr O'Flanagan's remark: 'the people have voted Sinn Féin. What we now have to do is explain to them what Sinn Féin really is'.[28] By the end of December, a joint session of the party and its elected representatives agreed on relations between Sinn Féin and the proposed Dáil. It also worked on a declaration of independence and a message to the international community.

Neither Unionist nor Irish Party attended the first Dáil on 19 Jan 1919 – with the exception of Laurence Ginnell, they went to Westminster. At Dublin's Mansion House, Cathal Brugha presided while Fr O'Flanagan opened the Dáil with a prayer in Irish. Those present (twenty seven, since the others were in prison) declared themselves parliament of the Irish republic. Adopting a provisional constitution, they reaffirmed the 1916 proclamation and endorsed the establishment of the Irish republic. A Democratic Programme was adopted with a strong commitment to provide for the physical, mental and spiritual wellbeing of the nation's children, to ensure that no child should 'suffer ... lack of food, clothing or shelter'. The rights of property were deemed subordinate to the public welfare. The Poor Law System was to be replaced by 'a sympathetic native scheme for the care of the nation's aged and infirm'. The development of the nation's resources were to be 'in the interest and for the benefit of the Irish people'. A major figure in drafting the Programme was Thomas Johnson – 'one of the best informed of the socialists on the fringe of the republican movement'. Johnson's original draft may have been softened by other influences (Michael Collins and Sean T O'Kelly). Even so, it impressively affirms the values of social justice and separatist republicanism. On food policy, on land redistribution, on attention to the people's welfare, the Programme reproduces O'Flanagan's primary concerns through the years. Even if the dawn of equality instanced by the Programme never reached fulfilment, yet it would not have been so bright were it not for those who like him had spoken loudly for radical social change.

In more recent times, during national emergencies, priests in Haiti and Nicaragua felt it their duty to accept public office in education, culture and foreign affairs. Had O'Flanagan stood for election in 1918, he would have succeeded in almost any nationalist constituency. This was not envisaged by him. Despite his conflict with ecclesiastical authority he was clear on his primary commitment as a priest. Yet he also believed that continued public service was demanded of him. As a close link remained between Sinn Féin and the Dáil government, many duties called for his attention. Sinn Féin committees replicated executive departments of the Dáil on national finances, public health, justice, foreign affairs and the Irish language. There was also a department for 'the reconquest of land'. Here, O'Flanagan worked either as a committee member or as Vice-President of the party. From January to May 1919 he attended the weekly meetings of the Sinn Féin executive committee. Likewise, his long standing interest in the co-operative movement initiated by Sir Horace Plunkett resulted in the publication (1922) of his pamphlet on Co-operative Movements.[29]

Reinstatement to Ministry at Roscommon

This reinstatement occurred in May 1919. As with the Callan Curates, an appeal to Rome was involved. Likewise, Archbishop Gilmartin of Tuam was an effective mediator. In any case, Fr O'Flanagan resumed parish duties, this time at Roscommon town. On his return, he articulated ten guiding

principles for republican land courts in the region. These en-
shrine the Judaeo-Christian idea that property rights are secondary to the right to life. Another principle re-echoes
O'Flanagan's earlier argument that the land was for the people rather than privileged individuals: 'when the land is not
being used so as to support a reasonable share of the population, the public has a right to bring about a change of ownership even by the use of force, if necessary'. This sounded too
radical even for the Dáil executive which retreated from earlier promises of its Democratic Programme.[30]

From summer 1920, General Sir Nevil Macready permit-
ted that strange assortment of ex-officers, the Auxiliaries, to
carry out a reign of terror. Alongside them, 'Black and Tans'
committed atrocities in Dublin and elsewhere. The bishops
of Galway and Clonfert directly charged the government with
murder when in November 1920, a young Galway curate, Fr
Griffin, was abducted. In Roscommon, Auxiliaries more than
once raided O'Flanagan's presbytery and threatened to shoot
him. After the first of these threats, O'Flanagan successfully
confronted their commanding officer but thereafter kept a
gun for self-protection.

'Black and Tan' atrocities disquieted·moderate opinion in
England – the Archbishop of Canterbury, George Bernard
Shaw, G. K. Chesterton and, allegedly, King George V. In
Oct 1920, General George Cockerill MP publicly urged a
truce and negotiations 'analogous to that of an International
Conference'. The proposal set in train moves ostensibly
aimed at securing peace terms. Initially, a series of intermedi-
aries shuttled between Dublin and London – an American
journalist John Steele, a Dublin businessman Patrick
Moylette, a British Labour leader Arthur Henderson and
eventually the archbishop of Perth, Dr Clune. It is difficult to
assess Lloyd George's strategy. Aiming at the defeat of Sinn
Féin while placating moderate opinion in England, he constantly shifted ground. On 6 December Fr O' Flanagan con-
tacted him by telegram: 'you state you are willing to make

peace at once ... Ireland also is waiting ... What first step do
you propose?'. A much publicised exchange of telegrams followed and, in January 1921, meetings with Lloyd George. To
the dismay of Michael Collins and the discomfiture of
Eamon de Valera, O'Flanagan undertook ill-co-ordinated initiatives which revealed a lack cohesion among the republican
leadership. De Valera was forced to say of O'Flanagan's initiative: 'it is unofficial ... Fr O'Flanagan speaks for the Sinn
Féin organisation on the spot, and not for the Irish
Parliament and the Irish Government'. Although O'Flanagan
later claimed he was calling Lloyd George's bluff, nonetheless
he had made an error of judgement. It is hard to avoid the
conclusion that he had acted precipitously and had conferred
the edge of advantage to the British side. His unilateral activity caused dissension among republicans, duly noticed by the
British leadership. Wryly, Collins put it: 'Possibly after his ad-
ventures, he will see things in their true perspective'. Brian
Murphy, a sympathetic commentator, admits that
O'Flanagan 'broke ranks with his closest allies, but while engaging in consultations, lacked the authority to enforce a policy decision'.[31]

Second Dáil

Although there were calls for censure of 'attempts at surrender', De Valera circumvented them. Fr O'Flanagan remained on the Sinn Féin executive. At this period of Anglo-
Irish negotiation his public speeches evidence a belief that the
future held 'a more bitter war than the war we have passed
through'. Those who were making the best preparations for
peace might well be those who are preparing 'to renew the war
if necessary'. O'Flanagan was centrally involved in a general
election fixed for May 1921. An issue was the Government of
Ireland Act (1920) which Sinn Féin candidates pledged to oppose. In the same anti-partition context, O'Flanagan wrote
for a short lived journal, *The Unionist*, arguing that partition
was a disservice to Unionists and Nationalists.[32]

'Irish Envoys' in America, Australia and Canada

By the end of the Anglo-Irish negotiations and a resultant treaty, Ml O'Flanagan was in the United States. Immediately after his re-election as Vice-President of Sinn Féin (Oct 1921), he was sent to America 'as an apostle to explain our cause ... that the Irish were simply fighting for their rights'. These words of De Valera mask the reluctance of some, notably Michael Collins, to endorse O'Flanagan's nomination for the task. Another instance of disagreement among the leadership is given by J J O'Kelly who later claimed that O'Flanagan expressed the fear that while he was in America the claims for an Irish republic would be mitigated by the official negotiators in London.[33]

In America, where opinion mirrored divisions in Ireland, O'Flanagan presented the case for an Irish republic.[34] As events unfolded, he adopted an anti-Treaty stance. He cast the treaty as perfidy on the part of British politicians and those in Ireland who collaborated with them. In Canada he criticised Irish bishops who had supported the treaty. As he put it, their judgement should be respected in religious matters; when, however, it came to politics, they were usually on the wrong side. In Australia, O'Flanagan documented the Free State offensive on republicans – 'the same old war under new guise ... the voice may be the voice of Cosgrave but the hand is the hand of Bonar Law'. Lenten pastorals of Cardinal Logue and Bishop Coyne, exported abroad, condemned anti-Treaty stances in virulent terms. When O'Flanagan publicly disagreed with these, Fr Wm Mangan, editor of the *Melbourne Tribune*, accused him of besmirching the good name of the Catholic priesthood. Terrorism, he claimed, was 'the gentle aim and object of Fr O'Flanagan'. In the three cities where O'Flanagan spoke (Melbourne, Sydney and Brisbane) he was opposed by Archbishops Kelly (Sydney) and Duhig (Brisbane) while Archbishop Mannix (Melbourne) made no secret of his support. Eventually, O'Flanagan and O'Kelly were arrested and after two months in prison were deported to the United States.[35]

Ireland again

In February 1925, Ml O'Flanagan returned to Ireland. Ostensibly, he had been recalled by de Valera to help in a series of by-elections. Ireland was now a changed place, ridden by the legacy of civil war. Republicans were harassed, precluded from employment and sometimes refused the sacraments of their church. Apologists for the Free State, lay and clerical, fulminated against its opponents. During a bitter election campaign, O'Flanagan's criticism of civil and ecclesiastical leadership alarmed the more timorous of his Sinn Féin colleagues. He argued that the Free State was the same old shop. Nothing had changed except 'the label over the shop door'. Behind the counter was 'the same old stuff'. As to the church, it had become an instrument 'to bludgeon the people into submission'. The sacraments had been abused by religious sanctions and, in such conditions, it was better to go without than receive them in degrading conditions.[36]

At the personal level, this was a difficult time for O'Flanagan. His mother's death occasioned a tribute to her support when Sinn Féin colleagues wanted him to capitulate to Dr Coyne. More publicly, a letter to the *Roscommon Herald* deemed him 'an evil germ in the political world as well as false to the obligations of his sacred calling'. The conservatism of the decade is exemplified in the rejection by a Sinn Féin candidate of O'Flanagan's criticisms of the hierarchy. Regarding them as an electoral liability, M J O'Mullane (Dublin South) added that '(O'Flanagan's) words could not but injure the deep religious feeling of the Irish people'. Then, there was Dr Coyne's re-imposition (April 1925) of earlier suspensions. The bishop cited a 'solemn and scathing denunciation' by Dr Duhig of Brisbane and claimed that O'Flanagan had given 'disedifying harangues to excited mobs at five places in the diocese of Elphin'. If Fr O'Flanagan had any intention of returning to parish ministry, that was now precluded.[37]

Social Critic

And so, perhaps reluctantly, O'Flanagan returned to Dublin where he lived in simple lodgings at Commons St. After poor results (Sinn Féin won two seats out of a possible nine), he seemed to have espoused a lost cause. At this stage, the closest socio-political analysis from a fragmented republican leadership is Art O'Connor's *Notes on National Economy*. With the emergence of *An Phoblacht* (1925), O'Flanagan wrote a series of articles from June to December. They contain socio-religious criticism of official life in the Irish Free State and clearly place him well to the left of the political spectrum. Long absence from the country and perhaps a certain distance from the leadership make his articles somewhat general though they remain typically challenging. Certainly, they provide valuable antidote to a reigning conservatism in Irish life during the mid-1920s.[38]

Split in Sinn Féin

Defeat in the by-elections of 1925 caused heart-searching in Sinn Féin. A change of direction was presaged by Sean Lemass's references in *An Phoblacht* to immobility besetting Sinn Féin. Lemass criticised those who sat by the roadside debating 'abstract points about a *de iure* this and a *de facto* that'.[39] Unless some moves were made, Sinn Féin's objectives would never be attained. On 6 January 1926, Eamon de Valera signalled his intention to enter Leinster House if the oath of allegiance were removed. He circulated a motion that entering either the twenty-six county or six county assemblies would become a question not of principle but of policy, 'once the admission oaths ... are removed'. Taken by surprise, Sinn Féin's executive declared the proposals were a personal initiative of the President. Ml O'Flanagan raised an amendment that 'it is incompatible with the fundamental principles of Sinn Féin ... to send representatives into an usurping Legislature set up by English law in Ireland'.[40] The debate continued until a special Ard Fheis on 9-10 March. Here, Fr

O'Flanagan's amendment was carried by a narrow margin
(223 to 218). On 11 March, De Valera resigned as President of
Sinn Féin. Thereafter, a steady trickle of resignations deprived
the party of figures such as Sean Lemass, Gerald Boland and
Constance Markievicz. In May, the Fianna Fáil party was
founded at Dublin's La Scala. Under the slogan of New
Departure, a nascent Fianna Fáil received approval of the IRA
and social radicals such as Peadar O'Donnell. When
O'Donnell assumed the editorship of *An Phoblacht* he expressed the hope that the realism of Sean Lemass and Patrick
Ruttledge would effect a much needed change in Irish political life.

Wilderness?

As to Sinn Féin, it became entrapped in a cul-de-sac of
dogmatism and recrimination. A tragi-comedy of squabbling
and neurotic concern for minutiae occupied its meetings. Old
colleagues of O'Flanagan like Thomas O'Deirg and Patrick
Ruttledge joined Fianna Fáil while people less congenial
dominated the standing committee. Some of these mistrusted
his sympathy with the social radicalism of Peadar O'Donnell
and George Gilmore. Likewise, they recoiled from his trenchant criticisms of the hierarchical church. At this period,
Sinn Féin was virtually a spent force in politics, concentrating
instead on educational, cultural and propaganda work.
Isolated in its Dublin head-office, its instruments were confined to what Peadar O'Donnell termed 'a rule book and a
typewriter'. Wordy communiques were issued to a largely indifferent press. The IRA, the military arm of the movement,
discounted the republican 'politicians'. The minutes of these
years show that energies were sapped on personal disputes,
e.g. Mary MacSwiney and Brian O'Higgins watched Ml
O'Flanagan suspiciously. When issues came up for practical
action (e.g. Peadar O'Donnell's proposals for opposition to
land annuities), the executive took refuge in broad generali-
ties but eschewed practical involvement.

The late 1920s became for Ml O'Flanagan a period of continuing frustration although he maintained a round of public addresses in Dublin and elsewhere. In a Glasgow address he singled out James Connolly's aspiration that the Irish people should be not merely 'the political rulers of Ireland but the economic owners of Ireland as well'(*An Phoblacht*, 4 June 1926). Personal dissensions between him and Mary MacSwiney emerged at the Ard Fheis of Dec. 1927 amid rumours that he was about to quit Sinn Féin. This did not happen although he refused nomination to the standing committee. For some months he devoted much time to editing the O'Donovan letters, a project which had for long been suggested by advanced nationalists.[41]

Fianna Fáil in Government

From 1927, Sinn Féin's political fortunes stood in inverse proportion to Fianna Fáil. Rigidity isolated it, even from groups pursuing the same objectives. A policy of non-cooperation with Fianna Fáil precluded activities which might have helped morale among the younger members. Work with the Anti-Imperialist League, agitation for release of political prisoners, even Bodenstown commemorations, were forbidden unless there were guarantees that no one 'associated with Leinster House' was involved. When Patrick Pearse's mother died in April 1932, Sinn Féin took no official part in the obsequies because of her support of Eamon de Valera. It should be noted that Fr O'Flanagan, once again a Vice-President of the party, did not endorse the absurd decision to stay away from Mrs Pearse's funeral. In regard to Wolfe Tone commemorations, an exasperated IRA leader wrote to the Sinn Féin executive: 'it is extraordinary that all republicans cannot join even in a matter as clear and simple as the pilgrimage to Wolfe Tone's grave ... what ought to be a national demonstration is being dragged down into a sectional affair'.[42]

Nonetheless, as the general election of 1932 approached, republicans sensed that the Cosgrave government could be defeated. For many, including Sinn Féin members, the priority was to unseat that administration. Mary MacSwiney, an apostle of non-cooperation with Leinster House, advised republicans to 'put out the murder gang', even if that meant voting for Fianna Fáil. With the help of some Sinn Féin members (it was later said that seventy five per cent of Sinn Féin members voted in the election) and the tacit support of the IRA, Fianna Fáil did come to power.[43] Among its first initiatives were release of political prisoners and acceleration of slum clearance. There were meetings with IRA leaders on future co-operation between the new government and republicans generally. In *An Phoblacht* (2 April), Peadar O'Donnell called on republicans to 'Give Fianna Fáil A Chance'.

As to the Sinn Féin executive, it relapsed into a witch-hunt of those who had either worked or voted for 'the newer Free State Party'. When this question was discussed at the 1932 Ard Fheis, Fr O'Flanagan argued that no one should be disciplined for what was not covered by rule. In other words, he did not agree with futile recriminations. Months later, when right-wing elements attacked Connolly House, the newly-founded Workers' College at Gt. Strand St., Ml O'Flanagan reprobated the 'mob hysteria masquerading as religion' which he believed was behind the attack.[44]

Work With Dept. of Education

A flexibility within republicanism in regard to the new government is disclosed by the claim of one younger member, earlier mentioned, that three quarters of the Sinn Féin party had voted in the 1932 election. As regards Fr O'Flanagan, it is notable that longstanding friends had become cabinet ministers, e.g. Tomas Ó'Deirg and Patrick Ruttledge. In Summer 1932, Ó'Deirg moved a Dáil vote on preparation of county histories for use in schools. Proposing Fr O'Flanagan as editor of the project, Ó'Deirg spoke of his proficiency in Irish as well as his long standing work on the O'Donovan and O'Curry letters. Ó'Deirg described Fr O'Flanagan as 'particu-

larly fitted to produce works having a national tone and particularly fitted for Irish pupils'. The proposal was carried despite oblique criticism from Frank McDermot and Brooke
Brasier (a Universities' representative). Thereafter, Fr O'Flanagan
worked at the National Library where with the help of a small
staff he completed eight volumes of county history.[45]

Perhaps the appointment reflects esteem of O'Deirg and
de Valera for O'Flanagan's long service in cultural-political
matters. It may also have been a delicate way of attending to
the priest's financial needs in the absence of any diocesan
stipend. For his personal circumstances it brought a security
lacking for many years and later he was able to buy a home in
Sandyford, Co Dublin. Besides, the project would, doubtless,
have interested his enthusiasm for local history as a valuable
educational aid. To use J. J. O'Kelly's phrase, the project was
'sufficiently valuable in the national sense to justify its prosecution even under the aegis of the Department of
Education'.[46]

Within Sinn Féin, things were different. Mary MacSwiney
fulminated against the deception – it was, she claimed, collaboration with the Free State administration. Albinia
Broderick's *Irish Freedom* was equally stringent. An American
correspondent to Sinn Féin's executive spoke of 'surrender to
England's traitorous Free State'. The same correspondent
called for expulsion from Sinn Féin of all who accepted pen-
sions from Leinster House or who voted in elections for either
Dublin or Belfast administrations.

President of Sinn Féin (Oct 1933)

A feature of republican politics of the early 1930s was the
mistrust of the IRA in regard to 'politicians'. Under this heading came the Sinn Féin party and the survivors of the pro-
rogued Second Dáil who claimed still to be the government
of the republic. To some degree, tensions in Sinn Féin reflect
these wider divisions. A socially radical wing, led by Peadar
O'Donnell, Frank Ryan and George Gilmore, moved towards

explicitly left wing politics (Saor Éire). A more traditional group, exemplified by Mary MacSwiney and Brian O'Higgins, feared that involvement in social questions would distract from republican objectives. It is notable that Fr O'Flanagan retained links with all groups, agreeing with O'Donnell on the need for practical politics yet taking no active part either in Saor Éire (1931) or the Republican Congress (1934). O'Flanagan's election as President (1 October 1933) indicates that republicans did not support the criticisms raised by MacSwiney, Broderick and O'Higgins. Almost immediately, he concentrated on revitalising the party. Heartened by the election, J. J. O'Kelly said the new president brought 'plenty of energy and no small degree of popularity in many places' – doubtless, this referred to O'Flanagan's standing among Irish republicans and in the US. At his first executive meeting, O'Flanagan proposed fund raising (in Ireland and America), employing a national organiser and publishing a weekly newspaper. As well, he proposed that Sinn Féin's policy should be 'to abolish the existing anti-Christian capitalist order and substitute in its place a social order based on Christian principles and their practical application as laid down in the teachings of James Connolly and James Fintan Lalor'.[47]

Throughout the year O'Flanagan combined work at the National Library with visits to local Sinn Féin cumainn in Ireland and Scotland. To some degree, his friendship with Maurice Twomey (IRA chief of staff) mitigated the distrust of IRA leadership in regard to 'political' discussions. In May 1934, talks between the IRA, Sinn Féin and the Second Dáil executive were held at Flemings' Hotel, Dublin. The IRA refused to place itself under political control and Second Dáil personnel feared that Sinn Féin might overshadow them. In these unquiet circumstances, the initiative came to nothing. Meanwhile, the emergence of proto-fascism and prevalent economic distress led Sean Edwards, Frank Murray and Michael O'Riordan to form the Irish Communist Party.

Protestant and Catholic workers in Belfast made common cause on social issues while a Protestant contingent attended Wolfe Tone commemorations at Bodenstown. An effort to harness these initiatives was made by O'Donnell, Gilmore and Ryan who organised an Irish Republican Congress at Rathmines in Sept 1934. Foreseeing tensions inherent to left-right wing politics, the IRA leadership opposed Congress – eventually, O'Donnell and Gilmore were expelled from the IRA. Minutes of Sinn Féin's executive record its fear of Congress's 'Marxist overtones'. Yet, the congress went ahead and tried to shape a new alignment in Irish politics. Although the congress did valuable work for more than a year, ideological dissensions led to its eventual dissolution.

These factors lie behind O'Flanagan's presidential address to Sinn Féin's Árd Fheis in Oct 1934.[48] He defines republicanism as service to the common good. As distinct from a monarchy (where the individual is a subject), in a republic the individual is a citizen with duties to the *res publica* and rights (not favours) which flow from citizenship. The address provides a significant narrative of the republican movement's development from 1917. Perhaps Fr O'Flanagan's most interesting observation is that the split within the movement 'was there from the start'. The Anglo-Irish treaty was simply 'the wedge that burst the sections asunder'. Thereafter, divisive tendencies became a flood when de Valera's New Departure caused 'the stampede of 1926'.

Throughout O'Flanagan's presidency, repeated attempts were made to repair tensions between Sinn Féin and the IRA. Although O'Flanagan and Twomey (IRA chief of staff) maintained cordial links, the IRA was now interested in setting up its own political network which might contest future elections. In the view of the IRA leadership, Sinn Féin's effectiveness had declined irrevocably. Thus, there was an element of dissimulation in repeated talks between the Sinn Féin leadership and some IRA delegates. The IRA alternative to Sinn Féin did eventuate in early 1936 but made no progress.

Perhaps this reality lies behind Sean McBride's observation in 1985 that by the 1930s the IRA had lost political direction and Sinn Féin had ceased to count.[49]

By the time of his November 1935 address to the Ard Fheis, Ml O'Flanagan had twice been hospitalised. Against medical advice, he attended the Ard Fheis although his speech was read by the vice-chair, Mrs Margaret Buckley. A note of disillusion is clear in his reference to the depression in the country. It was due to 'the panic of 1922' and 'the second great downwards plunge at the stampede of 1926'.[50] On the other hand, O'Flanagan believed the compromises made by Fianna Fáil in their accession to power were causing widespread disillusion. The tension between the ordinary membership and the leaders of Fianna Fáil was ever more noticeable at the party's Árd Fheiseanna. People attracted by the New Departure of 1926 were making their way back to Sinn Féin. Viewed with far hindsight, this presidential address contains several interesting arguments. There is some prescience to O'Flanagan's argument that the major political parties now had little to distinguish them. He also argued that, despite some changes in style and manner, the political-social system administered by Fianna Fáil remained the same as before. The higher levels of officialdom derived not merely from the Cosgrave administration but even from 'the days of undisguised British rule before 1922'. As outgoing president, O'Flanagan argued that if Sinn Féin held to its objectives, it would benefit from the inevitable swing away from the government party. His summation of these objectives included national independence, radical reform of the institutions of state, and resistance to partition.

Dismissal From Sinn Féin

In its various shapes, Ml O'Flanagan had been a member of Sinn Féin since 1910. Within the party, his forthright character and radical views aroused opposition and, sometimes, resentment. At various periods, individuals as diverse as

Michael Collins, Sean Lemass and Mary MacSwiney expressed reserves about his actions. Despite this, he had become a quasi-mythical figure in regard to republican politics and criticism of dominant institutions both civil and ecclesiastical. Therefore, the circumstances of his abrupt break with Sinn Féin are all the more difficult to understand.

Radio Éireann (2RN) proposed a documentary re-enactment of the First Dáil on 21 Jan 1936 – the presenter would be Noel Hartnett, a young barrister with republican sympathies. Survivors of the events were invited to re-enact their roles at the historic opening. Amongst those invited were Sean T O'Kelly, Piaras Beasley, Eamonn Duggan, J. J. O'Kelly. Count Plunkett and Fr Ml O'Flanagan. The Sinn Féin executive deemed this 'the latest attempt by the Free State authorities (to pose) as the successors of the first Dáil'. When O'Flanagan took a minor role in the documentary, the executive made an order that his participation 'automatically ends his connection with the Sinn Féin organisation'. Approached by the *Irish Independent*, Fr O'Flanagan remarked that something more than the Sinn Féin executive would be required to prevent him from repeating publicly the part he had taken in the events of 21 January 1919.[51]

It is difficult to accept that so trivial a matter could have effected such a break – perhaps O'Flanagan believed that by its option for isolation Sinn Féin was committing political suicide. Days after his 'expulsion', some members of the executive accused him of links with Cumann na Poblachta, a party mooted by the IRA leadership. The same accusers spoke of O'Flanagan's agreement 'to let the new organisation go ahead and after a reasonable time to hold a national convention (at which Sinn Féin would be represented) to christen the New Departure'. It is worth noting that Ml O'Flanagan did not take any public role in the short-lived venture of Cumann na Poblachta although he continued his friendly links with radicals such as Peadar O'Donnell, George Gilmore and Frank Ryan.

Civil War in Spain

The Spanish civil war erupted on 18 July 1936 when right-wing forces under the leadership of General Franco rose against the duly elected republican government. Traditional institutions – the army, the church and the aristocracy – massively supported Franco. On the other side was a coalition of militant workers, left-wing politicians, liberal intellectuals and some sections of the armed forces. The civil war became a theatre not only of Spanish conflicts but also a re-run of tensions across Europe and further afield. It revived many issues still unresolved in Irish society. The Catholic Church in Ireland, perhaps in its most conservative stage, made no secret of its support for General Franco. Similarly definitive was the Irish Christian Front (a version of the 'muscular Christianity' so often criticised by O'Flanagan) which eventually raised a volunteer contingent to fight 'the battles of Christianity against Communism'.[52] Many newspapers, notably the *Irish Independent* and the *Catholic Standard* resumed their old conservative stances and were rabidly pro-Franco. The *Irish Press* (reflecting de Valera's policy of neutrality) and the *Irish Times* preserved some objectivity. Even among Irish republicans opinion was divided – Tom Barry, now chief of staff of the IRA, forbade members to join either the O'Duffy or Ryan contingents of volunteers which were recruited to fight in Spain. The most vocal support for the Spanish republic came from the Irish Republican Congress. Although it seemed on the verge of extinction, its resistance to international fascism gave Congress new purchase on the fragile ground of Irish left-wing politics. Along with the Communist Party, it mustered opposition to conservative propaganda in the press and from the pulpit. Peadar O'Donnell and Frank Ryan emphasised the international threat of fascism. Although he later headed an Irish volunteer contingent, Ryan stressed that the Spanish trenches were in Ireland. Hanna Sheehy Skeffington, a supporter of the Spanish Republic, argued that 'eyes should be on Ireland and the fascist menace here'.[53]

By August 1936, Ml O'Flanagan had joined left-wing republicans in publicising the less popular cause. Appeals from
O'Donnell, Ryan and Gilmore found in him a ready listener.
Now, as earlier, he distinguished between adherence to
Christianity and support for oppressive regimes. For him, the
Spanish alignment of army generals, church hierarchy and
land owning aristocracy paralleled what he had for long contested in Ireland. Thus, in one of his first public interventions
he adverted to this line-up of powerful forces. Referring to
conservative enthusiasm for Franco, he criticised bishops and
right-wing Irish leaders in saying 'They Have Fooled You
Again'. Thereafter, in Ireland, in the US and, finally, in republican Spain, he argued that Catholicism is able to co-exist
with progressive, socially just policies. Conversely, the profession of Catholicism did not necessitate support for Franco. A
victory for Franco might herald more leverage for the church,
but not real religion. Even more trenchantly, he predicted
that with the defeat of the Spanish republic 'the old feudal
aristocracy of the church would again be entrenched in
power'. In America, where references to 'godless Russia' proliferated, O'Flanagan's arguments are remarkable for a
Catholic priest. He claimed that atheism in Russia was a reaction to distorted versions of Christianity. The people of
Russia had been shocked into infidelity 'by the evil deeds
which were done in God's name ... by those who prate about
God's name in order to cover up the iniquity of their actions'.
Speeches like this and, in particular, an address critical of the
Vatican's *realpolitik* initiated moves at the highest level of ecclesiastical authority to have him even further censured by his
church.[54]

Closer analysis of Fr O'Flanagan's arguments reveals his
conviction that the war in Spain was a class war, rather than
one of religion. He also believed that an alignment of land-
owning aristocracy, upper levels of the army and senior clerics
now stood against workers, peasants and social reformers. As
he saw it, justice and truth demanded opposition to that
alignment even at the cost of opprobrium within his church.

In practical terms, he chaired the Irish Foodship for Spain
Committee from its foundation in 1938. Later in that year, he
travelled to Barcelona and Madrid, then under siege. On his
return, he paid tribute to the selfless work in the besieged
cities of the Society of Friends. In more personal allusion, he
remarked that the 'red' government in Barcelona had facilitated
him in saying Mass – something denied him in Ireland since
1925. When the 'Connolly Column' returned to a very muted
welcome, he addressed them at a public meeting in Abbey St,
Dublin. In his fine book, *Connolly Column*, Ml O'Riordan
correctly divines O'Flanagan's motivation throughout the period – 'he put people first'.[55] This pattern had marked the
priest's activity throughout the decades from his ordination in
1900 – in any choice between the top echelons of society and
popular forces, he chose the interests of the rank and file of
the people.[56]

Quiet After Many Storms

Fr Michael O'Flanagan's many-sided personality brought
him beyond politics and social criticism. He had patented
several inventions during the late 1920s. His work in the
National Library occupied him from 1932 until his death – by
the time of his death, he had completed ten volumes of county
histories. A deep attachment to local history made him travel
widely in Ireland and he was named to a proposed Local
Placenames Commission in 1940. Despite his difficulties
with Sinn Féin, he maintained close links with republicans
throughout the country. And there is ample evidence that he
maintained contact with clerical colleagues in the diocese of
Elphin. Ironically, further moves to discipline him because of
his involvement in the Spanish cause led to his eventual reinstatement as a practising Catholic priest. Here, the influence
of the Papal Nuncio to Ireland, Dr Pascal Robinson, must be
acknowledged. It was through Dr Robinson's tact that his fac-
ulties as a priest were restored in April 1939. Thereafter, he
ministered as chaplain to the Carmelite nuns in Kilmacud,
Co Dublin.

People who remember Fr O'Flanagan in his closing years associated a premature ageing with the difficult circumstances of his nomadic life. More likely, it was the stomach cancer which caused his death in 1942 at the relatively early age of sixty-six. In July 1942 he entered a nursing home in 7, Mount St Crescent, Dublin. Almost daily he was visited by his one-time colleague and quondam political adversary, Eamon de Valera. Five days before his death, he wrote to a Cliffoney resident, Bernard Conway. In laborious hand, the letter sent greetings to friends in 'dear, dear Cliffoney ... and especially those who prayed for me in front of the church door'.

Early on the morning of 7 August 1942 Ml O'Flanagan died, attended by Fr McNevin of St Andrew's Church, Westland Row. His cortege, accompanied by a republican honour guard of Fianna Éireann (boys) and Clann na nGael (girls) was taken to City Hall where almost thirty years before he had spoken at O'Donovan Rossa's funeral. On Monday, 10 August, his funeral Mass was celebrated at the Franciscan Church on Merchants Quay. Ml O'Flanagan had been a member of the Franciscan Third Order and through the offices of a Franciscan, Dr Pascal Robinson, had been restored to active ministry as a priest. Old colleagues and friends, Eamon de Valera, Thomas Ó'Deirg and Sean McEntee attended. So did Jim Larkin, that legendary figure among Dublin's working people. At Glasnevin's republican plot a funeral oration was given by his life-long friend J. J. O'Kelly. O'Kelly paid tribute to Fr O'Flanagan's technical and scientific gifts but even more to his refusal to exploit any of the national causes with which for so long he was associated. Ironically, the *Catholic Standard*, one of the official newspapers so much mistrusted by Fr O'Flanagan, paid the most apposite tribute. The *Standard* compared him to Patrick Pearse in his sympathy for youth, to Tom Clarke in his resistance to oppression, to James Connolly in his concern for all who struggled against poverty. It is a worthy epitaph.[57]

Further Reading
Carroll, Denis, *They Have Fooled You Again*, Columba, Dublin 1993.
Greaves, C. Desmond, *Fr Ml O'Flanagan. Republican Priest*, Connolly
Association, London (undated).

CHAPTER TEN

TWO RADICAL CLERGYMEN OF THE CHURCH OF IRELAND

The Rev R.M. Hilliard (1903-1937) and The Rev Stephen Hilliard (1947-1990)

In Ireland, the 'fault lines' of religious division have reinforced socio-political disunity. As James Porter intimated in his *Billy Bluff and the Squire*, 'establishment' limited the freedom of Anglican clergy to criticise political exclusion of Dissenters and Roman Catholics. Yet, there are splendid exceptions. Dr Dickson, the bishop of Down, criticised military repression in the north during 1797-8. In Connacht, Dr Jeremy Stock (Bishop of Killala), tried to mitigate similar repression after the defeat of General Humbert and his Irish auxiliaries. Again, the heroism of many Anglican clergy during the Great Famine has been all too frequently overlooked. The introduction to this section noticed the contribution of Church of Ireland priests and laypeople to the Gaelic revival at the end of the nineteenth century.

On the other hand, an understandable tentativity marked the Church of Ireland's assessment of the new Irish state after the Anglo-Irish treaty. To refer again to Maurice Goldring's study, one asks if radical Protestantism had declined in the early twentieth-century because it chose 'the wrong side in the never ending Irish conflict'.[1] In an important essay, 'Protestantism Since The Treaty', W. B. Stanford remarked that since Ireland won independence 'with far less Protestant support or leadership than in any nationalistic rising for two centuries before, (this fact) was disastrous for the political prestige of the Church of Ireland in the new state'.[2] Stanford also remarks that Irish Protestants who might have joined the revolutionaries in other circumstances had been active in the 1914-18 war. When the new state was inaugurated, many Protestants left the country. Others became 'bitterly contemptuous of the new rulers'. While some were ready to co-operate in building the new state, the general policy was 'Lie low and say nothing, Wait and see'. Even today, Stanford's essay is an important comment in regard to the 1930s and 40s in Ireland.

On the other hand, several Church of Ireland contributors to the symposium of which Stanford's essay was the keynote, e.g. Lil Nic Dhonnchadha (Principal of Coláiste Moibhí) and Helen Chevenix (Women Workers' Union), had a more radically positive view of the Protestant contribution to life in the south. Helen Chevenix remarked that 'as far as the Trade Union and Labour Movement is concerned there is no sectarian barrier between those of us who profess a minority faith and our fellow-workers who belong to the Church of the majority'. Lil Nic Dhonnchadha, having remarked on the anti-Protestant attitudes of Catholic authority in the Dublin archdiocese, also observed that in many Irish-speaking districts there was no bigotry but only understanding.[3] In the same issue of *The Bell*, George Gilmore, a Church of Ireland layman and a radical voice in the 1920s and 30s, associated Irish republicanism with continued struggle for comprehensive social change. Gilmore's view was that Protestantism had nothing to fear from a co-operative struggle for social reform. Ostensibly, this is the tradition which the Reverend R. M. Hilliard entered during a full life which ended tragically at the battle of Jarama in the early days of the Spanish civil war.

Who was R. M. Hilliard?

Since Robert ('Bob') Hilliard was a man of action rather than of literary output it is difficult to offer the assessments made of Armour or O'Flanagan. According to Stephen Hilliard's fine tribute, R. M. Hilliard was 'a man of action, not, I think, a deep thinker'. A clergyman of the Church of Ireland, he was a distinguished athlete and a crusader in anti-Fascist causes both in Ireland and abroad. Among socialist republicans of the 1920s and 30s, 'the boxing parson' was noted as an example of one whose Christian faith enabled him to challenge inherited certitudes and to break conventional moulds.[4]

One of six children, Hilliard was born in Moyeightragh, Killarney, Co Kerry, to a successful business family. His secondary education was at Cork Grammar School and, later, Mountjoy School, Dublin. From a very early age he was interested in republican politics and had some association with local republican activists. Benefitting from a Read Sizarship, he commenced study at Trinity College Dublin where he maintained his links with republican activism. A colleague at Trinity later remembered his arrival there – 'a youth of seventeen, flaxen-haired and bubbling over with energy'. In 1944, a fellow student deemed him 'a Protestant and a fierce republican' who voted seventeen times against the treaty side in the 1922 general election.[5] (*Irish Times*, 13.5.1944). Hilliard's espousal of radicalism led him to become a Marxist in politics and an atheist in philosophical views. In Trinity, he was a founder member of the Thomas Davis Society, a society noted for its pro-republican stances.

The journal *T.C.D.*, reports Hilliard's frequent contributions to the Neophyte Debating Society, the College Historical Society. and the Classical Society. As reported, these are not especially radical and do not reflect the radicalism mentioned in colleagues' reminiscences. Doubtless, they have to be read in the summary, often humorous, tone of student minutes. Yet, they are indicative of Hilliard's enthusiastic participation in college activities. For instance, in 'an excellent maiden speech' to the Classical Society (8 December 1921) he argued that 'Virgil had the main qualification of a poet – love of nature'. At the Neophyte Debating Society (17 November 1921) he praised the tolerance of the Irish Party (? the Home Rule party) in a debate entitled 'A Plebiscite is Useless in Discovering National Opinion in Times of Crisis'. To the Historical Society he was heavily sarcastic about Free Staters and Republicans, Capital and Labour – arguing that 'the plain people' had the genius for orderly government (23 November 1922). At the same society in February 1922, he supported the motion that Egypt should have complete independence and cited Thomas Davis to strengthen his argument. Again, to the Historical Society (2 March 1922) he claimed that 'women alone were fit to conduct government'.[6]

Athletic Success

Hilliard's remarkable skill as a lightweight boxer is recorded from December 1922. Despite extreme myopia, courage and determination brought him notable success in the sport. He won an Irish Amateur Boxing Association championship in May 1923. This achievement resulted in his selection for the Irish team at the Paris Olympics of 1924 where, however, he was eliminated in the preliminary contests. Some years later, he returned to the sport and in 1931 won the Irish Featherweight championship. At this competition Hilliard was referred to by the *Irish Independent* (29 May 1931) as 'an old champion who was out of the game for some years'.

Expulsion from Trinity?

From summer 1925, Hilliard leaves the university scene – without a degree.[7] Although it is frequently claimed that republican activities led to his expulsion, there is no evidence for this in college records. More probably, it is that after his marriage to a Miss Robins of Grayshott, Surrey, he went to London for a career in journalism. He is reputed to have worked in various employments, including Basil Clarke's Editorial Services as well as *The Times*. He later claimed to have coined the advertising slogan for Tennant's beer, 'Great stuff this Bass'. There is an irony here – during the late 1920s, the Irish republican movement argued for a boycott of British imports and centred its campaign on the beer which Hilliard is reputed to have recommended.

Moral Rearmament

Although Hilliard had professed atheism while at Trinity, he now became associated with the Oxford Group (not to be confused with the earlier Oxford movement led by Edward Pusey). The Oxford Group was part of Frank Buchman's 'moral rearmament', founded as an international evangelistic movement. Its search was for moral absolutes and personal religious fervour. It is a further irony that, although Hilliard once professed Marxism, he was now part of an anti-Communist group which, according to some, had Nazi sympathies. Stephen Hilliard astutely observes that the version of Christianity he had adopted was narrow and pietistic, having little in common with his earlier socialist vision. Perhaps as a result of this association, he decided that his duty was to return to Dublin in order to enter the church.

Trinity Again

Just as R. M. Hilliard abruptly disappeared from college life in 1925, he equally abruptly re-appears from November 1931. Certainly, he had returned to Dublin before May 1931 since in that month he took the Irish featherweight boxing title. Once again, college societies and sporting achievement provide us with clues about his activities. Since he won the Irish featherweight championship in May 1931, it is somewhat of a surprise to note that in November he was defeated in the college bantamweight championship.[8] In the same term, he took a divinity testimonial which established his suitability for ordination as a clergyman. In 1931, he was made a deacon of the church and took what appears to be part-time employment as curate-assistant in Derriaghy parish, near Belfast. Yet, his association with Trinity College continued until 1933 when he took up full-time ministry at the Belfast Cathedral Mission Church.

At Trinity College, he prominently figured in the Theological Society, the Historical Society and the Gaelic Society. In minutes he is referred to as Reverend R. M. Hilliard, BA and, in October 1932, is accredited as R. M. Hilliard, MA. In view of his later development it is surprising that his theological views, as reported, are conservative. For example, he pleads that people should behave 'sensibly and seriously' if they wish to gamble. Later, he criticises the 'spiritual pride that engenders Pelagianism'.[9]

There were other engagements. At the Historical Society he argued that 'the Church of Ireland tended to look to Imperialism rather than to God for her safety and welfare'. To the Gaelic Society he read a paper on Jonathan Swift's work in Ireland. Evidence of non-conventionality is given by the student journal's allusions to his 'wearing strange suits' and being 'a cross between the hornpipe and the fugue, often of a wild nature'. A report on Hilliard's debating performance in March 1932 observes that his 'bright airy playfulness was not so much in evidence as usual, nor his wit, nor the other charming qualities which have so endeared him to the Society'. In May 1932, he proposed to the Historical Society a vote of confidence in the new Fianna Fáil government.[10]

Perhaps the most demanding activity of 1931-32 is Hilliard's editorship of *T.C.D.* A report of the Editorial Sub Committee (Trinity Term 1932) deems his editorship 'reasonable and well-informed, with the strange exception of an editorial on the Divinity school'. Despite this implied criticism, the sub-committee praised Hillliard's energy and recommended him 'for the best thanks of the company'. The offending article had appeared on 12 May 1932. It was a mixture of religious enthusiasm and astute political observation. There is a hint of Buchmanite absoluteness (Buchman was the founder of Moral Rearmament) in the claim that the divinity school needed firmer spiritual direction, a longer theo-

logical course and an update on psychology. Hilliard satirises
the pretension whereby 'a small bit of Greek gives even a
third-class man a superiority in the pulpit'. It is interesting to
note his observation that the Protestant layman in the south
no longer feels a stranger but 'was becoming nationally conscious'.[11]

Ministry in Belfast

As mentioned, Hilliard's priestly work commenced in 1933
at Belfast Cathedral Mission. With his wife and four children
he had entered a social context riven by poverty and long-
standing sectarian conflict. Hilliard's enthusiastic personality
and down to earth preaching drew large numbers to the
Mission. The prevalence of tuberculosis, bad living conditions and social exclusion touched him deeply. Relatives have
mentioned his energetically practical response in alleviation
of poverty. However, there is no evidence of any connection
with the radical political groups which at this stage were beginning to forge Catholic-Protestant co-operation on rent
strikes, etc. Later highlighted by Peadar O'Donnell's and
George Gilmore's Republican Congress, an evidence of this
collaboration is the presence of a contingent from the
Shankill Road at a pilgrimage to Wolfe Tone's grave in
Autumn 1934.

By late 1934, Robert Hilliard had resigned from the
Cathedral mission. Family difficulties may well have been a
factor in his sudden move away from wife and children.
Subsequent to his departure, a trust fund for the family was
set up by Hilliard's mother. Yet, one also asks if tension between a moralistic spirituality and a daunting social context
may have caused him to revise his religious views. The indi-
vidualistic piety of the Oxford group may have been insufficient for him to adopt what Stephen Hilliard calls 'a more
open catholic radicalism'. Perhaps even now he had doubts
about the religious ideology of Christianity and moved back
to his earlier Marxism. Given these uncertainties, it would be

unsafe to cast him in the role of Fr Camillo Torres (a Bolivian priest-sociologist who became a guerrilla fighter during the 1960s in his country's social struggle) or in the mould of other liberationist clergymen of the 1960s and 1970s.

London

London of the 1930s was the scene of conflicting movements. A right-wing organisation, headed by Oswald Mosley, was adopting pro-fascist and pro-Hitler stances. Likewise, many intellectuals saw communism as the ideology of the future. In this multi-facetted context, R. M. Hilliard set up a new home and worked, as earlier, on the fringes of journalism. On this period, Stephen Hilliard's remark is significant : '(he was) Accustomed to tread the edges of life where heroism and total commitment are to be found'. As did many generous spirits, he joined the Communist Party (founded in Ireland during 1934). The context of the time led many people of Robert Hilliard's idealism to adopt 'the simple dogmatic Stalinism of the 1930s'.[12]

The outbreak of the Spanish civil war convinced many radicals that anti-fascism was the great cause of the day and that Spain was the testing place of social commitment. From late 1936, volunteers went to Spain in a kind of latter-day crusade – on the one side were those who believed they were fighting for Christian civilisation; on the other were those who rejected the coalition of right-wing military, landowning aristocracy and the senior levels of the clerical hierarchy. An earlier chapter of this study has noticed in Ireland the massively pro-Franco response in pulpit and among right-wing Catholics.

Of especial interest here is the International Brigade which converged from Ireland, England, France, the U.S. and eastern Europe. The 15th Brigade (of which R. M. Hilliard was a member) was the 5th International Brigade organised almost immediately after the fall of Madrid to Franco's troops. The 15th brigade, formed in January 1937 at Albecete, can be de-

scribed as English-speaking in that its administration was carried out in the English language. At first, it was composed of a
British battalion (the Saklatovala, later the Clement Attlee
battalion), an American Lincoln-Washington battalion, a
Canadian MacKenzie-Papineau battalion and a Spanish battalion. Two other battalions were attached, viz the Dimitrov
and the Franco-Belgian. The Irish unit under Frank Ryan was
active in the Brigade almost from the start, commencing with
the British battalion and, after some difficulties, transferring
to the Lincoln-Washington battalion. The commander of the
15th brigade was Vladimir Copic, a Croat communist.[13]

In late 1936, R.M. Hilliard's battalion was recruited in
London. Jason Gurney, a veteran of the Brigade, later wrote
in somewhat bitter tones of the battalion's history.[14] They
were, says Gurney, a mixed bag of people from various backgrounds and with diverse motivations – 'Idealists, oppor-
tunists, doctrinaire Marxists, adventurers and plain rogues'.
This may not be fair to idealistic people like Hilliard who saw
in the Fascist advance throughout Europe a lethal threat to
social justice and a programme for oppression. Yet, Gurney's
remarks re-echo those of Frank Edwards in pointing out that
few had come to Spain for the reasons they stated.

From Albecete, the Battalion had travelled to Madrigueras,
a village in the plain of Murcia. Here, six hundred men
formed a training camp under the command of Wilfred
Macartney and an ex-officer of the British army, George
Nathan. Rudimentary training was given from 27 December
1936 until 6 February 1937 – a difficult period during which
the recruits lived in virtually intolerable conditions. Medical
and hygienic facilities were minimal. Military training was
poor and – at least according to Jason Gurney – leadership
was ineffectual.

Gurney's remembrance of the days at Madrigueras provides a clue to Hilliard's effect on his comrades: 'One of the
most amusing characters in Madrigueras was an ex-Anglican
parson, the Reverend R. M. Hilliard, who had become a

Communist. He was a great drinker and his friends were of all classes. They liked him for his sense of humour and his consistently cheerful attitude'.[15]

Very soon – on 12 February 1936 – the battalion was committed to halt the advance of Franco's troops along the Jarama river, south of Madrid. At the battle of Jarama, one of the most bitter of the whole war, Hilliard's battalion endeavoured to halt the advance of tanks and vastly more numerous troops. Despite the tone of his other comments, Jason Gurney pays full tribute to a handful of men preparing to charge into the face of Maxim guns and an unknown number of Moorish infantry. On 14 February, R. M. Hilliard was gravely wounded – one of a party of four men who fought advancing tanks with no suitable guns or even grenades. Despite this insufficiency, they managed to cover their colleagues' retreat. All of Hilliard's group were killed – he survived a mere five days in an improvised military hospital.[16]

Thus, Hilliard's many facetted life abruptly ended. Only the confused circumstances of the time explain why even left-wing Irish journals did not carry obituary notices of this brave man's death. His courage and generosity deserve to be remembered in an Ireland where his social vision comes under attack once again. R. M. Hilliard represents the best of a generation which gave practical expression to their idealism even at great cost to themselves. The all too few survivors of that period are witnesses to courage in opposing the threat of continental fascism.

Since Hilliard has left few writings, more theoretical questions about his biography are difficult to answer. His nephew's questions are rightly open-ended: Was he a Christian socialist? Or was he rather a socialist, then a Christian believer and then a socialist again?[17] In saluting Robert Hilliard and his colleagues one feels that these questions pale before his extraordinary life as a clergyman who maintained radical social commitments and dedication to generous ideals.

A note in the *Irish Times* after Hilliard's death paid tribute to his principled enthusiasm and concluded 'now he has given his life for something which he believed to be right. No man could do more'. In 1972, a veteran of the International Brigade presented to Derriaghy Church a communion chalice, paten and cruet to remember his fallen comrade at the battle of Jarama.

Reverend Stephen Hilliard – 1947-1990

In a tribute to R. M. Hilliard, Stephen Hilliard referred to himself as 'a Church of Ireland clergyman with a background of republican and socialist politics'. It was an apt description. Stephen Hilliard united exemplary dedication as a Christian priest with unremitting enthusiasm for a just and inclusive social order. An allusion in his *Resource* article to 'a more open catholic radicalism' further elucidates his own stance. His tragic death in 1990 is yet another link with his uncle.[1]

Stephen Hilliard grew to manhood in Rathfarnham, Co Dublin. He attended the High School, then located in Harcourt St. On finishing secondary education in 1966 he took a summer job as a street sweeper in London. Then, he attended Atlantic College where radio officers were trained for careers in marine service. Meanwhile, his particular interest was in journalism which, through the good offices of Douglas Gageby, he entered as a sub-editor with the *Irish Times*. Thus he became one of a group which a later editor termed 'bright and dedicated young people who came into the *Irish Times* in the late 1960s and early 1970s'.[3]

Night-time employment enabled him attend University College Dublin where he gained a degree in English and Irish in 1973. In that year he married Betty O'Doherty and set up home at Upper Rathmines Road, Dublin. Some years later, he worked as an external student with London University where he gained a degree in divinity. In 1983, he quit full time journalism to enter the Church of Ireland Theological College and in June 1986 was ordained a deacon. Thereafter, he worked with Archdeacon Gordon Linney in Glenageary and on the staff of the Christ Church parishes in central Dublin. While at Christ Church he devoted his journalistic talents to the parish magazine, *The Parishioner*, and also as a board member of the *Church of Ireland Gazette*. On 28 November 1989 he was installed as rector of St Saviour's Church with responsibility for Rathdrum, Laragh and Glenealy. Only six weeks later, an intruder to his house stabbed him fatally. Thus, his church and the broader Irish society lost both a radical Christian priest and a patriot in the very best sense.

Before turning to Stephen Hilliard's socio-political views it may be useful to note the estimation of his fellow journalists. These tributes are by no means prepared formulae, the required mead of praise, in face of a colleague's sudden death. Coming from a wide range of political views, they are a heartfelt eulogy of an exceptional personality. A common thread is Stephen Hilliard's individual qualities – cheerfulness, courtesy and infectious smile. Douglas Gageby's remark was typically generous – alongside intelligence, wide reading and professionalism, Gageby recalled Hilliard's 'marvellous smile which was like a ray of sunshine … he must have been a splendid pastor'. James Downey remembered his 'courage, kindness and humour'. Kevin Myers wrote that he was 'almost perpetually cheery … his loud shout of laughter could loosen plaster.' An appreciation by 'B O'C' speaks of a charming colleague whose very eccentricities were loveable. As a subeditor he was meticulous – after one edition a journalist remarked that he (Hilliard) would cut down a Shakespeare sonnet, to which the subeditor replied: 'I would, if it were more than 14 lines'. Two people adverted to Stephen Hilliard's stammer. Mervyn Taylor wrote that it matched 'his enormous enthusiasm but the enthusiasm always won out'. According to Kevin Myers, the impediment was overcome by his sheer communication of goodness.[4]

The appreciation by 'B O'C' is especially significant.

Evidently a friend from days at the *Irish Times*, 'B O'C' spoke of Hilliard's initial desire to minister in East Belfast – this was where R. M. Hilliard had briefly worked. The columnist also drew attention to Hilliard's qualities as an ecumenist, contemplative, scholar and socialist. Again, there is reference to his 'total if unostentatious' Christian commitment. Archbishop Donald Caird wrote that Stephen Hilliard had studied 'alternative philosophies with the predominant motive of his basic passion for justice'. Alongside this search for justice was a basic value of love 'as a commitment to the welfare and best interests of others'.[5]

The Irish Language

A long tradition in the Church of Ireland has served the language valuably and well. The tradition includes Bishop Bedell, Canon Hannay, Douglas Hyde, David Green, Lil Nic Dhonnachadha and, today, Archbishop Donald Caird. Thus, Stephen Hilliard's esteem of the Irish language should not be a surprise. His maternal grandparents, G. E. Hamilton and Beatrice Culverwell, were both members of Conradh na Gaeilge. Asked about his views on the language, Hilliard said: 'I love it. Its literature has opened up for me a whole world of Irish experience that ... would have remained closed to me'. For him. the Irish language was an inheritance of all the people, not of one cultural tradition. Again, he mentioned his enthusiasm for working out the meanings of placenames and how this second language enriched his life.[6]

Risteárd Ó Glaisne's moving article in *An tUltach* discloses Hilliard's interest in Irish culture even as he prepared to leave High School. In a first letter to the noted author, Hilliard made it clear that he rejected the view of Irish as 'a cultural backwater'. At the time (*1966*), his preferred authors were Brian O'Nolan (Myles na gCopaleen), Liam O'Flaherty and James Joyce. In the same letter, he sought guidance for a proposed article 'Why Protestants Should Learn Irish' in *The Erasmian*.[7] Ó Glaisne also tells of Hilliard's plan to acquire oral proficiency by visiting the Gaeltacht. Likewise, he took lessons with Conradh na Gaeilge and a new language movement – CARA – founded by P. A. Ó Síocháin. His plans were to publish in Irish language journals such as *Comhar*, *Feasta* or *Focus*. Later, Hilliard's journalism included contributions to the *Irish Times* column 'Beocheist' and a series entitled 'In Éirinn Trath'. Because of his premature death he could not fulfill his installation promise at Rathdrum to use the Irish language in his ministry.[8]

Early Journalism

After commencement with the *Irish Times* Stephen Hilliard's journalism includes an extended interview with Michael O'Riordan, an old comrade of R. M. Hilliard and general secretary of the Irish Workers' Party. To Hilliard's question whether students and workers of Ireland could unite to bring about a socialist state, O'Riordan with characteristic directness replied: 'The national question is a social question and the only incorruptible inheritors of the struggle for freedom in Ireland is the working class'. In March 1969, Hilliard's article on Credit Unions in Dublin's Liberties supports those battling against parlous housing conditions. Citing James Connolly's dictum that without economic freedom there was no real freedom, Hilliard wrote: '... people in the Liberties can and will fight to enforce their right to live in security in their own home area. Credit Unions, since they are a genuine community effort, are an effective barrier to those who for profit would reduce a people to submission by exploitation and economic oppression'. There were other pieces – book reviews, letters in favour of sanctions against South Africa, an article on a strike at the jewellery manufacturers, Thomas O'Connor and Sons. Another *Irish Times* series – 'U.C.D. Notes' – occasionally discloses Hilliard's own egalitarian views. Writing on the failure of U.C.D. students to support a strike by college attendants, he reported: 'The reaction by the students to the strike was a mixture of snobbery, apathy and wilful ignorance about an issue which does not concern them directly – intelligent consideration of the issues, involved total and unquestioning support for the strikers.' In an article written in Irish, Hilliard gave sympathetic treatment to the opening of a campaign by the tenants's organisation (ACRA) against ground rents.[9]

Articles on East Germany

Stephen Hilliard recurrently described himself as a Christian socialist. In an unpublished paper he argued that capitalism, no matter how it is modified is 'inherently immoral and exploitative ... a peculiarly unsuitable instrument for establishing justice'. Nevertheless, while he was unapologetically sympathetic to socialism, he retained an ability to pose critical questions. He believed that Socialism was true to its origins only when it remained democratic and humanitarian. In several contexts he admitted that no existing Socialist regime had avoided deviation and, even, corruption. Along with other Christian socialists, he was aware that no political system attained perfection. After his death, Mervyn Taylor remarked that many of Hilliard's stances were 'vindicated by the dramatic events of 1989'. An example of enthusiasm tempered by realism is his review of Jose Miranda's *Marx And The Bible*. Welcoming Miranda's critique of Western interpretations of the bible, he insisted that Marxist thought helps to interpret the bible's most important insights. Unambiguously, Hilliard avows his own conviction that liberation theology would free Christianity 'to resume its historically destined task of bringing the good news of liberation to the oppressed of the world'. Yet, at the end of his review, he reminds the reader of the distinction between propaganda and theological scholarship. Good intentions cannot substitute for real scholarship. Without claiming to be a professional biblicist, he suggests that *Marx And The Bible* is a book of real scholarship. Provocatively, he concludes: '... my guess is that if our professional exegetes in the Church Establishments ever took *Marx and the Bible* in their hands, they would get some surprises'.[10]

In late 1976, Stephen Hilliard visited the German
Democratic Republic. On return, he wrote a series of three
articles for his newspaper which combined realistic observation with sympathetic assessment. A sub-text of the articles,
hinted rather than laboured, is an uneasiness at state authori-
tarianism. On the other hand, Hilliard argues that a radical
alternative to arrogant capitalism is under way in the German
Democratic Republic. One article expresses his own long
standing question: can Socialism and Christianity co-exist?
He cites the then leader of the Christian Democratic Union
(CDU) as a hopeful instance: 'The best argument (for socialism) we can give is our example .... We try to give a Christian
witness in socialism and to show that as Christians we have
equal rights and duties with other citizens'. While he unfail-
ingly documents less pleasant aspects of his surroundings –
ubiquitous policemen and dour officials – Hilliard is scrupulously fair in making comparison with capitalist countries. If
housing was dingy with dark hallways and peeling walls, it
was 'just as in Dublin and other capitalist cities'.[11]

This search for evenhandedness emerges in his *Church of
Ireland Gazette* article on the Church in Russia. The Irish
Council of Churches had sponsored a visit by churchmen
from the then Soviet Union who had lectured in Belfast and
Dublin. Hilliard's report/article humorously notices the hearers 'who meekly sat there, troubled eyes lowered, hands fold-
ed on their laps ... and dutifully laughing at witticisms'. In a
nuanced way, Hilliard's article detailed the good and bad sides
to church life in Russia, while signalling the rather evasive answers of Metropolitan Filaret. Typically, Hilliard sought deeper answers than those given by the patriarch. Instead of bland
assurances on church-state relations, Hilliard wanted to know
how Christians in the Soviet Union 'experience the gospel'.
Likewise, he criticised the 'western form of myopia known as
anti-sovietism' and the conventional emphasis on 'underground churches'. Shortly before his death Hilliard spoke of
his interest in Russia – its literature, politics religion and way

of life. He had attempted with little success to learn Russian but hoped to make another try.[12]

Christians for Socialism

Founded in February 1977, this inter-church group believed that Christianity and socialism could mutually enrich each other. It aimed to spread knowledge of socialism among Christians and to enable socialists better to understand Christianity. In its early days, it maintained close links with the Student Christian Movement and other bodies with a radical social agenda. The immediate genesis of Christians For Socialism was a Drogheda conference on liberation theology, held in December 1976. A Marx Study Group headed by the Dublin academic, John Maguire, was its first project which lasted through several months of 1977. Initially termed Christians and Social Action Group, it later became Christians for Socialism. In title and focus it reflected events in Latin America where radical Christians motivated by liberation theology opted for socialism at great cost to themselves. Stephen Hilliard was the first chairman of Christians for Socialism, later to be succeeded by Fr Michael O'Sullivan, a Jesuit priest. Active members included Betty Hilliard, Fergus Brogan, Brenda O'Riordan, Lorcan McDermott, John Heffernan and Peadar Kirby, several of whom had experience in Latin American politics. A particular interest of the group was Christian-Marxist dialogue then conducted by J. R. M. Tilliard, the English Slant group (Fr Herbert McCabe, Laurence Bright, Terry Eagleton) with Marxist intellectuals such as Roger Garaudy and Ernst Bloch.

From 1977 to 1982, Christians for Socialism initiated meetings with various left-wing groups in Ireland, ranging from Sinn Féin to the Irish Communist Party. The group participated in May Day processions in Dublin alongside other groups from left-wing politics. A manifesto, drafted by Stephen Hilliard, John Maguire and Michael O'Sullivan, spoke of transforming Ireland into a society where resources would be brought under communal ownership and democratic control. Letters to the national papers were composed, often by Hilliard himself. In June 1977, the group invited Irish Christians to support left-wing parties in the general election – although Ml O'Riordan, when consulted, opposed the interjection of confessional distinctions into Irish politics even if this were to benefit the left. Nonetheless, the group specifically recommended candidates of the Communist Party, Sinn Féin the Workers Party, the Socialist Party as well as independent left-wing candidates. On this basis grew a subsequent trust between the group and left-wing parties. During its first year Christians for Socialism took public stances on issues like development aid, community schools, the Ferenka closures at Limerick and, in international context, on repression in Chile.

On 28 April 1979, representatives of Christians For Socialism took part in a T.C.D. symposium on Marxism, Atheism and Christianity. Here, Dr Helena Sheehan of the Communist society warned against 'sham dialogue' between Marxists who no longer believe in class struggle and Christians who no longer believe in God.[13] Ml O'Sullivan argued that belief in God need not be an alienation since the dialectic of love is a liberative force for Christian believers. Although Marxism might have begun as the antithesis of religion, the time had come to move to a higher synthesis. Another event later organised by Christians For Socialism was a seminar on the Irish economy in which six left-wing groups discussed their differences. Entitled 'the Ballymascanlon of the Left', the symposium numbered representatives of Sinn Féin the Workers' Party (Eamon Smullen), the British and Irish Communist Organisation (Fergus O'Rahilly), the Irish Marxist Society (Paddy Carmody), the Communist Party of Ireland (Eoin O'Murchu), the Socialist party (Seamus Ratigan) and the Socialist Labour Party (Alan Matthews).

On the controverted question of the relation between nationalism and socialism, Irish socialists adopted changing stances. After 1969, the majority of socialists favoured British withdrawal from the north of Ireland and the unification of the country. However, from the late 1970s they tended to argue that traditional nationalism was an obstacle to socialist development. They moved towards a 'two nations theory' and even denied that the Northern Ireland state was fundamentally based on sectarian domination. Instead, they argued that discrimination was 'a typical effect of the unregulated uneven development of capitalism'. Linking Protestant Unionist fear of nationalist aspirations with economic analysis, they put it that northern unionists had a valid case for self-determination. As an addendum, they claimed that nationalism was not a satisfactory way to 'mobilise a socialist movement'. Thus, the task was to guarantee the status of Northern Ireland as a separate entity and to move into the mainstream of British politics so that sectarian tensions might 'wither away' to be replaced by 'the more vital issues of class politics'. To a degree there is an analogy to Fr Ml O'Flanagan's attempt to address 'the national question'. Like O'Flanagan's *Leader* articles, there was a noticeable omission – the new socialist analysis contrasted southern Irish nationalism and northern Irish unionism without sufficient reference to the nationalists/republicans in Northern Ireland. Writing after the 'Good Friday agreement' of 1998 one adverts to the shortcomings of the 'two nations theory' and the injustice of excluding an alienated minority in an already tiny state.

How far Stephen Hilliard accepted the newer socialist analysis of the late 1970s is difficult to determine. Certainly, he opposed the Anglo-Irish Agreement of 1985 on 'democratic grounds'. He argued that the citizens of Northern Ireland had 'never been allowed to participate on equal footing with the rest of the UK'. As he saw the matter, Northern Ireland was disadvantaged in democratic terms because the parties which governed them were 'in no way answerable to the Northern Ireland electorate for their policies on Northern Ireland'. Expressing the highest regard for the people of Northern

Ireland of both traditions, he avowed 'I have no desire whatever to bring them under Dublin rule'.[14]

In 1981, the H Blocks hunger strikes reminded everyone that radical stances can be tested by immediately current events. In a letter to the group, a Long Kesh prisoner enquired about Christians For Socialism and praised it as a progressive body. Having mentioned the churches' failure to condemn root causes of injustice, the writer asked the group for public support of the hunger strikers. Stephen Hilliard wrote an extended reply, noteworthy both for its courtesy and firmness. In human terms, the letter expressed sympathy with those 'cut off from your families and suffering daily for your principles as you see them'. Nevertheless, Hilliard expressed the inability of his group to give public support. The reasons were both political and moral. Politically, Hilliard claimed to reflect the views of Irish socialists that the Provisional Republican Movement was 'actually holding back the development of socialist mass struggle' and militated against 'the interests of the Irish working class'. From the moral standpoint, he argued that the Provisional IRA was risking the lives of innocent people. He referred to 'placing bombs in public places (with the risk) of killing and maiming and bringing tragedy to ordinary working-class people who have committed no crime whatsoever'. The letter is remarkable for two other features. One is its emphasis that Christians for Socialism was ready 'to strike up a dialogue' to explain why the group could not support 'the struggle of your movement'. The other feature is a sensitive understanding that it was all too easy for people in the Republic to homilise prisoners who were undergoing daily suffering. Thus, firmness of moral purpose and reluctance to judge others came admirably together.

About this time, reviewing a new book on the bible and non-violent revolution, Hilliard wrote: 'Before reading the book I was not really a pacifist. Now I am more inclined to think that pacifism is enjoined on the Christian'.[15]

Christians For Socialism continued to enjoy the hospitality of Stephen and Betty Hilliard at their home on Rathmines Road. Likewise, the group met at the Jesuit Institute at Milltown Park. In 1982, as leading members went to other assignments, it dissolved. Questions arise about the group. Politically, one asks if it was a belated reaction to the slogan 'The Seventies Will Be Socialist'? Some members had been in the Labour Party and, when that Party seemed to move to the right, quit for other more satisfying involvements. It is also the case that a certain naïvete marked some of its initiatives. This could be said of its eagerness to recommend that Irish Christians vote for left-wing parties at general elections. As already mentioned, Ml O'Riordan, a veteran of left-wing politics, is reputed to have advised against that course of action on the grounds that the lessons of Irish history should discourage confessional voting. Theologically, one notices a quasi-evangelical fervour among Christians For Socialism in regard to faith and politics. In a substantial article for *The Christian Left Review*, Hilliard wrote that Christians For Socialism was a conservative movement in that 'We try to base our thoughts and actions on what God is saying to us in the Bible and in the traditions of the Church Fathers'.[16]

Theological Work For the Ministry

Alongside political radicalism, Hilliard's writings show a deep spirituality. Perhaps it is this strain which caused 'B O'C' to note in an obituary tribute that Stephen Hilliard's life was a 'sacrament'. Interviewed by *The Parishioner* some months after his ordination, he spoke of 'attending to God in the stillness and bringing that stillness with us into our everyday life'.[17] Certainly Stephen Hilliard's interest in Julian of Norwich and Dietrich Bonhoeffer argues to a spirituality in the midst of political engagement. Likewise, his decision to commence study for a theology degree evidences a perception that if 'everything is politics, politics is not everything'. In an article on Christian Socialism, he had stressed the necessity for personal conversion, 'regeneration', prayer and meditation alongside social engagement.[18] It is coherent with this emphasis that in 1983 Hilliard commenced training for the Church of Ireland ministry. Living near the Theological College, he carried out full-time studies while resident with his wife and daughter. As already mentioned, he was ordained a deacon in June 1986 and commissioned to work in the Christ Church group of parishes.

At this period Stephen Hilliard's pastoral work demanded much of his time and energy. In *The Parishioner* interview already cited, he spoke of duties 'exhausting though deeply satisfying and varied'. As a curate in St Paul's, Glenageary, he was ordained priest in 1987. Two years later – in November 1989 – he was installed as rector of the Rathdrum group of parishes. Colleagues and parishioners speak of a comprehensive gracefulness in his dealings with people of all ages, backgrounds and convictions. One such remembrance speaks of his 'genuine enjoyment of people and irrepressible good humour (which) turned even the briefest encounter with him into a moment of grace'. Here one thinks of 'B O'C's reference to his life as a 'sacrament': a outward sign of an inner reality. Yet, like R. M. Hilliard, his involvement in socio-political reflection demanded costly sacrifices for the good of others. The family had moved into the rectory on Dec 18th 1989. Three weeks later, Stephen Hilliard was stabbed during a break-in at the house in the early hours of January 9 1989. The person later convicted was a young man who was already in some trouble. The irony is that had he come to the rectory door he would have received help without question – this is the view of Betty Hilliard who accompanied Stephen's last moments. A letter received after his death made the same point – 'if any one could have helped that young man it was stephen.'[19]

NOTES TO PART I

INTRODUCTION

1. A resolution of Dublin Corporation (Sept 1792) defined Protestant Ascendancy in these exclusively Anglican terms. The triple ranking in eighteenth-century Ireland of Protestant (Anglican), Dissenter (Presbyterian) and Catholic is described in *The Mighty Wave*, (eds. D. Keogh and N. Furlong), Four Courts Press, Dublin, 1996, p 10.

2. L de Paor, 'The Rebel Mind: Republican and Loyalist' in *The Irish Mind. Exploring Intellectual Traditions* (ed. R. Kearney), Wolfhound Press, Dublin, 1985, pp 157-187, especially p 163.

3. For an extensive description of 18th century Ireland cf Roy Foster's, *Modern Ireland 1690-1922* (especially pp. 167-286). For a fascinating glimpse of a forgotten happening in eighteenth-century Irish life, viz the great frost and subsequent famine (1739-41) cf David Dickson's, *Arctic Ireland*, The White Row Press, Belfast, 1997.

4. Brendan Clifford, *Billy Bluff and The Squire. A Satire on Irish Aristocracy*, Athol Books, Belfast, 1991, p 79.

5. R.B. McDowell, *Ireland in the Age of Imperialism and Revolution*, Clarendon Press, 1979, p 430. For an excellent treatment cf Daire Keogh, *The French Disease*, Four Courts Press, Dublin, 1993. More generally Vincent J. McNally, *Reform, Revolution and Reaction. Archbishop Troy and the Catholic Church in Ireland 1787-1817*, University Press of America, 1995.

6. R.R. Madden, *Antrim and Down*, Burns, Oates and Washbourne, London, (Cameron and Ferguson edition, no date) p 212.

7. B. Clifford, *Thomas Ledlie Birch, The Causes of the Revolution in Ireland 1798* (by Thomas Ledlie Birch), Athol Books, Belfast, 1991, p 13.

8. Thomas Moore's satire 'Intolerance', in *The Poetical Works of Thomas Moore*, Yardley and Hanscomb, London, no date, pp 174-177.

9. For a description of Belfast in the 1790s cf Marianne Elliott, *Wolfe Tone Prophet of Irish Independence*, Yale University Press, 1989.

10. Elliott, *Wolfe Tone*, p 119 et seq.

11. Denis Carroll, *The Man From God Knows Where*, Gartan, Dublin, 1995, p 26.

12. Cited in Daire Keogh and Nicholas Furlong (eds.), *The Mighty Wave*, p 41.

13. A.T.Q. Stewart, *The Narrow Ground. The Roots of Conflict in Ulster*, Faber, London, 1989, p 101.

14. Russell's Journal for mid-July 1793. cf National Archives, Rebellion Papers 620/20/33.

15. Charlemont Papers, cited by Ruan O'Donnell in *Irish Times*, 30 Dec 1997.

16. Re Presbyterian ministers' independence of spirit cf B. Clifford, *Birch*, pp. 14-15. A.T.Q. Stewart cautions against exaggerating their radicalism in his *Summer Soldiers*, Blackstaff, Belfast, 1995, p179.

17 Re these 'Ascendancy protests' (all the more significant for that) cf. Charles
    Dickson, *Revolt in the North: Antrim and Down in 1798*, Clonmore and
    Reynolds, Dublin, 1960, pp 104 et seq. Also W.H.F. Lecky, *A History of
    Ireland in the 18th Century* (5 vols), London, 1892, esp. vol 4. pp 265-274.
18 McDowell, I*reland in the Age*, p 611. citing 'Eumenes' *Thoughts on the Present
    Rebellion 1798*.
19 McDowell, *Ireland in the Age*, p 612.

CHAPTER ONE

FR JAMES COIGLY

While this chapter was being prepared, Fr Raymond Murray's splendid contribution to *Protestant, Catholic and Dissenter: The Clergy and 1798* (Columba Press,
Dublin, 1997) appeared. The present author wishes not only to salute this work
but also to acknowledge his indebtedness to Fr Murray's article. A poignant element to research on Fr Coigly is *The Life of the Reverend James Coigly: an Address
by him to the People of Ireland, as written by himself during his confinement in
Maidstone Gaol.* In the months after his death it was published at London with an
extended introduction by Valentine Derry, a friend and distant relative. The
memoir, hereafter referred to as *Life*, suffers from the circumstances in which it
was composed. Yet, it provides very interesting details on Fr Coigly's motivations
as well as on the circumstances of life in Ireland during the 1790s.

1   Re. position of Catholics in late eighteenth-century Ireland cf. Arthur Young,
    Tour of Ireland, vol 2, Dublin, 1780, p 37. Re. schools and freehold land cf.
    Patrick J. Corish, T*he Irish Catholic Experience*, Gill and MacMillan, Dublin
    1985, p 138.
2   cf Liam Swords, *The Irish–French Connection, The Irish College Paris, 1978*,
    esp chapter three, pp 44-62.
3   M. Elliott, 'Irish Republicanism in England: the First Phase' in Bartlett, T.
    and Hayton, D.W. (eds.) *Penal Era and Golden Age 1690-1800*, Ulster
    Historical Foundation, Belfast, 1979 pp 204-221, reference at p 208.
4   cf Coigly's own *Life*. Also, Swords, *The Irish-French Connection*, p 59.
5   Swords, op. cit., p 53. Lecky wrote of the French educated Irish priests: 'they
    brought with them a foreign culture and a foreign grace which did much to
    embellish Irish life' (cf. Swords, op. cit., p. 52).
6   Brendan McEvoy, 'Fr James Quigley', *Seanchas Ard Mhacha* (1970), pp 247-259.
7   Samuel Simms believes that Capt. Quigley was the brother of Fr Coigly.
    Others, notably Raymond Murray, claim the relationship was that of cousins.
8   Louis M. Cullen, 'The Internal Politics of the United Irishmen' in Dickson,
    Keogh and Whelan (eds.), *The United Irishmen*, Lilliput Press, Dublin, 1993,
    pp 176-196. Reference at pp 178-9.
9 Denis Carroll, *The Man From God Knows Where*, pp 106 et seq.

10 S. Simms, *Rev James O'Coigly, United Irishman*, Belfast, 1937, pp 99-100, citing McNeven's *Pieces of Irish History*.

11 Richard Musgrave, *Memories. of the Rebellion in Ireland*, 3rd ed. (2 vols), Dublin, 1802, p 194. (Recently re-issued in 4th edition, Stephen W. Myers and Dolores McKnight, Duffry Press, Enniscorthy, 1995).

12 Brendan McEvoy, art cit, p 257. Louis Cullen, 'The Internal Politics of the United Irishmen' in Dickson, Whelan and Keogh, *The United Irishmen*, p 193.

13 'An Observer', *A View of the present state of Ireland with an account of the origin and progress of the disturbances in that country, and a narrative of facts addressed to the people of England by an observer.* London, 1797. From internal evidence, Raymond Murray offers strong arguments that the 'Observer' is in fact James Coigly (cf. Murray's essay 'Father James Coigly', in *Protestant, Catholic and Dissenter: The Clergy and 1798*, p. 133). Louis Cullen argues (although Raymond Murray disagrees, art cit., footnote 13) that Fr Coigly also wrote a pamphlet, published in 1792, entitled 'Impartial account of the late disturbances in the county of Armagh since the year 1784 down to the year 1791 by an inhabitant of the town of Armagh'.

14 Daire Keogh, *The French Disease*, p 188.

15 D. Keogh, op. cit., p 190.

16 Reamonn O Muiri, 'The Killing of Thomas Birch, United Irishman, 3 March 1797 and the Meeting of the Armagh Freeholders, 19 August 1797' in *Seanchas Ard Mhacha* (1982), pp 267-320. For James Hope's reference cf R.R. Madden, *The Lives and Times of the United Irishmen* (3rd series), vol ii, Appendix 6, p 392.

17 M. Elliott, 'Irish Republicanism in England' *Penal Era*, p 208.

18 M. Elliott, ibid., p 209

19 M. Elliott, ibid., p 210

20 A.T.Q. Stewart, *The Summer Soldiers*, p 273.

21 M. Elliott, *Wolfe Tone*, pp 366-382.

22 Archives des Affaires Etrangeres, Correspondence Politique Anglais, 592, folio 43, folios 161-6 and 220. For more detailed analysis, cf M Elliott, *Wolfe Tone*, p 367 re Muir's argument for a French expedition to Scotland.

23. National Archive, Rebellion Papers 620/52/207 re Coigly's arrest. Also PRO (London) PC 1/51/A 143.

24 B McEvoy, art cit, p 268.

25 National Archives, Rebellion Papers 620/36/192.

26 cf Fr Coigly's *Life*, also B. McEvoy, art. cit. p 265.

27 Re Lord Holland cf W.J. Fitzpatrick, *The Secret Service Under Pitt*, London, 1892, p 21.

28 ibid., p 22.

CHAPTER TWO

THE REVEREND JAMES PORTER

1   R.B. McDowell, *Ireland in the Age of Imperialism and Revolution*, p. 171.

2   Pieter Tesch, 'Presbyterian Radicalism' in Dickson, Whelan and Keogh, *The United Irishmen*, pp 33-48.

3   Classon Porter, *Irish Presbyterian Biographical Sketches*, Belfast, 1883. Also Charles Teeling, *History of the Irish Rebellion 1798*, Irish University Press, Dublin, 1972, pp 204 et seq.

4   Nancy Curtin, *The United Irishmen*, Clarendon Press, Oxford, 1994, p 175.

5   Letter 10 April, 1794, PRO (London) HO 100/46/150-1.

6   R.R. Madden, *Antrim and Down*, p 214.

7   Classon Porter, Thomas Witherow and Brendan Clifford argue thus. Nevertheless, in the *Dictionary of National Biography* Alexander Gordon claims Firebrand is Hugh Montgomery, owner of Greyabbey estate.

8   Re Johnston's report cf *Pratt Papers*, U 140, 0 146/3 (May 1795). Re report on Porter cf National Archives, *Rebellion Papers* 620/26/105 and 620/20/53.

9   Thomas Russell's Journal, April 1793, *Rebellion Papers*, 620/20/33.

10 cf Charles Dickson's *Revolt in the North*, pp 104 et seq.

10a The text of 'Wind and Weather' can be found in Brendan Clifford's *Billy Bluff and The Squire*, Athol Books, Belfast, 1991, pp 70-78.

11 Re Mary Ann McCraken's assessment of the rising of 1798, cf *Rebellion Papers* 620/16/3.

12 Re Porter's disapproval of the form of the rising cf *Porter Mss.* PRONI D/3579; re account of events at Greyabbey cf Stewart, *The Summer Soldiers*, p 191.

13 National Archives, *Rebellion Papers* 620/2/15/54. For another account, *Dictionary of National Biography*, p 181. Re trial cf *The Summer Soldiers*, p 252.

14 B Clifford, *Billy Bluff*, p 85.

15 *The Summer Soldiers*, p 254.

CHAPTER THREE

MYLES PRENDERGAST OSA

1   John Cooney argues that the correct date is 22 August and not 23 August 1798 as claimed in Flanagan's *Year of the French*. cf Cooney's article in *Sunday Tribune* 4 Jan 1998.

2   L.W. Carr, *Connaught Telegraph*, 5 July 1941

3   Augustinian Archives (Ballyboden, Dublin) C.F.A. 3. My thanks to Fr O'Mahony and Rev Professor F.X. Martin for permission to consult this archive.

4   S.J. Connolly, *Religion, Law and Power*, Oxford, 1992, p 249.

5   D. Keogh, *The French Disease*, pp 186 and 199.

6   *Dublin Evening Post*, 29 Nov 1798

7   Such, at least, is the tradition dramatised in Leon O'Broin's *Slán Le Muirisg* (Oifig an tSolathair, Dublin, 1944). Years later, Fr Prendergast's order secured remission of the automatic suspension from exercise of his priesthood in shooting the unfortunate Brighouse. When it was discovered that the prison guard was a Catholic, the remission, it is said, was revoked!

8   Report from Capt. Taylor (Galbally) to Colonel Littlehales, 23 March 1799, National Archives, *Rebellion Papers*, 620//46/83.

9   *Rebellion Papers*, 620/7/76/7 and 620/1/197.

10 British Museum Ms 35730. Also L.W. Carr's *Connaught Telegraph* article.

11 Re Humbert's desire to return to Ireland cf J. Cooney, *Humbert's Expedition – A Lost Cause?* Humbert Bicentennial Committee (n.d.g.).

12 *Rebellion Papers*, 620/14/189/3 and 620/14/189/4.(13)

13 *Rebellion Papers*, 620/14/189/1; 620/ 14/188/6 and 620/14/189/5

14 Daire Keogh, *The French Disease*, p 184 and especially footnote no 133.

15 cf Augustinian Provincial Archives, C.F.A. 3.

16 Henry McManus, *Sketches of the Irish Highland*, Hamilton Adams, London, 1863.

CHAPTER FOUR
WM. STEEL DICKSON

1   cf. Brendan Clifford's *Scripture Politics* (Athol Books, Belfast, 1991), p 12. Clifford's valuable work gives a widespread selection of Dickson's writings and sermons. Chapter 1 (pp 11-38) and chapter five (pp 83-108) give valuable extracts from Dickson's own Narrative of his work and motivations (*A Narrative of the Confinement and Exile of William Steel Dickson, D.D. with an Appendix*. Stockdale, Dublin 1812).

2   re Francis Hutcheson cf. P. Tesch 'Presbyterian Radicalism' in Dickson, Whelan and Keogh, *The United Irishmen*, especially p 38.

3   Clifford, *Scripture Politics*, p 14.

4   In an Appendix to the *Narrative* Dickson remarks favourably on Alexander Stewart's foundational role at Mount Stewart. This is all the more remarkable in view of his good reasons for hostility to Robert Stewart, Lord Castlereagh.

5   cf Tesch, 'Presbyterian Radicalism', op. cit., p. 43 et seq.

6   ibid., p 44.

7   A.T.Q. Stewart, *Narrow Ground*, p.54 citing Dickson's *Narrative*.

8   Clifford (p.60) describes the purpose of these sermons as 'an amalgamation of politics, philosophy and theology which was the world outlook of Presbyterian Ulster'. The texts of the sermons are at Clifford, pp 63-82.

9   The Echlinville sermon can be found in Clifford, *Scripture Politics*, pp 52-59.

10 Sermon One, *Scripture Politics*, p.68.

11 Sermon One, ibid., p 73.

12 Tesch, 'Presbyterian Radicalism', op. cit., p 45. Re Lord Rutland's comment, cf. Rutland Mss., vol. 5, p. 421, Also Stewart's *Narrow Ground*, p 107.

13 Cf. Elliott, *Wolfe Tone*, pp. 173 et seq.

14 cf *Narrative*, for Dickson's modest account of his contribution.

15 *Scripture Politics*, pp 23–24.

16 Elliott, *Wolfe Tone*, p 54: 'A number of the country corps withdrew before the end of the debate – a withdrawal interpreted by some as a sign of their disgust at the sentiments expressed in the address, by others as necessitated by their long march home. Whichever way there can be no doubt that opposition to the address would have been greater had the County Down Volunteers remained. As it was, the document had no easy passage.'

17 Clifford, *Scripture Politics*, p 24.

18 Journal entry, late April–early May 1793 National Archives, *Rebellion Papers* 620/20/33.

19 Letter from Neilson to Drennan 17 February 1793, cf *The Drennan Letters* (D.A. Chart editor), Belfast, 1931. letter 390a.

20 Musgrave, op cit., p 124.

21 Clifford, *Scripture Politics*, p 25.

22 cf. Russell's letter to the *Northern Star* (30 august 1793).

23 Clifford, *Scripture Politics*, p 23.

24 For text of sermons cf. Clifford, *Scripture Politics*, pp 63–82.

25 Clifford, *Scripture Politics*, p 75.

26 Dickson's Christmas Day sermon is remarkable for its endeavour to quell such carefully planted rumours of discord. For his pains in identifying such 'malicious whisperer's artful tale, the base insinuations of the crying sycophant and the false representations of the officious partisan', Dickson was deemed by loyalists 'a papist at heart' . cf Keogh and Furlong, *The Mighty Wave*, p 41.

27 Clifford, *Scripture Politics*, p 79.

28 ibid., pp 81 and 82.

29 cited in W.E.H. Lecky, *A History of Ireland in the 18th Century*, vol 4, 1892, p 52.

30 cf. *Scripture Politics*, p 26.

31 Martha McTier to Wm. Drennan, *The Drennan Letters*, pp 236-7, letter 621.

32 National Archives, *Rebellion Papers*, 620/28/5.

33 cf. Clifford, op. cit., p 27.

34 Downshire to E. Cooke 20 February 1797, *Rebellion Papers*, 620/28/288.

35 Musgrave, op. cit., p 124.

36 Re Magin's allegations cf PRONI Lytton-White Papers, D 714/2/13; also PRONI McCance Papers (Black Book of the Rebellion) D 272/1.

37) Mary McNeill, *The Life and Times of Mary Ann McCracken*, Blackstaff, 1988 (republished), pp 184 and 189.

38 Clifford, *Scripture Politics*, p 35.

39 The Kilmainham conversations, not to be confused with events in the career of C.S. Parnell, are a series of meetings between Dublin Castle officials and

United Irish prisoners then held at Kilmainham and Newgate. In return for information of a general kind, the lives of Oliver Bond and Wm. Byrne were to be spared while other leaders such as Neilson and Addis Emmet were to be exiled. Cornwalis and Castlereagh spearheaded these talks from the official side while Neilson, Addis Emmet, Arthur O'Connor and Wm McNeven spoke for the 'state prisoners'.

40. Clifford, *Scripture Politics*, p. 89.

41 *Narrative*, cf Clifford, *Scripture Politics*, pp 104 and 98.

42 Earl Annesley to Marsden, 4 August 1803, *Rebellion Papers*, 620/64/65.

43 Letter to the Catholic Citizens of Dublin on the convention Act and the Conduct and Motives of the Catholic Committee, Dublin, 1811. For further treatment cf. Vincent McNally, *Reform, Revolution and Reaction*, pp 166-185.

44 W.D. Bailie, 'William Steel Dickson', *The Bulletin of the Presbyterian Historical Society of Ireland*, No 6, May 1976, p 28.

45 *Narrative* (2nd edition), Dublin, 1812, p 312.

46 Bailie, op, cit., p 31. Attention is drawn to Bailie's article on Dickson in L. Swords (ed.), *Protestant, Catholic and Dissenter. The Clergy and 1798*, Columba Press, Dublin, 1997, pp 45-80.

NOTES TO PART II

INTRODUCTION

1 Darrel Figgis, *AE (George Russell)*, Kennikat Press, New York and London (2nd ed), 1970, p 123.

2 Brendan Clifford, *Scripture Politics*, p 7.

3 Samuel Neilson, writing from Fort George, 21 July, 1799. cf. R.R. Madden, *Lives and Times of the United Irishmen*, 4th Series (2nd ed), 1860, pp 105-6. Re Hussey's remark cf Madden Mss (TCD), 873/197.

4 Cited in B. Clifford, *Scripture Politics*, pp 6-7.

5 More extensively considered in J.W. Good, 'Two Ulster Patriots', *Studies*, June 1921, pp 239-253. citation at p. 253.

6 P.J. McLoughlin, 'Richard Kirwan', *Studies* (XXIX), 1940, pp 281-300. citation at p 281. cf also Hubert Butler 'The Big House After the Union' in *Escape From The Anthill*, Lilliput, 1986, pp 46-56. Also E O hAnluainn, 'Irish Writing' in *Field Day Anthology of Irish Writing. Prose, Fiction and Poetry 1966-1986*, ed S. Deane, vol 3, pp 814 et seq.

7 Ordnance Survey Memoirs (R.I.A.) (8/11/1, p. 22); also *A New History of Ireland* (ed. W.E. Vaughan), vol. i (*Ireland Under the Union*, 1801-1870) Clarendon, Oxford, 1979.

8 cf *The Banner of Ulster*, 4 June 1868.

9 A.T.Q. Stewart, *The Narrow Ground*, p 101.

10 R.R. Madden, *Lives and Times of the United Irishmen* (3rd. series), vol. 1, p. 222.

11 Keogh and Furlong, *The Mighty Wave*, p. 32.

12 V. McNally, *Reform, Revolution and Reaction*, p 184 and 183 – re Troy's comment and 1811 pamphlet.

13 D. Carroll, *They Have Fooled You Again*, Columba Press, Dublin, 1993, p. 180.

14 M. Elliott, *Wolfe Tone*, p 19.

15 For a good account cf. P.J. Corish, *The Irish Catholic Experience*, pp 156-7.

16 B O Cathaoir in *Irish Times*, 8 Sept 1997.

17 Corish, op. cit., pp. 153-154. Also L De Paor 'The Rebel Mind' in *The Irish Mind*, R. Kearney (ed.), pp 157-187.

18 Roy Foster reviewing Fintan O'Toole's *The Traitor's Kiss* in *Irish Times*, 8 Nov 1997.

19 Editorial reflection in *The Tablet*, after Tony Blair's 'apology' re the Great Famine.

20 For a good account cf. Robert McCarthy, T*he Great Famine. A Church Of Ireland Perspective*, A.P.C.K., Dublin, 1996, p 10.

21 *Irish Times* (Famine Diary), B O Cathaoir, 24 May 1997.

22 Garrett Fitzgerald, *Irish Times*, 16 Nov. 1996.

CHAPTER FIVE

FR JOHN KENYON

1 Louise Fogarty, Fr John Kenyon. *A Patriot Priest of '48*, Whelan and Son, Dublin, 1920. Citation at pp. 7 and 8. Fogarty's work (hereafter, *A Patriot Priest*) is more a compendium of Kenyon's writings than a critical biography in any sense. However, it provides a valuable introduction to the issues in which Fr Kenyon immersed himself and an extensive corpus of his articles, speeches and letters.

2 *A Patriot Priest*, pp. 7 and 8. John O'Leary, *Recollections of Fenians and Fenianism*, Downey, London, 1896, vol. I, p. 14. Also John A. O'Shea, in *A Patriot Priest*, pp 158-165.

3 cf John Gleeson, *History of Ely O'Carroll*, Gill, Dublin, 1913. Re Thomas O'Brien's comment, cf. Larcom Papers (NLI) Ms 7636.

4 *A Patriot Priest*, pp. 131 and 30.

5 For a good account of this tension, cf. John N. Molony, *A Soul Came Into Ireland. Thomas Davis 1814-1845.* Geography Publications, Dublin 1995, pp. 176-182.

6 R.B. McDowell, *Public Opinion and Government Policy in Ireland*, 1801-1846, London, 1952, p. 254; Oliver McDonagh, *The Life of Daniel O'Connell*, 1775-1847, London, 1991, p. 574.

7 It was Sir Robert Inglis who, speaking in the House of Commons, described

mixed education as 'a gigantic scheme of Godless education'. Cf Molony, *A Soul Came Into Ireland*, p.302. Re the memorandum presented for Archbishop Crolly's attention at Marlborough St, Dublin by Fr Kenyon and Fr C.P. Meehan, cf. Donal Kerr's *A Nation of Beggars*, Clarendon, Oxford, 1994, p. 163.

8   Re the remarks of Daniel and John O'Connell, cf. Molony, op. cit. p.284. Also *The Nation*, 5 April 1845.

9   *The Nation*, 9 Aug. 1845. cf also Molony, op. cit., p 285.

10 Cited in *A Patriot Priest*, p. 134.

11 Richard Davis, *The Young Ireland Movement*, Gill and MacMillan, Dublin, 1987, pp. 123-4. cf also W. Dillon, *Life of Mitchel*, vol 2, p.44.

12 *The Nation*, 19 Jan. and 13 Feb. 1847 re Kenyon's letters on the question of slavery.

13 Re secession and related issues, cf. F.S.L. Lyons, *Ireland Since the Famine*, pp. 105 and 107.

14 B. O Cathaoir, *Irish Times* (Famine Diary), 3 Aug. 1996. Also Lyons, op. cit, p. 106.

15 Re Kenyon's argument in *The Nation*, cf. *A Patriot Priest*, p. 32. Re Frs O'Carroll and Durcan, cf. *Irish Times* (Famine Diary), 3 Aug. and 7 Dec. 1996.

16 There was a lack of cohesion which led many priests to withhold their names from the petition.

17 Roy Foster, *Modern Ireland*, p. 316.

18 cf. *A Patriot Priest*, pp 25-27 for text.

19 O. McDonagh, *Life of Daniel O'Connell*, p.576. also *A Patriot Priest*, p. 31.

20 D. Kerr, *A Nation of Beggars*, p. 163.

21 cf. *A Patriot Priest*, p. 88.

22 cf. *A Patriot Priest*, pp. 164 et seq.

23 For text cf. *A Patriot Priest*, pp. 77, 81 and 96-7.

24 E. Hobsbawm, *The Age of Capital, 1848-1875*, pp 25 and 30.

25 F.S.L. Lyons, op. cit., p. 109.

26 For text of Kenyon's letter cf. *A Patriot Priest*, pp. 87-88, also R. Davis, *Young Ireland*, pp 140-1.

27 R. Davis, *Young Ireland*, p. 146.

28 *A Patriot Priest*, pp. 126-128.

29 D. Kerr, op. cit ., pp. 163-4.

30 Ignatius Murphy, *Diocese of Killaloe, 1850-1904*, Four Courts Press, Dublin, 1995, p. 201.

31 *A Patriot Priest*, p. 121.

32 F.S.L. Lyons, op. cit ., p 110.

33 Philip Fitzgerald, *A Narrative of the Proceedings of the Confederation of 1848*, Duffy, Dublin, 1868, p. 25.

34 Fitzgerald, op. cit., pp. 28 and 31.

35 Ignatius Murphy, op. cit., p.205; *A Patriot Priest*, p.2.

36 Ignatius Murphy, op. cit., p 164.

37 Ignatius Murphy, op. cit., p 200.

38 *A Patriot Priest*, p. 120.

39 Cited in Ignatius Murphy, op. cit., p.202.

40 *Cork Examiner*, 5 March 1851. cf also Ignatius Murphy, op. cit, p.236.

41 James O'Shea, *Priests, Politics and Society in Post–Famine Ireland*, Wolfhound, Dublin, 1983, p. 147.

42 O'Shea, op. cit., p. 52.

43 Gleeson, *History of Ely O'Carroll*, p. 201.

44 For text, cf. Gleeson, *History of Ely O'Carroll*, pp. 200-203.

45 cf. O'Leary, *Recollections of Fenians and Fenianism*, vol 1, p. 158. Also, *A Patriot Priest*, p. 150.

46 Cited in T. O'Shea, op. cit., p. 155.

47 *A Patriot Priest*, p. 160.

48 Cited in *A Patriot Priest*, p. 57.

49 Richard Davis, *Young Ireland*, p. 160.

CHAPTER SIX
THE CALLAN CURATES

1 Published (1994) by Callan Heritage Society, and edited by Michael O'Dwyer. Hereafter *Callan Tenant Protection*.

2 *Callan Tenant Protection*, p. 58-9.

3 ibid., p. 3.

4 ibid., p. 47.

5 ibid., p. 19.

6 ibid., p. 15.

7 ibid., pp. 13-14.

8 ibid., pp.16 and 17.

9 ibid., pp. 18 and 19.

10 ibid., pp 19 and 20.

11 ibid., p. 23. Also pp. 32 and 33 re political actions.

12 ibid., p. 32.

13 ibid., p. 34.

14 ibid., p. 36.

15 *Banner of Ulster*, 24 Oct. 1854.

16 *Callan Tenant Protection*, p. 39. cf Edward Lucas, *Life of Frederick Lucas*, London, 1886, p 185 .

17 Charles Kickham, 'Pulpit Denunciation – Priests in Politics' Irish People, no 44. Cited by John O'Leary in *Recollections of Fenians and Fenianism*, p. 53.

18 cf. J. Kennedy, 'Thomas Shelly and Callan' in *Old Kilkenny Review*, 1988, pp 492-502.

19 Ed. Lucas, *Life of Frederick Lucas*, p. 206.

20 Letter 9 April 1855. Cited by Gavan Duffy in *My Life in Two Hemispheres*, Fisher Unwin, London, 1898 vol. 2, p. 102.

21 *Callan Tenants Protection*, p. 43.

22 ibid., p. 44.

23 Gavan Duffy, op. cit., vol. 2, pp 253-4.

24 cf. E. Larkin, *The Consolidation of the Roman Catholic Church in Ireland, 1860-70*, Gill and MacMillan, Dublin, 1987, pp. 612 et seq.

25 David Thornley, *Isaac Butt and Home Rule*, p. 59.

26 *Callan Tenants Protection*, p. 48.

27 *Kilkenny: History and Society*, eds. W. Nolan and K. Whelan, Geography Publications, Dublin, 1990, p. 523.

CHAPTER SEVEN

THE REVEREND ISAAC NELSON

1 cf. notice in *Northern Whig*, 12 Oct 1916 citing George Gilfinnan's *Remoter Stars in the Church Sky*. Gilfinnan remarks that Nelson was termed 'the Ismael of the Church in Ireland'.

2 J.C. Beckett, *Belfast: The Making of the City 1800-1914*, Appletree, 1988, p. 141.

3 My thanks to Reverend Alfred Williamson, Belfast, for this reference in a letter of 15 Oct 1996.

4 *Northern Whig*, 12 Oct. 1916.

5 *N. Whig*, 29 April 1847.

6 Re Gilfinnan's remark, cf. *N. Whig*, 12 Oct 1916.

7 cf *N. Whig* from 18 Nov. to end December 1847.

8 Report in *Banner of Ulster*, 13 July 1854.

9) *The Northern Whig* (8 March 1888) opined that Nelson's disappointment left 'a broken arrow in his bosom which was never extracted, and his faith was broken in the ministry and work of the General Assembly'

10 J.B. Armour to John Megaw, 6 Feb. 1862, in PRONI, D 1792/A 2/7.

11 *N. Whig*, 17 April 1845.

12 Letter was printed in pamphlet form by J. Gadsby, Manchester, 1846.

13 *N. Whig*, 20 Jan. 1846.

14 cf. *N. Whig*, 20 Jan 1846; 9 July 1846; 15 July 1847; 30 Aug. 1847.

15 Re Edinburgh meeting, cf. U.S. Library Catalog NN 010 5684; re *American War in Relation to Slavery* (lecture 24 Nov. 1863) cf US Library Catalog NN 0105679 MN IU

16 cf. David Hempton and Myrtle Hill, *Evangelical Protestantism in Ulster Society, 1740-1890*, Routledge, London and New York, 1992, p.60.

17 re J. B. Armour's phrase 'circus riders in the Tory hippodrome' at the Presbyterian General Assembly in 1893, cf J.B. McMinn, *Against The Tide*, p xlii.

18 J. McCosh, *The Ulster Revival and its Physiological Effects*, Belfast, 1859.

19 Wm. Gibson, *The Year of Grace. A History of the Ulster Revival of 1859*, Edinburgh and Belfast, 1860.

20 Pamphlet: US Library Catalolg: CsaTNN 0105680

21 *Banner of Ulster*, 12 Nov. 1864.

22 *N. Whig*, 3 Dec. 1864. F.S.L. Lyons, I*reland Since The Famine*, p. 152.

24 *N. Whig* 27 Feb. 1874.

25 At General Assembly, June 1893, cited in J.D. Houston and J.B. Dougherty, *Are Irish Protestants Afraid of Home Rule?*, London, 1893, pp. 10-11.

26 Letter from John Martin, sec. of Home Rule League, in outletter book of Home Rule Association and League, PRONI D 213, pp 108 et seq.

27 Lecture on 16 April 1874. For text cf. *Collins Pamphlets*, vol 9, no.11 (TCD library NN 010 5682 I u).

28 T.W. Moody, *Davitt and Irish Revolution 1846-82*, Clarendon, Oxford, 1981, pp. 334–5. Re 'Appeal to the Irish Race' cf. Irish Times, 22 Oct. 1877.

29 Report in *N. Whig* 26 May 1880.

30 The service is reported in extenso by *Northern Whig*, 31 May 1880.

31 Hansard, 253, Coll 248-9.

32 Hansard, 253, col. 1681; Hansard 257, coll. 1729 and 1912.

33 Hansard, 269, coll 1305–6.

34 Hansard, 254, col. 122.

35 July 1882. Hansard, 272, coll. 859-60.

36 F.S.L. Lyons, op. cit., p. 171.

NOTES TO PART III

INTRODUCTION

1. Sean Connolly, *Religion and Society in 19th Century Ireland, Economic and social History Society of Ireland*, Dundealgan Press, Dundalk,1985, p 34.

2. Maurice Goldring, *Belfast: From Loyalty to Rebellion*, Lawrence and Wishart, London, 1991, citation at p 99.

3. F.S.L. Lyons, *Ireland Since The Famine* , pp 315 et seq.

4. Desmond Fennell, 'Irish Socialist Thought' , in *Heresy. The Battle of Ideas in Modern Ireland* , Blackstaff, Belfast, 1993, pp 9-37.

5. cf J.A. Gaughan, *Memoirs of Senator Joseph Connolly*, Irish Academic Press, Dublin, 1996, p 69 for biographical note on Dr Irwin.

CHAPTER EIGHT
ARMOUR OF BALLYMONEY

1   Wm. B. Armour, Armour of Ballymoney, Duckworth, London, 1934. Reference is at p. 50; cf, also foreword, pp. xv and xvi. This book by J.B.

Armour's son is now rare. It is at once an enthusiastic biography of Armour and a valuable compendium of his addresses and writings. Cf. also, J.B. McMinn's *Against The Tide* (PRONI, 1985) for a detailed biography and a scholarly presentation of Amour's letters. An interesting memoir on Armour's life is given in Len Snodgrass, *Armour's Meeting House 1885-1985*, Ballymoney, 1985, pp 41-59.

2   Ordnance Survey *Field Memoirs for Ballymoney*, PRONI, M 1C6/13/4.

3   cf. J.D.. McMinn, *Against The Tide*, p. xv. also PRONI D 1792/A2/11, for letter of 4 Nov. 1863.

4   *Against The Tide*, pp. lx and xvi.

5   cited in Len Snodgrass, *Armour's Meeting House 1885-1985*, p. 45.

6   Fr. H. E. Plunkett, cited in *Armour of Ballymoney*, p. 382.

7   *Against The Tide*, p. xx.

8   ibid., p xx, note xi.

9   *Armour of Ballymoney*, pp. 58 and 40.

10 *Armour of Ballymoney*, pp. 28-31.

11 Re speech at Ballynure cf. *Against The Tide*, footnotes at p. xlv. For Armour's speech of 12 Feb. 1873, cf. *Armour of Ballymoney*, p. 37. Re inclusion of 'day labourers' cf. McMinn, 'The Land League in North Antrim', The Glynns (XI), 1983, pp. 35-40.

12 At Town Hall, Ballymoney, 23 Jan. 1880. For text cf. *Armour of Ballymoney*, pp. 41 et seq.

13 For text cf. *Armour of Ballymoney*, pp. 41 et seq.

14 ibid., pp. 43-44.

15 Speech in Spring 1892, for citation cf. *Armour of Ballymoney*, p. 88.

16 Dervock speech, *Armour of Ballymoney*, pp. 42 and 44.

17 *Armour of Ballymoney*, p. 275.

18 ibid., p. 67.

19 ibid., p. 73.

20 *Witness*, 18 June 1886.

21 F.S.L. Lyons, *Ireland Since The Famine*, p. 142, argues that from 1865 Gladstone moved steadily to a dominant position among 'that medley of Whigs and Radicals, churchmen and non-conformists, bourgeoisie and working men, out of which a great Liberal party was to be fashioned'. Thus, argues Lyons, he could turn at last 'to look in the face and work through the problems Ireland still presented'.

22 For a major speech to General Assembly 1893, cf. *Armour of Ballymoney*, p. 102.

23 *Against The Tide*, p. xxi and p. 21 (especially footnotes).

24 *Armour of Ballymoney*, p. xix.

25 J.D. Houston at General Assembly 9 June 1893; cited in J.D. Houston and J.D. Dougherty, *Are Irish Protestants Afraid of Home Rule?*, London, 1893, pp. 10-11.

26 *Armour of Ballymoney*, p. 351-2.

27 PRONI, D 1792/A3/6/31.

28 At General Assembly June 1891; cf. *Armour of Ballymoney*, pp. 60-1.

29 *Armour of Ballymoney*, p. 174.

30 ibid., pp. 373-4.

31 *Against The Tide*, pp. x-xi.

32 Snodgrass, op. cit., p. 54.

33 *Against The Tide*, pp. viii and xi.

34 ibid., pp. xx-xxi and *Witness* 15 June 1886; 1 May 1908.

35 *Armour of Ballymoney*, p. 215 (re Celtic studies); ibid., pp 210-3 (re Scholastic philosophy).

36 ibid., p. 219.

37 ibid., p. 247.

38 ibid., p. 193,.

39 Letter 23 June 1886, cf. PRONI D 1792/A2/22.

40 *Against The Tide*, pp xxxii and xxxix.

41 ibid., pp x and vi. Also *Ballymoney Free Press*, 30 June 1892.

42 *Against The Tide*, p. x.

43 To an unnamed correspondent, PRONI, D 1792/A2/22.

44 F.S.L. Lyons, op. cit., p. 202.

45 PRONI, D 1792/A1/1/9.

46 Lyons, op. cit., p. 202.

47 Lyons, op. cit., p. 301.

48 Interview *Daily News* 3 Jan 1911. Armour reiterated these views in *The New Irish Constitution*, ed. J.H. Morgan, Hodder and Stoughton, London, 1912.

49 *Armour of Ballymoney*, p. 248.

50 ibid., p. 255.

51 *Against The Tide*, p. lvii.

52 *The Times*, 23 Oct 1913.

53 *Armour of Ballymoney*, p. 263.

54) Re Armour's call for the government to retain its nerve, cf. letter of Wm. B. Armour, 30 July 1914. PRONI, D 1792/A3/5/20.

55 To Jane McMaster, 17 March 1914. PRONI, D 1792 A3/13/14.

56 *Armour of Ballymoney*, pp. 209–303.

57 op. cit., p. 306.

58 op. cit., p. 307.

59 op. cit., pp. 309-316.

60 op. cit., p. 312.

61 op. cit., p. 304.

62 op. cit., p. 302.

63 op. cit., p. 305.

64 Letter, cf. *Against The Tide*, p. 186.

65 *Armour of Ballymoney*, p. 312.

66 ibid., p. 307.

67 ibid., p. 320 re speech to General Assembly, 1920

68 ibid., pp 320 et seq.

69 ibid., p. 333.

70 Snodgrass, op. cit., p. 63.

71 *Against The Tide*, pp. 187 and 183.

72 *Armour of Ballymoney*, p. 373.

73 Dean Victor Griffin, at Donaghpatrick church, Ceannanais (Kells), bv 15 March 1996. cf *Irish Times* 19 March 1996 and 21 March 1996. For the tribute cited above, cf. *Irish Book Lover* 23 1935, pp 100-101.

CHAPTER NINE

FR MICHAEL O'FLANAGAN

1 For fuller treatment cf D. Carroll, *They Have Fooled You Again*, Columba, 1993. Citation re O'Flanagan's hostility to the 'war effort' is in Carroll, op. cit., p.82.

2 I wish to thank Mary O'Flanagan (Fr Michael's niece) for showing me these letters at Castlerea during the summer of 1992.

3 Letter 1 April 1916, cf. Irish College Rome Archives. The letter is cited in P J Corish, *History of Maynooth College*.

4 *Irish Phonetics*, Brown and Nolan, Dublin, 1904. Also E O hAnluain, *The Field Day Anthology of Irish Writing*, Field Day Publications, Derry, 1993, ed. Seamus Deane, vol 3, p 814. O hAnluain points out that Pearse's editorship of *An Claidheamh Solais* addressed 'the new problems of spelling, grammar and style ... that would take years and much controversy to resolve'.

5 *The Sligo Champion*, Sesquicentennial Edition, pp 37 and 41. Also, Carroll, op. cit., pp. 21-3 for specific references.

6 This phrase 'rank and file of the people' recurs throughout O'Flanagan's writings and speeches. At first sight, one thinks of rudimentary populism. Yet, Fr O'Flanagan's political thought contained a noticeable strand of Catholic social teaching and, in many instances, of socialism.

7 For what follows cf. *Diarmuid O'Donovan Rossa. Funeral Souvenir Edition*, Dublin, 1915 (available at National Library of Ireland). Also, *They Have Fooled You Again*, pp 29-33.

8 *Souvenir Booklet*, p 34.

9 For more extended treatment, cf, Carroll, op. cit., pp 33-39.

10 A lengthy report is given in *Sligo Champion*, 16 Oct 1915.

11 For what follows cf Carroll, op. cit., 40-41. Also *Cork Examiner*, 13 Jan 1916; Cork Constitution, 13 and 17 Jan 1916; *Intelligence Notes* (ed. B Mac Giolla Choille), Oifig an tSolathair, Dublin, 1966, pp 213 and 225.

12 Re O'Flanagan's letter to O'Hagan cf Irish College Rome Archives, also P J

Corish's *History of Maynooth College*. For an account of Biggs Davison's argument cf Brian Murphy, *Patrick Pearse and The Lost Republican Ideal*, Duffy, Dublin, 1991, pp 51-56.

13 In 'Fr O'Flanagan and his Critics', *The Leader*, 2 Sept 1916.

14 *The Leader*, 23 Sept 1916.

15 For O'Flanagan's text and a hostile assessment of it cf *Freeman's Journal*, 8 Sept 1917. For a subsequent discussion, *Freeman's Journal*, 11, 14 and 15 Sept 1917.

16 *Freeman's Journal*, 8 Sept 1917.

17 cf Carroll, op. cit., pp 57-59.

18 cf Peadar O'Donnell, *Not Yet Emmet*, pp 6-7.

19 cf *Irish Times*, 10.2.1917 and *Roscommon Herald*, 24 February 1917.

20 Letter is dated 29 April 1917. Text appears in *Roscommon Herald*, 5 May 1917. For Fr Tom Flanagan's remarks, cf. *Roscommon Herald*, 27 Oct1917.

21 Ml Laffan, 'The Unification of Sinn Féin', Irish Historical Studies (XV11), March 1971, pp 353-379, citation at p 379. Also Brian Murphy, *Patrick Pearse and the Lost Republican Ideal*, pp 91 and 105.

22 In *The Strength of Sinn Féin*, Dublin 1934. O'Flanagan's presidential address to the Ard Fheis.

23 During April 1925 Fr O'Flanagan composed an extended memorandum on his difficulties with Dr Coyne. Here, he sets forth his own motivations in his socio-political activities to date. The memorandum, for long in the possession of J J O'Kelly (Sceilg), is now in the possession of Fr Brian Murphy, O.S.B., Glenstal Abbey.

24 From Fr O'Flanagan's Ballyjamesduff speech. Censored by the civil authorities, the speech was published as a four-page pamphlet by the Sinn Féin standing committee. It is now somewhat of a rarity.

25 For Ml O'Flanagan's tribute to his mother, cf. *Roscommon Herald,*24 Jan 1925.

26 cf. *Roscommon Herald* 15 Dec 1918. For fuller account of the election campaign, cf. Carroll, op. cit., pp 88-99.

27 Cited by P.S. O'Hegarty in his *The Victory of Sinn Féin*, Dublin,1924, p 32.

28 *Co-Operation*, Cumann Leigheacht an Phobail, Series C, Dublin 1922.

29 An extensive report is given in *Roscommon Herald*, 13 Sept 1919.

30 Text of telegram is given in the national dailies for 6 Dec 1920. Re de Valera's remark, cf. *Daily Sketch*, 7 Dec 1920. Also Ml Collins to Art O'Brien (London) 15 January 1921. A remarkable dossier on the affair is in the de Valera papers at Franciscan House, Killiney, Co Dublin. Cf. also Brian Murphy's *Patrick Pearse and the Lost Republican Ideal*, p 126.

31 9 Oct 1921 at Ballinalee, Co Longford (reported in *Roscommon Herald*, 15 Oct 1921).

32 J.J. O'Kelly, *Cathal Brugha*, Gill and Son, Dublin, 1942, p 260. Re Collins on the nomination, cf. de Valera papers, letters 15 and 16 Oct 1921.

33 Under J J McGarrity, the AARIR were anti-Treaty, while the *Friends of Irish Freedom*, under John Devoy, supported Collins and Griffith.

34 For extended account of the visit to Australia, cf. Carroll, op. cit., pp 143-147.

35 cf *Roscommon Herald*, 28 Feb 1925 for text.

36 *Roscommon Herald*, 24 Jan 1925. Re the memorandum cf footnote 23 above. Re O'Mullane's comment cf *Irish Independent*, 11 March 1925. Re the personal attack on Fr O'Flanagan, cf *Roscommon Herald*, 28 Feb 1925.

37 *An Phoblacht* carried several articles by Fr O'Flanagan through 1925: 21 Aug ('Fr O'Flanagan Asks Questions'); 28 Aug ('A Bolshevik Ireland'); 4 Sept ('Socialism Or Anarchy?'); 18 Dec 1925 ('Sturdy Republicanism'). A two part article also appeared on 28 Aug and 4 Sept ('Great Hearted Irishmen').

38 Re the Lemass articles cf. *An Phoblacht*, 18 Sept and 23Oct 1925; Also 22 Jan, 29 Jan and 5 Feb 1926.

39 *An Phoblacht*, 19 Feb 1926.

40 During 1927 and 1928 Fr O'Flanagan and a devoted team of helpers edited these letters at the Ordnance Survey Office. The completed work was made available to the National Library and several Universities. The edition/publication of these letters had been a project of Ml Davitt and Tim Healy when imprisoned in England for Fenian activities. It is interesting to note that Edward Carson had been willing to back the project during the closing years of the 19th century.

41 Read at Standing Committee Sinn Féin 17 May 1932. Text of the committee meetings are in the legal documentation of the Sinn Féin Funds litigation at the State Papers Office, 2B, 82, 117.

42 D MacSuibhne in *An Phoblacht*, Feb 1934 re pattern of Sinn Féin voting in the February 1932 general election.

43 *An Phoblacht*, 15 April 1933.

44 cf Dail Debates, July-Aug 1932, Coll. 853-862.

45 J J O'Kelly to Mary MacSwiney, in MacSwiney Papers, U.C.D., P 48a 59/42 and 59/37.

46 Standing Committee, 6 Oct 1933, cf Sinn Féin Funds Case, State Papers Office, PROD 2B, 82, 1199.

47 *The Strength of Sinn Féin*, Dublin, 1934.

48 In Uinseann MacEoin, *Survivors*, Argenta Publications, Dublin,1980. p 122.

49 Text in Sinn Féin Funds Case File, State Papers Office, PROD 2B,82, 119, document 1751.

50 Sinn Féin Standing Committee notes for 20 Jan 1936. PROD 2B,82 116.

51 Fr Myles Ronan wrote in the *Irish Press* 18 Dec 1936 on 'Ireland Remembers Her Debt To Spain' while Dean Ryan of Cashel praised those who fought 'Christianity's battles against Communism'.

52 I wish to thank Patrick Byrne for his generous help in regard to this period of Fr O'Flanagan's life. Along with Ml O'Riordan, Paddy Byrne is a link with

Ml O'Flanagan's courageous stance when it was exceedingly difficult for a priest to question the positions adopted by many of his colleagues and the hierarchical leadership.

53 For a more extended treatment of O'Flanagan's addresses in the United States cf Carroll, op. cit., pp 219-234.

54 Ml O'Riordan, a veteran of the Spanish Civil War has written a fine study of the Irish contribution to the republican cause in Spain. His *Connolly Column*, (New Books, Dublin, 1979) is a fitting tribute to men who braved opprobrium at home and, in Spain, the dangers of war. Ml O'Riordan pays loyal tribute to Fr O'Flanagan's encouragement of the republican spirit, this time in Spanish context. Cf *Connolly Column*, pp 67-68, 8, and 139.

55 This reference is to an interview with Nora Harkin, a veteran of Irish solidarity with Republican Spain committees.

56 J J O'Kelly's Glasnevin oration was later published in pamphlet form by National Aid Auxiliary Committee, 1942. Cf also *The Catholic Standard*, 14 August 1942.

CHAPTER TEN

TWO RADICAL CLERGYMEN

REVEREND R.M. HILLIARD

1 Maurice Goldring, *Belfast: From Loyalty to Rebellion*, Lawrence and Wishart, London, 1991, p 99.

2 cf symposium in *The Bell*, June 1944, pp 218-232.

3 ibid., pp 230 and 231.

4 cf. 'The Boxing Parson', an article by Stephen Hilliard in *Resource*, Spring 1988, pp14-15. Also generous references are made to R. M. Hilliard in Ml O'Riordan's *Connolly Column*, New Books, Dublin, 1979. Jason Gurney's *Crusade in Spain*, (Faber and Faber, London, 1974), gives some outline of Bob Hilliard's period in Spain. Cf also Wm Rust, *Britons in Spain*, Lawrence and Wishart, London, 1939. (This book is now a rarity).

5 The Sizarship was for students from Co Kerry and, at the time Hilliard received it, was awarded from entrance examination results. The reminiscence of a student colleague is in an *Irish Times* note written after Hilliard's death. I am indebted to Mrs Betty Hilliard for access to this source.

6 The following reports in the student journal *T.C.D.* give a flavour of R. M. Hilliard's contributions to various societies: *T.C.D.*, 8.12.1921; 23.11.1922; 2.3.1922.

7 For much of the following I am indebted to Stephen Hilliard, 'Boxing Parson', *Resource*, Spring 1988. Also I express my thanks to R. M. Hilliard's nephew, Martin Hilliard, for his courteous help. A short note, evidently from the *Irish Times*, mentions Hilliard's work in London and also his marriage.

8   *T.C.D.*, 5.11.1931, p 22.

9   *T.C.D.*, 12.11.1931 and 26.11.1931 (reports on Theological Society Proceedings). In the latter report Hilliard is referred to as The Reverend R. M. Hilliard, B.A. In another report, this time by the Editorial sub-committee of *T.C.D.* journal (27. 11. 1932) the reference is to R. M. Hilliard, M.A.

10 *T.C.D.*, 18.2.1932, p 101; 3.3.1932, pp 122 and 127; 26.5.1932, p 3. The chairman of the last mentioned debate was Senator Joseph Connolly, a member of de Valera's new cabinet.

11 Re Editorial Sub committee report, cf *T.C.D.*, 27.10. 1932, p 3. Re Divinity School article, cf *T.C.D.* 12.5.1932, pp145-46.

12 Both citations are from 'The Boxing Parson', op. cit., p 15.

13 Cf Frank Graham, *The Book of the XV Brigade*, Newcastle-Upon Tyne, 1938, esp pp 23 et seq.

14 Jason Gurney, *Crusade in Spain*, Faber and Faber, London, 1974, p 66.

15 ibid., p 61.

16 Gurney, op cit., pp 66 et seq. Gurney cites 14 February 1937 as the date when Hilliard was mortally injured. Stephen Hilliard, however, mentions 13th February.

17 'The Boxing Parson', *Resource*, p 15.

REVEREND STEPHEN HILLIARD

1   'The Boxing Parson', *Resource*, Spring, 1988, p 14.

2   After his ordination, Stephen Hilliard gave an extended interview to *The Parishioner*, the journal of the Christ Church group of parishes. The reference here is to the Autumn 1986 edition, no 25, pp 78.

3   In the days after his death, Stephen Hilliard's colleagues paid handsome tribute to his memory. Many of the subsequent references in this section are to these tributes. The immediate citation is from Conor Brady's note in the *Irish Times*, 10.1.1990.

4   Douglas Gageby and James Downey wrote in the *Irish Times* on 10.1.1990. Kevin Myers' article appeared the following day. In regard to 'B Ó'C' there is internal evidence that the appreciation is written by scholar and journalist, Breandan Ó'Cathaoir. The piece has a remarkable depth of feeling and breadth of vision. Mervyn Taylor wrote a fine appreciation in *The Irish People*, 19.1.1990. The jocose reference to editing a Shakespeare sonnet was made in conversation with Deáglan de Bréadúin, a friend and colleague of Hilliard.

5   Archbishop Caird, to whom I am indebted for guidance, is cited in the *Irish Times*, 11.1.1990.

6   *The Parishioner,* Autumn, 1986, p 8.

7   Risteard Ó Glaisne, the noted Gaelic scholar, philosopher and writer, wrote a fine piece in *An tUltach*, March, 1990. I am indebted to Ó Glaisne for much guidance in repeated telephone conversations. *The Erasmian* is the journal of the High School, in which Stephen Hilliard published at least one poem.

8   Deáglan de Bréadúin, *Irish Times*, 10.1.1990.

9   *Irish Times*, May 1968 for the interview with Ml O'Riordan. *The Liberties*, vol i, no 4, March 1969, p 6 for citation re the housing question. The articles on the German Democratic Republic appear in *Irish Times*, 2.12.1971.

10 M. Taylor in *The Irish People*, 19.1.1990. Review in *The Christian Left Review*, Autumn, 1981.

11 *Irish Times*, 30.11.1971; 1.12.1971 and 2.12.1971.

12 *Church of Ireland Gazette*, 18.2.1983, pp 8-11.

13 Extended report in *Irish Socialist*, June/July, 1979, p 4.

14 cf Stephen Hilliard's interview in *The Parishioner*, Autumn 1986, p 6. I have found typewritten notes (presumably of a lecture), among some papers of Stephen Hilliard, which expound the 'newer' thinking of socialists on 'the national question'. I am unable to attribute the analysis.

15 My thanks to Betty Hilliard for the opportunity to read this letter and for considerable help in preparing these pages. Stephen Hilliard's review in the *Church of Ireland Gazette* (November 1982) is of John Ferguson's *The Politics of Love*.

16 *Christian Left Review*, No1, 1980, pp 11-13. Only two issues of the *Review* appeared.

17 *The Parishioner*, Autumn, 1986, p 8.

18 *Christian Left Review*, November 1980, p 13.

19 Ironically, the last issue of *Resource* – to whose work Stephen Hilliard had generously contributed – paid a superb tribute, cf *Resource*, Summer 1990, p 27.

Index of Persons